Sharing Environmental Risks

Sharing Environmental Risks

How to Control Governments' Losses in Natural Disasters

Raymond J. Burby

with Beverly A. Cigler, Steven P. French,
Edward J. Kaiser, Jack Kartez,
Dale Roenigk, Dana Weist,
and Dale Whittington

Westview Press
BOULDER • SAN FRANCISCO • OXFORD

Westview Special Studies in Public Policy and Public Systems Management

Copyright © 1991 by Westview Press, Inc.

Published in 1991 in the United States of America by Westview Press, Inc., 5500 Central Avenue, Boulder, Colorado 80301, and in the United Kingdom by Westview Press, 36 Lonsdale Road, Summertown, Oxford OX2 7EW

Library of Congress Cataloging-in-Publication Data
Burby, Raymond J., 1942–
    Sharing environmental risks : how to control governments' losses
in natural disasters/Raymond J. Burby with Beverly A. Cigler . . .
[et al.].
        p.   cm.—(Westview special studies in public policy and
public systems management)
    Includes bibliographical references.
    ISBN 0-8133-1172-1
    1. Natural disasters—Economic aspects—United States.
2. Disaster relief—United States—Cost control.   3. Insurance,
Disaster—United States.   4. Risk (Insurance)—United States.
5. Natural disasters—Economic aspects.   6. Disaster relief—Cost
control.   7. Insurance, Disaster.   8. Risk (Insurance) I. Title.
II. Series.
HC110.D45B87   1991
368.1'221'0973—dc20   90-20869
                                                                CIP

Printed and bound in the United States of America

The paper used in this publication meets the requirements
of the American National Standard for Permanence of Paper
for Printed Library Materials Z39.48-1984.

10   9   8   7   6   5   4   3   2   1

Contents

PART 2
HOW TO CONTROL LOSSES

PART 3
FOUR ISSUES IN SHARING
ENVIRONMENTAL RISKS

Tables

Figures

Preface

The havoc, personal suffering, and massive financial losses caused in 1989 by Hurricane Hugo in the Caribbean and Carolinas and by the Loma Prieta earthquake in the San Francisco Bay region of California have drawn the nation's attention once again to our vulnerability to the forces of nature. This book summarizes the results of an extensive study of public losses from natural disasters during the decade of the 1980s and how those losses can be controlled through reforms in federal, state, and local policy. The study was initiated in 1986 under the direction of Dr. Raymond J. Burby, principal investigator, and co-principal investigators Beverly A. Cigler, Steven P. French, Edward J. Kaiser, and Dale Whittington, at the University of North Carolina at Chapel Hill, with support from the National Science Foundation.

The study is the most comprehensive investigation of public losses in natural disasters yet undertaken. It would have been folly, however, to approach the research as an effort to provide a complete analysis of the public's vulnerability to natural hazards or of all of the ways governments can deal with that problem. Such a goal is illusive under ideal circumstances and is clearly unrealistic given the immense number of issues to be addressed. Instead, our objective has been to provide a carefully conducted study that documents the magnitude and character of public losses in over one hundred and thirty natural disasters, describes a range of policy options for dealing with those losses, and evaluates opportunities for and constraints on innovation and reform in this policy arena.

This book is the product of a collaborative effort by the eight co-authors, who brought to the effort the perspectives—economics, planning, political science, public administration, and public finance—of their respective disciplines. To coordinate our efforts, we jointly developed and shared new data sources—case studies, newly available federal records on losses to public property, and information from national surveys of risk managers and other local government officials—and we met regularly in seminar sessions to discuss the progress of our research and our findings.

Each coauthor took the lead for one or more of the chapters reported here. Raymond J. Burby prepared Chapter 1 on the overall policy framework for the study, Chapter 2 on disaster losses, and Chapter 6 on current policies and practices, and he collaborated in the preparation of the remaining eight chapters. Dana Weist prepared Chapter 4 on financial planning strategies and Edward J. Kaiser Chapter 5 on physical planning strategies. Steven P. French directed the case study of the Whittier Narrows earthquake, reported in Chapter 3, and undertook the work on technical issues in measuring governments' vulnerability to loss, reported in Chapter 7. Dale Whittington developed Chapter 8, which provides an economic perspective and guide to policy choices. Jack Kartez prepared Chapter 9, which analyzes attitudinal factors that ease and also limit governments' ability to cope with natural hazards, and he assisted with the preparation of Chapter 2. Beverly A. Cigler took the lead in preparing Chapter 10, which deals with political and institutional considerations in implementing risk coping strategies. Finally, Dale Roenigk drafted Chapter 11, which pulls together our findings and suggests new directions for public policy.

A number of people have helped us with this study, and we would like to acknowledge their assistance. They include our colleague David Brower of the University of North Carolina Center for Urban and Regional Studies; project research associates Scott Bollens and Robert Paterson; research assistants Lori Glosemeyer Dutra, Timothy West, Philip Averell, Harrison Greene, Christine McIntyre, and Suzanne Aucella; and members of the Center for Urban and Regional Studies administrative and secretarial staff, Carroll Carrozza, Carolyn Jones, and Barbara Rodgers.

Local officials in Los Angeles, Santa Ana, Laguna Beach, Garden Grove, and Orange County, all in California, met with us early in the study and helped shape our understanding of local governments' approaches to and perspectives on losses from natural hazards. Officials serving governments that suffered extensive losses in the Whittier Narrows earthquake of October 1987—Alhambra, Los Angeles, Los Angeles County, Monterey Park, Pasadena, and Whittier—provided a wealth of information about the consequences of that disaster. Hundreds of other local officials responded to our requests for help by returning the mail survey questionnaires we asked them to complete during 1987 and again in 1988. Officials of the Federal Emergency Management Agency and U.S. Department of Transportation have been very thoughtful in helping us retrieve information from federal records on losses to state and local governments in disasters.

An important source of guidance and consultation was made possible by the study's Advisory Committee, drawn from experts in state and local government, risk management, public finance, and public administration. They include: William Anderson, National Science Foundation; Michael Buckley, Government Finance Research Center; Neal Evans, City of Richmond, Virginia; Gerald Hoetmer, International City Management Association; Henry Hulme, Arlington County, Virginia, and American Public Works Association Council on Emergency Management; Howard Kunreuther, University of Pennsylvania; Bradley Jacobs, Orange County, California; Larry Larson, State of Wisconsin; Elliott Mittler, University of Southern California; William Petak, University of Southern California; Lawrence Pierce, Government Finance Research Center; Claire Rubin, George Washington University; Patricia Stahlschmidt, Federal Emergency Management Agency; Frank Thomas, Federal Insurance Administration; James Wright, Tennessee Valley Authority; Larry Zensinger, Federal Emergency Management Agency; and Rae Zimmerman, New York University. While we are grateful for their help, it goes without saying that none of the Advisory Committee members bears responsibility for the findings and opinions expressed here, which are solely those of the authors.

Finally, we would like to acknowledge financial and other aid from the universities with which we have been associated during this study: California State Polytechnic University, San Luis Obispo (French); University of North Carolina at Chapel Hill (Burby, Kaiser, Kartez, Weist, Whittington); North Carolina State University (Cigler); Penn State Harrisburg (Cigler); Stanford University (French); and Washington State University (Kartez). We also thank the National Science Foundation, which supported this work through research grant No. ECE-8517265.

Raymond J. Burby

1

Natural Hazards
and Infrastructure

Every year state and local governments in the United States lose nearly $1 billion as a result of damages to public facilities from floods, hurricanes, earthquakes, and other natural hazards. Most of those losses are not covered by insurance, and most are not absorbed by the federal government through disaster assistance, even though public losses in natural disasters cost the U.S. Treasury hundreds of millions per year.

This book is about policies to ease the perennial hardships states and localities suffer as roads, water and sewer systems, storm drainage, recreational facilities, and other infrastructure important to the lives of their citizens are put out of action by seemingly random acts of nature. State and local governments have four choices. They can continue to assume a majority of the risk of loss, as they do now, and recover from the effects of catastrophic events as best they can using available resources. There are three other choices, however. Two—risk elimination and risk reduction—minimize damages by locating infrastructure out of harm's way (or even abandoning some highly vulnerable locations) or by retrofitting existing facilities (and designing new ones) so they are less susceptible to damage. Those options can reduce losses, but they are expensive. A fourth option involves transferring risk to other levels of government and to the private sector. For very large catastrophic events, a controversial transfer mechanism—federal disaster assistance—is already in place. It covers up to three-fourths of public losses in Presidentially declared disasters. Another means of transferring risk—insurance—is available for some hazards for some classes of infrastructure, but it is used infrequently.

In this book we analyze those state and local policy choices and the federal policies that affect them. We explore the nature of losses governments experience from natural hazards, and we examine in detail each of the four approaches governments can employ to reduce the costs of disasters. In deciding how to cope with losses, governments confront a number of issues, some political, some economic, and others technical. We devote chapters to each of those aspects of risk management. We also explore some basic behavioral factors that in the past have limited individuals' and governments' ability to cope successfully with natural hazards. Thus, our aim is to lay out the choices natural hazards pose for the public sector, identify factors that will affect those choices, and recommend courses of action for consideration by federal, state, and local policy makers.

In this introductory chapter we lay the foundation for the remaining chapters of the book by looking briefly at the magnitude of public losses in natural disasters and the policy issues they pose for the public sector. We show that current policies are flawed in three ways. First, costs are not contained adequately. Second, policies provide insufficient incentives for governments to adopt measures to prevent, or at least minimize, increases in exposure to losses. Third, policies are inequitable, rewarding governments for imprudent behavior and redistributing tax resources from poorer to wealthier states. We conclude this chapter by examining briefly the organization of the book and the ways we address those three issues.

Disasters' Toll on Infrastructure

The problem addressed in this book is serious. Between 1980 and the end of 1985, for example, 145 disasters received Presidential declarations, enabling stricken states and localities to receive federal assistance for disaster recovery and reconstruction. The federal expenditures stemming from those events, summarized in Table 1.1, were substantial, totalling some $4.5 billion. While the lion's share of aid went to the private sector in the form of grants, loans, and federal insurance payouts to individuals and firms, a substantial amount ($1.3 billion) went to state and local governments to help them recover the costs of debris clearance and rebuilding public facilities. Precise measures of losses in disasters of more limited scope (and which did not merit a Presidential disaster declaration) are not available, but one source estimates that national losses annually from such smaller events are three times as large as those experienced in Presidentially declared disasters. (Petak and Atkisson 1982: 244) Over the six-year period summarized by data in Table 1.1, therefore, national infrastructure losses may have been as great as $5 billion.

When disasters strike, many communities experience a number of problems in repairing and reconstructing damaged infrastructure, although in the past substantial outside assistance has enabled most to

TABLE 1.1
Federal Costs Associated with Presidentially Declared
Disasters, January 1, 1980 - December 31, 1985

Federal Program	Aid Provided	% from Each Source
Federal Aid to State and Local Government[a]		
President's Fund (FEMA)	$ 898,620,000	20%
Secretary's Fund (USDOT)	381,122,000	8%
Subtotal	$ 1,279,742,000	28%
Federal Aid to Private Sector[b]		
President's Fund (FEMA)	$ 398,533,000	9%
Other Federal Loans and Grants (SBA/USDA)	1,516,920,000	33%
Flood Insurance Payments (FEMA	1,351,060,000	39%
Subtotal	$ 3,266,513,000	72%
Total Federal Cost of Disasters	$ 4,546,255,000	100%

[a] Does not include a small amount of aid available
through the U.S. Army Corps of Engineers, U.S.
Environmental Protection Agency, and U.S. Department
of Education.

[b] Note that some portion of flood insurance payments
were made to state and local governments to reimburse
them for losses to public buildings; since the
majority of insurance is carried by the private
sector, all flood insurance payments are included
here.

Source: Federal Emergency Management Agency and U.S.
Department of Transportation.

recover fully. The success of long-term recovery efforts has been documented by Wright, Rossi, Wright and Weber-Burdin (1979) and by Friesema, Caporaso, Goldstein, Lineberry, and McCleary (1979). As explained below, however, factors that in the past eased disaster recovery (in particular, 90 to 100 percent federal assumption of losses to state and local public facilities and ready availability of financing for infrastructure at low interest rates) are less likely in the future to aid recovery.

Recent evidence also points to a number of short-term difficulties and hardships communities have encountered in rebuilding damaged public facilities. Rubin, Saperstein and Barbee (1985), for example, studied communities that experienced natural disasters during the late 1970s and early 1980s and found that many had problems finding funds to repair and replace damaged public facilities. May (1985) studied the recovery from the Mount St. Helens disaster and also noted difficulties local governments had experienced with the recovery process. In addition, he documented intergovernmental political problems that resulted when localities looked to state government for help, but found the State of Washington unwilling to meet all of their needs.

The problems states and localities experience in reconstructing public facilities will be magnified in the future by the infrastructure crisis that has drawn national attention over the past decade. According to the report of the National Infrastructure Advisory Committee to the Joint Economic Committee of Congress (1984: 2):

> The United States faces a serious . . . problem related to the condition and adequacy of its basic infrastructure—surface transportation, water supply and distribution, sewage collection and treatment facilities. Nationally a gap exists between anticipated revenues and basic infrastructure needs approaching 450 billion dollars through the year 2000. All states face substantial infrastructure needs and insufficient revenue with which to meet them.

The committee went on to recommend that with considerable uncertainty about the federal role in funding new investment in infrastructure, "state and local governments assume primary responsibility with respect to infrastructure management, financing, and development" (p. 3). In order for states and localities to keep up with infrastructure demands, the committee noted they must make increasing use of new financial mechanisms, including greater reliance on user charges and special dedicated revenue sources (also see American Planning Association 1980). According to Settle (1985: 106), however, "Because of limited tax base and reserves, community governments' options of financing disasters are very restricted."

The Federal Policy Dilemma

Localities' problems in restoring public facilities damaged in floods, hurricanes, earthquakes and other natural disasters pose a dilemma for federal policy makers. On the one hand, state and local governments may need (and almost always demand) assistance in recovering from disasters, and such assistance may be essential to the restoration of lifelines vital to local and regional economies and social well-being. In response to those needs, federal disaster relief has increased substantially over the past four decades. On the other hand, past efforts to aid in recovery and reconstruction have led to charges that federal relief policy is costly (as we've just shown), inefficient (since such aid may encourage governments to ignore hazards in designing and locating public facilities), and inequitable (due to alleged flaws in criteria used to define state and local governments' need for aid). (Comptroller General of the United States 1980, 1982; May and Williams 1986; Petak and Atkisson 1983; White and Haas 1976)

Thus, the federal policy dilemma is this: How can the government meet legitimate needs for assistance, while at the same time it minimizes the drain on the federal treasury, fosters prudent behavior among state and local governments, and distributes aid equitably? Providing an answer to that dilemma is one of the goals of this book. Here we briefly describe the evolution of federal disaster relief policy and examine the basis for the three criticisms—cost, efficiency, and equity—of that policy.

Federal Disaster Relief Policy

Review of federal policy over the past four decades reveals the increasing largess of Congress, mounting costs of relief, and consequent attention in recent years to limiting those costs by encouraging states and localities to adopt loss prevention measures. The history of federal disaster relief legislation, however, shows little Congressional interest in the efficiency or equity effects of federal policy.

The Era of Increasing Federal Largess: 1950–1970

Prior to 1950, individuals and local governments could obtain federal help in recovering from a natural disaster, but aid was distributed only on a case-by-case basis. If victims of natural disasters wanted federal aid, they had to petition the government for assistance through their state or local representatives. Specific Congressional authorizations of aid—128 were enacted between 1800 and 1949—were necessary before federal agencies could help with recovery. The hit-or-miss nature of that system and failure to achieve a timely and coordinated federal response led to reform in 1950.

The Disaster Relief Act of 1950 (PL 81-875; signed September 30, 1950) established a new system for relief—one that bypassed the need for specific Congressional authorizations after every natural catastrophe. Under the new (but now familiar) arrangement, a permanent relief fund (initially only $5 million) was created so that federal agencies could quickly come to the aid of stricken states and local governments. Governors seeking assistance were to petition the President for relief; the federal government would then step in to provide emergency services without Congressional consultation.

But, not much aid was authorized by the 1950 legislation. Federal resources were available only for "making *emergency* repairs to and *temporary* replacements of public facilities damaged or destroyed." (emphasis added). (Senate Report Accompanying HR 8396, The Disaster Relief Act of 1950, Report Number 2571, September 14, 1950) The bill specifically *did not* authorize the permanent restoration of state or local facilities with federal monies and Congressional floor managers took pains to make that point clear. A proposed grant program was dropped by the House Public Works Committee because of its potential cost. Opponents of the grant approach believed permanent reconstruction of public facilities was the responsibility of local authorities. Federal relief was confined solely to "the development of emergency measures for the preservation of life and property." (House Public Works Committee Report on HR 8396, The Disaster Relief Act, Report Number 2571, July 25, 1950)

Only very limited discussion of the need to mitigate or reduce future disaster risks accompanied passage of the 1950 Disaster Relief Act. Congressman Judd of Minnesota noted during House debate on the bill that "the right thing to do is to make preparations in advance . . . rather than wait until the last moment and then try to figure out some sort of improvised relief." (Congressional Record, August 7, 1950: 11899) Generally, however, the Congress was satisfied at that point with establishing a more efficient system for dealing with disasters once they occurred.

The 1970 Disaster Relief Act—passed in the wake of Hurricane Camille in 1969—sharply expanded the federal role in reconstructing public facilities damaged in catastrophic events. Federal support of local public facility rebuilding efforts no longer had to be confined to temporary replacements but could also include the reconstruction of permanent structures. To implement this new approach, the Congress created a federal grant program under Public Law 91-606 (signed December 17, 1970). Communities that had suffered a "substantial" loss of real personal and property tax revenues were eligible for grant assistance for up to three years after a disaster. Grants were limited at most, however, to making up the difference between the communities' average revenues in the three years prior to a disaster and the average revenues after the disaster occurred.

The Emergence of Cost Containment: 1968–1974

While expanding federal aid to states and localities, Congress also began to pay serious attention to the need to contain costs. A start in that direction occurred in 1968 with passage of the National Flood Insurance Act. The insurance program was designed, in part, to shift federal costs for relief to the private sector and state and local government by requiring them to pay insurance premiums and to reduce their exposure to losses by adopting building and land use regulations to prevent flood damages to new construction.

Hazard mitigation efforts were tied to federal disaster relief programs for the first time by the 1970 Disaster Relief Act. Section 221 authorized the President to take action "to avert or lessen the effects of (an imminent) disaster before its actual occurrence." Federal resources could therefore be extended in advance of a formal declaration that a major disaster had occurred. Noted the House Report, "Emphasis (in the act) is properly given to preparedness measures and to the prevention of disasters."

While Congress believed that passage of the Disaster Relief Act of 1970 had set in place a long-term program for disaster assistance, rising program costs—spurred by almost $1 billion in federal relief for the 1971 San Fernando Earthquake and 1972 destruction wrought by the Rapid City flash flood and later in that year by Hurricane Agnes—renewed legislative interest in the program. More directly, however, Congressional concern was sparked in 1972 by allegations that hundreds of fraudulent disaster relief claims had been paid by the Small Business Administration. As a result of the SBA scandal, the Congress called for the President to report in 1973 on ways to improve the program and prevent the misuse of benefits.

Based on that Congressionally mandated study, President Nixon submitted the Disaster Preparedness and Assistance Act to Congress on May 8, 1973. The bill proposed ways to reduce claim fraud, but more importantly, stressed that overall program costs could best be controlled by "protecting people and property against the effects of disaster *before* they occur." To improve disaster mitigation work, the bill specifically proposed to fund state disaster planning grants of $250,000. Although comprehensive revision of the federal disaster program was not to come until the next year, the mitigation emphasis of the Nixon bill clearly drove Congressional efforts to craft new disaster relief legislation in the 93rd Congress.

Favorable consideration of Nixon's disaster mitigation concept was also eased by concurrent Congressional debate on revisions to the 1968 National Flood Insurance Act (NFIA). In Senate Housing and Urban Affairs Subcommittee hearings on the NFIA in June, 1983, for example, Administration witnesses such as Federal Insurance Administrator George K. Bernstein stressed the importance of requiring improved land use regulations as part of the Act's core revisions. Other influential witnesses, such as John Sammon of the National Association of Realtors, broadened the debate by recommending that land use controls be linked to all aspects of the federal disaster relief program. The Congress, said Sammon, should "make disaster relief policy congruous with land use policy, and in particular coordinate any disaster relief legislation with the closely related land use legislation now before the Senate."

That is precisely what the Congress did in 1974. The 1974 Disaster Relief Act (PL 93-288) made it easier for states and local communities to receive disaster assistance, and it fostered loss prevention. Eligible states or local communities could choose to receive 100 percent of the cost of rebuilding facilities on a project-by-project basis or to receive a block grant of 90 percent of the estimated cost of total public facility damage in the entire locality. Grants were also made available, for the first time, to rebuild educational and recreational facilities. Construction cost estimates for either option were to be made by the federal government, however, to provide an element of cost control.

To further control costs, Congress stipulated (under Section 314) that states and local governments obtain insurance adequate to protect against future loss for any disaster-damaged property that had been "replaced, restored, repaired, or constructed with federal disaster funds." Without such insurance, no public applicant for federal assistance could receive aid for any future disaster-related damage.

The 1974 amendments contained several provisions designed to promote loss prevention, reflecting Congressional intent in Section 101 (b)(5) to "encourage hazard mitigation measures to reduce losses from disasters, including the development of land use and construction regulations." These provisions largely paralleled those first outlined in the Senate bill, S.3062. S.3062 had been developed by the Senate Public Works Committee following extensive field hearings that looked at the rebuilding effort in Mississippi necessitated by Hurricane Camille. After witnesses at those hearings pointed out the relationship between unwise development and hurricane vulnerability, the Committee added language encouraging hazard mitigation planning and improved land use and construction practices. These measures—supported by the Red Cross— were eventually adopted by the Congress as a whole.

Section 201 (b), for example, directed the President to "provide technical assistance to States . . . for hazard reduction, avoidance and mitigation." An additional impetus to state and local mitigation efforts was added when House and Senate conferees included language that allowed states to use their $250,000 state disaster planning grant (authorized in Section 201 (c) of the bill) for "disaster prevention" planning—as well as emergency response planning. Thus, the 1974 bill came to closely reflect the earlier Nixon proposal from 1973. The heart of the bill's emphasis on disaster mitigation, however, was contained in Section 406, which stated, "As a condition of any disaster loan or grant made under the provisions of this Act . . . the State or local government shall agree that the natural hazards in the areas . . . shall be evaluated and appropriate action shall be taken to mitigate such hazards, including safe land use and construction practices."

The Cost Containment Issue

In the fifteen years since passage of the 1974 disaster relief bill, succeeding administrations have tackled the job of implementing the intent of the legislation to control costs. Federal policy makers have attempted to limit liability for disaster assistance in four ways: by establishing eligibility criteria for receiving disaster relief, by requiring cost sharing by state and local governments, by tying relief to requirements for state and local adoption of loss prevention measures, and by shifting some costs from the federal government to state and local governments and the private sector through the National Flood Insurance Program. Each of those efforts has been controversial. Whether they have been successful or not is examined later in this book in Chapters 2 and 6.

While making it easier for state and local governments to obtain federal disaster relief to rebuild damaged infrastructure, the 1974 disaster relief legislation reasserted the principle, first established with the 1950 relief act, that federal aid should be supplementary in nature. That is, the federal role is to supplement, not supplant, state and local government resources in responding to disasters. Accordingly, one way the federal government has limited its exposure to disaster relief costs is by providing aid only in those cases where states and localities cannot recover satisfactorily on their own. It does that in two ways: by limiting initial eligibility for aid to only those communities that suffer losses in a major, Presidentially declared disaster and by requiring state and local governments to share in the costs of restoring and reconstructing damaged public facilities. Controversy has centered on the criteria the government uses for determining what level of losses and local incapacity to recover merit a Presidential disaster declaration and on the appropriate extent of state and local cost sharing.

Disaster Declaration Criteria

About four of every ten requests by governors for Presidential disaster declarations are denied by the Federal Emergency Management Agency, which administers the disaster relief program. (Comptroller General of the United States 1981) In deciding whether a disaster worthy of federal assistance has, in fact, occurred and a Presidential declaration should be made, FEMA takes into account a variety of factors, such as the extent of damages, prior disaster history, existence of surplus state funds, and threats to public health and safety, which it weighs subjectively on a case-by-case basis. In December of 1981, the opaque nature of that decision process led the General Accounting Office to criticize FEMA for apparent inconsistencies in deciding which disasters merited federal aid. (Comptroller General of the United States 1981) FEMA responded by trying to standardize the background data it received from states seeking a disaster declaration and by establishing uniform procedures for gauging state and local governments' fiscal capacity to recover without federal aid. Based on an analysis of per capita income, FEMA concluded that state governments could afford disaster response and recovery costs of about $1 per resident (approximately one-tenth of one percent of the estimated General Fund expenditures of the states) for disaster response and recovery, and it suggested losses of that magnitude, adjusted by the ratio of the state's per capita income to average per capita income in the nation, be used as a criterion for federal disaster declarations. (Settle 1990) When the agency presented that proposal to Congress, however, it was strongly opposed by state and local officials and was rejected. Thus, the determination of what constitutes a disaster continues to be based on the subjective judgment of federal officials.

Cost Sharing

Presidential disaster declarations make aid available for losses within counties defined as disaster areas. In keeping with the supplemental intent of federal disaster assistance legislation, FEMA had to establish criteria for determining what portion of losses within those areas is within the fiscal capacity of state and local governments and what portion is to be borne by the federal government. The law itself provided little guidance about that, requiring only that states and affected local governments commit a "reasonable" amount of their funds to disaster response and recovery. FEMA's initial approach was to require states, as a condition for receiving federal aid, to enter into a Federal-State agreement about cost sharing and to negotiate the state and local share on a case-by-case basis. Because of difficulties in securing what it considered to be adequate commitments from the states, the agency changed that approach beginning with the Mt. St. Helens disaster, for which it limited federal assistance to 75 percent of eligible costs for debris removal and reconstruction of public facilities. As might be expected, that cost-sharing requirement has drawn considerable criticism from state and local governments, who believe that limitations on what FEMA defines as an eligible expense already require them to shoulder a large share of the burden of natural disasters. (Comptroller General of the United States 1981)

By limiting aid to large disasters and requiring cost sharing the federal government has reduced expenditures on disaster relief from what they might otherwise have been, but as summarized in Table 1.1 earlier, those costs are still substantial. After passage of the Gramm-Rudman-Hollings anti-deficit law in 1985, FEMA again looked for ways to reduce the federal burden of disaster relief costs. In 1986, the agency proposed reducing the federal contribution to state and local governments from 75 percent to about 50 percent of total eligible costs by instituting a deductible provision in which aid would not become available to states until losses exceeded $1 per capita and to local governments until losses exceeded $2.50 per capita. For losses greater than the deductible amount, FEMA proposed to pay for 75 percent of eligible costs for losses up to $10 per capita, and (to ease financial burdens on the most hard-hit localities) 90 percent of eligible costs for losses over that amount. (Settle 1990) That proposal fared no better in Congress, however, and in 1988 amendments to the disaster relief legislation (the Stafford Act) Congress cemented 75 percent federal cost sharing into law.

The failure of FEMA's attempts at reform leaves open the question of what constitutes a real need for assistance among states and localities and what level of cost sharing can be required without creating local hardships. In the research reported in this book, we provide some answers to that question based on our estimates of individuals' willingness to bear losses and also on local governments' own statements about what levels of loss would be beyond their capacity to respond. Comparison of those estimates with actual losses experienced indicates that many state agencies and local governments are receiving federal aid they probably do not need to recover adequately from natural disasters. Thus, in our opinion federal disaster relief costs could be cut drastically with little adverse effect on local governments or their citizens.

Hazard Mitigation Requirements

While balking over increased state and local cost-sharing, the Congress has had little difficulty buying the proposition that hazard mitigation measures should be fostered to contain losses and consequent federal relief expenditures. That comes through clearly in the hazard mitigation planning assistance provisions of the 1974 disaster relief legislation, and it is reflected in the support FEMA has received for subsequent efforts to implement those provisions. To increase states' attention to hazard mitigation planning, the agency uses the Federal/State Disaster Assistance Agreement as a lever. States that want federal aid have to agree to develop and implement hazard mitigation plans for the disaster-stricken areas where the aid will be applied. To increase localities' attention to mitigation, in July 1980 FEMA secured interagency agreements for the formation, after every flood disaster, of Interagency Hazard Mitigation Task Forces that would work with local governments to identify hazard mitigation needs.

In 1982 concern for continuing losses to infrastructure in hurricanes (see Sheaffer and Rozaklis 1980) led Congress to enact the Coastal Barrier Resources Act, which prohibited federal aid, including disaster assistance and flood insurance, to development on designated barrier islands. Most recently, in the 1988 Stafford Act Congress added additional inducements for local adoption of mitigation measures. In Section 409 it required localities, as a condition for receiving disaster assistance, to evaluate hazards and take appropriate actions to mitigate them. In Section 404, it authorized the use of up to 10 percent of federal disaster assistance funds for 50/50 matching grants to localities for projects to prevent future losses.

The issue with hazard mitigation is thus not with Congressional intent or federal agency willingness to foster mitigation, rather it is with state and local governments' willingness to comply with that federal mandate. In 1982, for example, the General Accounting Office reported,

> State government officials told us that although hazard mitigation plans have been prepared under various initiatives, the long-term prospects for implementing effective hazard mitigation measures are limited . . . only limited resources are available for implementing recommendations resulting from such plans. They believe that to make an substantial long-term progress, FEMA or some other Federal agency will have to provide Federal funds. (Comptroller General of the United States 1982)

New funding made available through provisions of the Stafford Act may help overcome the financial barriers to mitigation discovered by the GAO, but a number of other issues remain open.

The most basic hinges on the shared governance characteristics of hazard mitigation and the federal policy dilemma that presents. That is, to reduce losses federal policy must affect not only federal agencies' behavior but also the behavior of states and localities. The dilemma arises because while federal officials may believe that mitigation is important, local governments frequently do not (e.g., see Burby and French et al. 1985; Drabek 1986; Nilson and Nilson 1981; Rossi et al. 1982; and Turner et al. 1980). May and Williams, who studied the shared governance dilemma, put it this way,

> The indirect influence of federal policy over subnational governments and individuals presents an implementation dilemma for hazard mitigation and preparedness policies. On the one hand, federal officials have a strong stake in promoting hazard mitigation and preparedness but little direct control over the effectiveness of such efforts. On the other hand, in the aggregate, subnational governments and individuals owning property in hazardous areas directly control the effectiveness of mitigation and preparedness policies, but for the most part actions consistent with such policies are low on their list of priorities. (May and Williams 1986)

To date, federal policy has dealt with this dilemma by mandating mitigation through eligibility criteria for disaster assistance and for participation in the National Flood Insurance Program, and by offering to share some costs for mitigation work after a disaster. Those approaches have inherent weaknesses. Tying mitigation requirements to disaster assistance has the advantage of imposing the mitigation mandate when, after a disaster, mitigation should be most salient to local officials. But, that does little to foster mitigation among the thousands of local governments that have not experienced a disaster. Furthermore, research indicates that the ability of a disaster to heighten the political salience of mitigation is short-lived; thus, it may do little to stimulate sustained attention to mitigation. Mitigation requirements related to the NFIP have two weaknesses: They apply only to new construction and existing structures damaged more than 50 percent in a disaster, and they apply only to public buildings, which we show in Chapter 2 account for only a small portion of public facility losses in most disasters.

In this book we document local governments' past inattention to hazard mitigation, adding substantial new data to previous hearsay evidence (such as that gathered by the GAO) of local neglect. We systematically analyzed those data to identify factors—including present federal policy—associated with local attention to mitigation. By explaining scientifically why some governments pay attention to mitigation while most ignore it, we provide clues for finding a truly effective solution to this important federal policy dilemma.

Insurance

Insurance provides a fourth way—in addition to disaster declaration procedures, cost sharing criteria, and hazard mitigation requirements—for containing federal disaster relief costs. If losses to state and local infrastructure are covered by insurance, obviously federal liability for disaster losses will be reduced accordingly. With that in mind, the Disaster Relief Act of 1974 stipulated that localities could receive federal aid once for flood losses to uninsured structures, but after that any future insurable losses would not be eligible for federal aid. That "first bite free" policy was eliminated by the 1988 Stafford Act, which provided that flood losses that could have been covered by insurance would not be reimbursed through federal disaster relief.

In this book we question whether federal requirements for insurance are likely to have the desired effect. Specifically, we provide evidence that a number of disaster-stricken governments failed to comply with the 1974 relief act requirement that they buy insurance. If disaster-stricken governments that had used up their "one free bite" did not purchase insurance, there is little likelihood that taking away that free bite will affect the behavior of governments that have not experienced a disaster. While demonstrating the likely ineffectiveness of present policy, however, we also point out steps the government can take to make insurance a more effective cost-containment device.

We also document a number of limitations of insurance, as presently available, as a cost containment tool, beyond the issue of localities' failure to insure themselves adequately. In particular, by disaggregating infrastructure losses into their component parts, we show that available insurance (flood and earthquake insurance for public buildings) would cover only a small portion—less than 5 percent—of state and local government losses. Thus, even with 100 percent local government subscription to insurance, federal disaster relief costs would not be affected substantially.

The limitations of the present approaches to disaster insurance raise the question, which we address in this book, of whether the federal government should extend the flood insurance program so that it addresses a full array of natural hazards and so that it covers not just buildings but all infrastructure at risk in natural disasters. The U.S. General Accounting Office has argued for such an approach, stating its belief that,

Insurance is the most efficient and equitable method of providing disaster assistance . . . insurance programs are inherently more consistent over time than loans, whose availability is triggered by, and whose terms are the result of, political decisions. Thus, the principles that should guide formulating disaster policy indicate that both in theory and in practice insurance is more appropriate than loans and grants. In practice, insurance produces lower differences in incomes and wealth distribution among victims and between victims and taxpayers. (Comptroller General of the United States 1980)

Insurance, as a substitute for disaster assistance, has been argued for by other disaster policy analysts as well. Petak and Atkisson (1982), for example, note several advantages of insurance over a relief program: it provides assurance to participants that their losses will be covered and thus avoids the uncertainties of the federal disaster declaration process; it should stimulate policyholders' attention to risk reduction, since that should result in reduced premiums; it should improve equity (see below), since governments with similar risks will be treated in a similar manner; and it should be easier to administer than disaster relief.

More recently, the U.S. insurance industry, concerned about its exposure to losses from a catastrophic earthquake, has proposed expansion of the National Flood Insurance Program to cover earthquake hazards through the creation of a Federal Catastrophic Insurance and Reinsurance Corporation. Because of its uncertain fiscal consequences, however, that proposal has yet to advance very far in the Congress.

Summary of Cost Containment Issues

Efforts to contain the escalation in federal disaster relief costs thus have taken a number of tacks, each of which has serious limitations. The extent to which states and local governments should bear responsibility for such costs is still unclear, but further efforts to require greater local cost sharing, although logical, seem doomed politically. Cost reduction through hazard mitigation has fared better politically at the federal level, but mitigation suffers from an apparent lack of state and local political viability. Insurance, which many argue is a preferable alternative to disaster relief, is undersubscribed by local governments and, for many types of infrastructure at risk in natural disasters, is simply unavailable. In this book, we examine those limitations and other barriers to effective federal policy for dealing with the consequences of natural disasters for state and local government infrastructure. Based on that analysis, we suggest a number of revisions in current policies that should improve their performance.

Efficiency and Equity Issues

The two other federal policy issues examined in this book—inefficiency and inequity—have received less attention from Congress than the cost containment questions just considered. Nevertheless, they too bear close examination.

The inefficiency issue is this: provision of disaster assistance may lead decision makers to ignore hazards in deciding where to locate public facilities, and it may also hinder the adoption of mitigation measures and purchase of insurance. Kunreuther (1974) noted, for example, that federal aid reduced incentives for persons who suffered losses in the Alaska earthquake of 1964 to take steps to protect themselves from future losses. As a result, vulnerability to loss after reconstruction was in many cases as great as before the earthquake. Similarly, White (1974) noted,

> If victims of a disaster were forced to bear the costs themselves, it has been shown . . . that they would have a larger incentive to protect themselves against future catastrophes. Current federal policy encourages individuals not only to continue to ignore these events in future but actually to take steps to profit from the next earthquake or flood.

Whether conclusions based on studies of individuals' adjustments to natural hazards can be generalized to local governments is explored in this book.

The answer is obviously important. If federal relief policy is leading to inefficiencies in facility location and design, then steps should be taken to counteract that effect. To some degree, in fact, the federal government has been doing just that. The Interagency Hazard Mitigation Task Forces assembled by FEMA following disasters, for example, should stimulate local governments' attention to mitigation and may minimize the tendency noted by Kurnreuther and White for relief to hinder mitigation work. We looked at that and found that the task forces were having some effect, which to us indicates that their use should be continued and expanded. The Stafford Act's repeal of the previous "first bite free" policy and refusal to extend aid to uninsured structures also is designed, in part, to counteract the adverse effects of relief—in this case on insurance coverage. As we noted above, however, we don't believe that new policy will be very effective.

The equity issue has been raised by Petak and Atkisson (1982). They note that disaster relief can be inequitable to the extent that individuals and governments living in areas that receive Presidential disaster declarations receive aid, while similarly situated people and governments in other areas, who may experience just as great a loss from a flood or other natural hazard, do not receive aid. We examined that issue in the research for this book and found that there is much to it: a number of local governments—more often than not located in sparsely populated rural areas—have experienced sizable losses in disasters that affect only a small area and do not result in a Presidential disaster declaration. We thought that experiencing such an event would lead governments to adopt more self-protective measures than were being adopted by governments that received federal aid, but that hasn't occurred. Thus, governments in disaster stricken areas that do not receive Presidential disaster declarations are losing in two ways: they get little or no help with recovery, and their vulnerability to loss from future disasters generally remains high. In this book we address that problem and suggest revisions in federal policy to deal with it.

The equity issue has another dimension as well. Disaster relief and tax deductions of losses experienced in natural disasters represent a massive transfer of income—estimated at from $2.7 to $5.8 billion annually in 1970 dollars by Petak and Atkisson (1982)—from people who have not exposed themselves to hazards to those who were less prudent in their choice of locations. To the extent that people and governments are benefiting from hazardous locations and federal relief and tax policy allows them to avoid paying for those benefits, those policies are inequitable. Insurance has been proposed as one way of improving equity, since costs to beneficiaries in the form of insurance premiums are proportional to the degree of the hazard to which they have exposed themselves. But, insurance on private buildings does not compensate local governments for many of the social costs of disasters, such as losses to infrastructure, and it will not improve equity if it is not available or not used. In this book we show that those problems limit the present use of insurance to right inequities in federal policy, and we suggest ways that insurance could be used more effectively in the future.

The State and Local Policy Dilemma

To this point we have focused on a number of issues facing federal policy makers as they try to cope successfully with the threats to infrastructure posed by natural hazards. Local officials face an equally serious policy dilemma, since in the end it is their property that is damaged in natural disasters and their constituents that suffer from those losses. The local dilemma, termed the "land use management paradox" by Burby and French (1981), is this: until local exposure to losses in natural disasters becomes serious, traditional regulatory approaches to hazard mitigation, such as building standards and zoning, lack sufficient political salience to be enacted. After localities have allowed a hazardous situation to develop and the adoption of such measures becomes politically feasible, however, the measures no longer work very well. They are preventive in nature and do not do much to reduce losses to development after it has occurred.

Federal mandates requiring local adoption of hazard mitigation measures, such as the eligibility requirements attached to the National Flood Insurance Program, can help local policy makers resolve that dilemma, but those mandates have limitations. They include localities' frequent failure to employ appropriate (e.g., remedial and well as preventive) land use management measures (Burby and French 1981); less than complete implementation of federally mandated regulations by local government (Hutton et al 1979); difficulties in enforcing federal standards (Comptroller General of the United States 1975; 1982); and the continued susceptibility of development to hazardous events that exceed normally accepted and utilized design standards (Sheaffer et al. 1976 estimate such storms account for over two-thirds of national flood losses). Certainly one key additional factor is an imbalance in the incentives and disincentives for development in hazardous locations. As long as much of the social cost of location in hazardous areas is borne by the public sector through subsidized insurance programs, disaster relief programs, and engineering structures funded from general tax revenues, there is a built in incentive for property owners to make economically unwarranted use of hazardous locations and to evade regulatory requirements.

A number of observers have argued that the next step in the management of hazardous areas must be the employment of measures that, while allowing continued use of hazardous areas where such use is economically beneficial, internalize more of the social costs associated with such locations so that property owners and developers make efficient choices regarding the location and design of new development (for expressions of this viewpoint see Slovic, Kunreuther and White 1974; James 1977; and Milliman 1983). That was one of the basic rationales for the National Flood Insurance Program (Task Force on Federal Flood Control Policy 1966), but the need to subsidize insurance for existing development, the establishment of insurance rates in coastal areas that, until recently, did not reflect the true likelihood of experiencing losses, and the failure to insure the infrastructure associated with new development have all served to diminish the intended economic efficiency effects of that program.

If local governments can assume increased responsibility for funding losses to infrastructure from natural disasters, that would help correct observed deficiencies of the flood insurance program, and it would internalize more of the social costs of hazards such as earthquakes and landslides that are not covered by national insurance programs. In addition, if increased requirements for local funding of disaster losses led localities to shove those costs back onto the beneficiaries of hazardous locations—for example, through the use of benefit assessment districts or other devices—that might improve the effectiveness of existing regulatory-based hazard management programs as well. Baker and McPhee's (1975: 112) work on the use of land use management measures in hazard mitigation noted that public finance policy should be employed more frequently in managing hazard area development. According to Thomas (1983: 163–168), "Properly conceived, tax laws could promote sound planning for flood-prone lands with a minimum of public expense and legal uncertainty," but, although "we routinely couple financial incentives and disincentives with a number of land-use regulations, . . . we have not explored adequately how tax policies can be used best to mitigate damages."

In this book we show how local governments can assume more responsibility for managing the risk to infrastructure from natural hazards, and, finding that few local governments, in fact, are using those methods, we analyze the effects of current federal policies and additional technical, economic, and political factors that affect the feasibility of the new approach to local hazard management we advocate. Basically, we argue that obstacles do exist, but that they can be overcome. We show how localities can deal with various problems that in the past have limited their ability to deal effectively with losses to infrastructure, and we show what the federal government can do to help. Thus, our attention to federal policy has two elements. We address the cost containment, efficiency and equity issues discussed earlier in this chapter, and we also address what federal policy makers can do to help local governments be more effective partners in stemming disasters' annual toll on public facilities of all types.

A Look Ahead

The book has four parts. In Part 1 we establish the magnitude of public sector losses in natural disasters and answer the question: "What is a disaster to local governments?" Chapter 2 uses newly obtained data from federal records to dissect local governments' loss experiences during the seven-year period from January 1, 1980, through mid-1987. We show who lost what due to what types of disaster agents, we analyze the extent to which those losses truly constituted a "disaster" for stricken local governments, and we document a number of flaws in current federal insurance and disaster relief policies. Many governments, for example, suffer loses that can't be covered by insurance and many receive federal aid for trivial losses they easily could cover from already budgeted contingency funds. The illogic of federal policy and hardships that creates for local governments is emphasized even more in Chapter 3, where we use data from a case study of the October 1987 Whittier Narrows earthquake to demonstrate the wide variation in losses nearby governments experience in a large Presidentially declared disaster. As currently written, federal disaster relief legislation treated each of those governments equally. We show, however, that their needs were not equal and that much more cost sharing may occur in a disaster than meets the eye. That is, while federal policy pegs the federal share of relief costs at three quarters of the damage experienced, in practice the federal share may be much less. Thus, while some governments receive aid they don't need, others may not receive nearly enough help in recovering from a disaster.

Part 2 has two purposes. One, developed in Chapters 4 and 5, is to present a course of action local governments can take to assume greater responsibility for protecting themselves from the threats to infrastructure posed by natural hazards. The second, presented in chapter 6, is to evaluate the impact of federal policies on local governments' adoption of protective measures. In Chapter 4 we describe five financial strategies available to local government: risk identification, risk elimination, risk reduction, risk assumption, and risk transfer. In Chapter 5 we show how a number of the financial strategies we propose can be linked to a community planning program, which provide one avenue for easing their adoption. In Chapter 6 we use a comparative survey of local governments—some of which experienced disasters and received federal aid, some of which experienced disasters and were denied aid, and some of which have yet to experience a disaster—to examine the extent to which disaster relief and other federal policies have stimulated or stifled local governments' efforts to cope on their own with natural hazards.

Part 3 of the book raises and evaluates four sets of issues—with a chapter devoted to each—that must be resolved before progress toward local adoption of the risk management strategies we advocate can occur. Chapter 7 examines the technical feasibility of identifying and evaluating the risk of loss to public facilities. Chapter 8 takes a hard look at whether it is rational, from an economic perspective, for local governments or the federal government to bear the lion's share of losses in natural disasters. Chapter 9 reports on local officials' willingness to insure against losses from floods and earthquakes and at their attitudes toward other policies we propose. Chapter 10 looks at those policies in the context of the shared governance that characterizes our federal system and the obstacles that poses to strategies that depend on intergovernmental cooperation.

In Part 4 (Chapter 11) we conclude our analysis of catastrophic losses to public property. We summarize the constraints to reform revealed by the preceding chapters and propose changes in federal and state policies that seem necessary if the nation is to address public losses from natural hazards in a more efficient and equitable manner.

PART 1

Public Losses
Under the Microscope

2

Losses to the Public Sector in Natural Disasters

In 1980 the net stock of fixed assets (structures and equipment) owned by state and local governments in the United States totalled over $2,034.8 billion. New investment is increasing that stock at the rate of about 3 percent per year. (U. S. Bureau of the Census 1983: Table No. 455) Every year, however, state and local governments lose hundreds of millions of dollars in public property damaged as a result of floods, hurricanes, earthquakes and other natural disasters. In this chapter, we use newly assembled data from federal records and our own survey research to look more closely at the nature of those losses and how governments recover from them. Prior to this research, only sketchy information has been available about public losses in natural disasters. As a result, the formulation of policies to deal with disasters has occurred in an information vacuum.

Specifically, in this chapter we examine eight sets of questions:

1. What is the magnitude of losses to the public sector in natural disasters? Are losses large enough in the aggregate to warrant national concern about them? Are losses widely distributed enough among state and local governments to generate support among those governments for risk management measures?
2. What proportion of losses result from repetitive events (disasters striking more than once in the same community)? Are repetitive losses high enough to suggest that retrofitting infrastructure to make it more loss-resistant would be a prudent course of action?
3. To what degree are different types of state and local government infrastructure—buildings, roads, drainage, utilities, parks—being damaged by natural hazards? Does the locus of losses suggest that public policy should focus on one or another type of infrastructure?

To what extent are the types of infrastructure damaged insurable against such losses?

4. Who owns infrastructure damaged in natural disasters—state government, cities, counties, special districts? How are damages distributed among those governmental units? Do states or do localities bear the greatest share of losses attributable to natural disasters? What do ownership patterns imply for loss mitigation policy?

5. What sources of funds have state and local governments used to finance losses they have incurred in natural disasters? In disasters which receive a Presidential declaration, the federal government provides funds to cover approximately 75 percent of eligible losses to public property. But, how is the remainder paid for? Are localities borrowing to cover their share of the losses, or can they be met from funds on hand? What does that imply for federal disaster relief policy?

6. To what extent are losses experienced by local governments truly "disastrous" to those governmental units? What, in fact, is a disastrous loss? How many governments experience such losses? What does that imply for federal efforts to contain relief expenditures?

7. To what extent is federal disaster aid being distributed in an equitable manner? Are similarly situated local governments receiving similar amounts of federal assistance?

8. To what extent is federal disaster assistance being distributed in an efficient manner? What proportion of losses covered are large enough to warrant the expense of distributing aid?

In answering those questions, we address many of the policy issues raised in Chapter 1, while at the same time we provide readers with a better understanding of the nature of public sector losses in natural disasters.

Sources of Data

We tapped a number of sources of data to answer the questions posed in this chapter. Specifically, data on losses to the public sector in natural disasters prior to 1980 were obtained from a search of previous literature on disaster losses; data on disaster losses since 1980 were obtained from unpublished records of the Federal Emergency Management Agency and U.S. Department of Transportation. Data on sources of funding for local recovery came from a survey of disaster-stricken localities we conducted in 1987. Data on local officials' perceptions of losses and the meaning of the term "disaster," as well as information on the equity of federal relief policy came from a second survey we conducted during the summer of 1988. That survey obtained data from three groups of local government officials: one group served governments that experienced a disaster during the 1980s and received federal aid; a second group served governments that experienced a disaster and did not receive federal aid; and the third group served governments that had not experienced a disaster during the 1980s. Each data collection procedure is described briefly.

Data on Public Sector Losses in Natural Disasters Since 1980

Unpublished records of the Federal Emergency Management Agency provided information to measure losses to the public sector in natural disasters that received Presidential disaster declarations and in some smaller events that were denied federal assistance. FEMA provided us with a computer tape containing over 20,000 logical records for federal disaster assistance obligations incurred as a result of 131 Presidentially declared natural disasters during the seven and one-half years from January 1, 1980, through July 31, 1987.[1] Those disasters included earthquakes, floods, hurricanes, landslides, and various combinations of those disaster agents.

Our data do not include losses from tornadoes, which account for about 20 percent of expected average annual losses in natural disasters (Petak and Atkisson 1982: 208). In addition, the data do not include damages from an extremely large (e.g., 7.9 or greater on the Richter scale) earthquake in California (which did not occur during the period studied), and they do not include losses not eligible for federal assistance. Thus, our total loss data are conservative. They understate damages by about 20 percent because of the exclusion of tornado losses, they do not include some losses the federal government refuses to reimburse, and they understate potential damages by some unknown amount because a catastrophic earthquake did not occur during the period studied. Nevertheless, the data do tell us a lot about the nature and distribution of losses that, year in and year out, are typical of the disaster experience of state and local governments across the United States.

The FEMA data tape provided a separate record for each of nine categories of loss incurred by each government within the 131 designated multi-county disaster areas. For example, the loss data for a government that experienced damages to roads (Category C), public buildings (Category E), and public utilities (Category F) were provided on three separate records, one for each category of loss. We reorganized those data on individual obligations, sorting them by recipient governmental units (N = 8,380), so that the losses experienced by those governments could be analyzed.

The data obtained from FEMA include all public-sector losses funded by the President's Disaster Assistance Fund; public costs of disasters not covered by that fund are losses to federal aid highways (recovery is financed by the U.S. Department of Transportation), schools (recovery is financed by the U.S. Department of Education), and some emergency flood fighting aid provided by the U.S. Army Corps of Engineers and U.S. Soil Conservation Service. Data on losses to federal-aid highways were obtained from the U.S. Department of Transportation, which gave us computer data files of losses reported by state highway departments and funded by DOT between 1980 and mid-1987. The Department of Education, Corps of Engineers, and Soil Conservation Service do not maintain computerized files of disaster assistance, and, therefore, we could not obtain accurate data from those agencies. Agency officials, however, indicated that their expenditures on disaster relief were not large in comparison to costs borne by the Federal Emergency Management Agency and U.S. Department of Transportation.

Data on Sources of Funds
Used to Recover from Disasters

We obtained information on local governments' sources of funding for disaster recovery from a random samples of 189 city and county public works departments in metropolitan cities and counties that experienced a Presidentially declared natural disaster between 1980 and 1986 and from 159 city and county finance and risk management offices, in the same sample of metropolitan localities. The local government surveys were undertaken in the spring of 1987. The nine-page public works questionnaire was returned by 49 percent of the public works departments we queried (189 responses from 389 agencies surveyed) and the thirteen-page risk management questionnaire was returned by 41 percent of the finance/risk management departments queried (159 of 389 agencies surveyed). Copies of the survey instruments are provided in Appendix B.

Data on Local Officials' Perceptions of Disasters

To answer questions related to the amount of losses that truly constitute a disaster from the perspective of local officials and to explore issues related to disaster mitigation and recovery policy, we conducted a second survey during the summer of 1988. In this case, we obtained data from local officials serving three groups of local governments: 133 cities that experienced a disaster between 1980 and 1986 and did not receive federal disaster assistance; 178 cities that experienced a disaster during that period and did receive federal aid; and 170 cities that had not experienced a natural disaster during the 1980s. The response rate for this survey was 60 percent (481 of 800 jurisdictions surveyed). A copy of the survey instrument is provided in Appendix C.

The Magnitude of Losses

The data assembled on losses to the public sector from all sources show that the problems disasters create are both large and widespread. Losses to state and local governments in Presidentially declared earthquake, flood and hurricane disasters from January 1, 1980, through July 1987 were almost $1.8 billion. Those losses are lower than those estimated in previous decades, but they are nevertheless substantial. Over six thousand state agencies and local governments, located in 45 of the 50 states, experienced losses in Presidentially declared disasters over that seven-and-a-half-year period. We estimate during the same period state and local governments lost an additional $5.4 billion in smaller disasters that did not merit a Presidential declaration. Thus, the answer to the first question posed in this chapter is clear: public losses in natural disasters are a serious problem, that problem is shared widely, and its resolution should be an important concern of the federal government, states, and localities.

Losses to the Public Sector
in Natural Disasters Prior to 1980

Prior to the formation of the Federal Emergency Management Agency in 1979, no agency of government maintained detailed records of losses the public sector experienced in natural disasters. Nevertheless, some data are available on the amount and nature of disaster losses to public property before the initiation of detailed federal record keeping.

Dacy and Kunreuther (1969: 50–51), for example, surveyed eight disasters occurring in the 1950s and 1960s and found that damage to public facilities accounted for from 7 percent to 75 percent (median of 25 percent) of total damages experienced. Sheaffer et al. (1976: 24) calculated average annual flood damages to infrastructure (highways, bridges, culverts, water supply and sewerage systems, but not public buildings) at about 25 percent of total damages from flooding in urban areas. In a later study of 23 communities, they estimated that flood losses to public facilities (again excluding public buildings) would average about 16 percent of total losses (Sheaffer and Roland, Inc. 1981: 113). Finally, Petak and Atkisson (1982: 243) estimated expected (based on exposure levels) losses to public facilities (including public buildings) in 1970 from earthquakes, hurricanes, wind, landslides, riverine flooding, storm surge, tsunami, and tornadoes) at almost $2 billion. That estimate includes all loss events; they estimated that losses in Presidentially declared disasters would be about a quarter of that total or $500 million per year. Thus, prior to 1980 it appears that public-sector losses accounted for about one quarter of all losses experienced in natural disasters and, based on Petak and Atkisson's (1982) estimates, that public sector losses in Presidentially declared disasters could have been as large as $500 million per year in 1970 dollars.

Losses to the Public Sector in Disasters: 1980–1987

Losses from the 131 Presidentially declared disasters we examined are summarized, by state, in Table 2.1.[2] The distributions of losses among states and across disaster-stricken local governments within states are highly skewed. Fifty-seven percent of the losses we identified fell on just five states—California, West Virginia, Utah, New York, and Connecticut. The first three of those experienced serious flooding, while New York and Connecticut experienced large losses from hurricanes. California, with a high level of vulnerability to floods, earthquakes, and landslides, had nine Presidentially declared natural disasters and absorbed more than a third of national losses. At the opposite end of the spectrum, five states and several Pacific island territories had no losses.

Over 500 governmental units experienced extremely large losses of $500,000 or more, and over 1,800 had serious but less severe losses of between $50,000 and $500,000. For two thirds of the governments with loss events (and that received federal disaster assistance), however, the magnitude of the loss was under $50,000, and in 22 percent of the cases the loss was under $5,000. We look at the implications of those small losses for the efficiency of federal disaster relief at a later point in this chapter and again in Chapter 8.

Losses from Repetitive Events

A small proportion (22 percent) of state and local governmental units experienced losses in more than one Presidentially declared disaster (multiple loss events). Those governments, however, account for a majority (57 percent) of the total losses that occurred over the seven-and-one-half-year period we studied. (See Table 2.2.) That high concentration of repetitive losses indicates that repetitive-loss communities should be a target of federal efforts to reduce losses and that retrofitting infrastructure may be a cost-effective way to reduce future losses.

TABLE 2.1
Total Damages to Public Facilities From Presidentially Declared Natural Disasters,
1980 - 1987, by State and Territory[a]

State	Number of Disasters	Total Damages (in millions) Amount	Pct.	Number and Percent of Loss Events Experienced by Governmental Units				
				Number	Under $5,000	$5,000-50K	$50K-500K	$500K+
California	9	$ 599.9	34%	1,444	14%	40%	34%	12%
West Virginia	3	137.4	8	247	33	36	22	9
Utah	3	129.2	7	239	9	40	37	14
New York	6	69.8	4	509	17	55	24	4
Connecticut	3	65.1	4	321	15	41	40	4
Arizona	3	60.5	3	111	15	29	41	15
Texas	5	56.8	3	287	18	39	36	7
Oklahoma	7	46.9	3	300	25	33	34	8
Virginia	2	36.3	2	109	26	31	35	8
Puerto Rico	3	35.6	2	127	3	36	47	14
Idaho	2	31.6	2	21	5	14	43	38
Massachusetts	2	30.7	2	428	15	49	35	10
Michigan	3	30.2	2	336	33	38	25	4
Illinois	4	28.3	2	777	24	61	14	1
Pennsylvania	5	28.2	2	253	20	53	23	4
Oregon	4	27.5	2	8	0	0	25	75
Arkansas	2	26.4	2	117	31	33	28	8
Hawaii	3	22.8	1	27	27	11	30	37
Nevada	1	22.4	1	46	11	23	47	19
Colorado	2	21.4	1	83	17	36	39	8
Alaska	2	18.7	1	27	11	26	37	26
Florida	2	18.4	1	101	15	41	40	4
Mississippi	5	18.3	1	142	30	36	21	3
Washington	4	18.0	1	62	13	40	32	15
New Jersey	1	17.9	1	247	14	58	26	2
Alabama	4	17.4	1	70	24	43	24	9
Louisiana	1	16.4	1	87	17	40	34	9
Maine	1	16.0	1	250	20	64	14	2
Missouri	4	12.2	1	142	30	46	21	3
South Dakota	2	11.5	1	493	50	44	5	1
North Carolina	1	11.0	1	39	36	33	23	8
Kansas	3	10.7	1	120	31	52	11	6
Indiana	1	9.7	1	23	22	35	35	8
Kentucky	1	9.2	*	80	30	42	24	4
Montana	3	9.1	*	82	13	41	40	6
Tennessee	2	8.8	*	32	31	25	38	6
New Mexico	3	8.3	*	95	36	37	23	4
Nebraska	1	7.1	*	56	12	42	42	4
Rhode Island	1	6.8	*	67	21	37	37	5
Vermont	1	6.3	*	51	12	43	39	6
Virgin Islands	2	5.4	*	27	33	30	26	11
Wisconsin	2	5.2	*	72	36	43	17	4

TABLE 2.1 (Continued)

State	Number of Disasters	Total Damages (in millions) Amount	Pct.	Number and Percent of Loss Events Experienced by Governmental Units Number	Under $5,000	$5,000- 50K	$50K- 500K	$500K+
American Samoa	2	4.9	*	6	0	67	0	33
Iowa	2	4.8	*	29	0	0	1	0
Ohio	3	3.4	*	130	35	54	11	0
Wyoming	1	2.3	*	10	20	30	20	30
N. Mariana Is.	1	1.2	*	1	50	50	0	0
North Dakota	1	0.5	*	6	17	33	50	0
Georgia	1	0.5	*	1	0	0	0	100
D.C.	1	0.2	*	1	0	0	100	0
Delaware	0	0.0	0	0	0	0	0	0
Maryland	0	0.0	0	0	0	0	0	0
Minnesota	0	0.0	0	0	0	0	0	0
New Hampshire	0	0.0	0	0	0	0	0	0
South Dakota	0	0.0	0	0	0	0	0	0
Guam/Other Pacific Is.	0	0.0	0	0	0	0	0	0
Totals	131	$1,178.2	100	8,522	22	45	27	6

Source: Unpublished records of the Federal Emergency Management Agency and U.S. Department of Transportation.

[a]Includes damages from coastal storms, earthquakes, floods, hurricanes, and landslides in the following categories: debris removal; emergency protection; roads and streets; water control facilities; public buildings; public utilities; parks and recreational facilities. Does not include losses to educational facilities.
*< 0.5

Types of Infrastructure Damaged

Almost half of all losses incurred by state and local governments were associated with damages to highways, roads and streets ($925 million). (See Table 2.3.) Clearance of debris ($263.9 million) and emergency protective measures ($199 million) rank second and third among the eight categories into which we grouped losses. Other facilities that incurred substantial losses include water control facilities (e.g., storm drainage channels, dikes, levees), public utilities, public buildings, and parks and recreational facilities.

Our data on losses to public utilities and public buildings are net losses after receipt of insurance payments. In analyzing federal liabilities from natural disasters, Petak and Atkisson (1982: 247) assumed that 50 percent of losses to private buildings and utilities were covered by insurance. If we assume the same market penetration for public buildings and utilities, the loss figures reported in Table 2.3 for those two categories would double (public utilities from $106.2 million to $212.4 million and

TABLE 2.2
Governments Experiencing Repetitive Losses in
Natural Disasters, January 1, 1980 - July 31, 1987

Number of Loss Events	Governmental Units		Losses (millions)	
	Number	Percent	Total	Percent
1	5,336	78%	$564.377	43%
2	1,215	18	484.450	37
3	233	3	220.995	17
4	27	<1	28.987	2
5 or more	5	<1	5.961	1

Source: Unpublished records of the Federal Emergency
Management Agency and U.S. Department of
Transportation.

public buildings and equipment from $35.1 million to $70.2 million). The addition of $141.3 million in losses, however, would add only about 10 percent to the estimate of total losses incurred in Presidentially declared disasters.

The types of losses to which state and local governments are exposed vary by type of hazard, as shown in Table 2.3.[3] Highways and streets, for example, are much more likely to suffer losses in floods than in earthquakes and hurricanes. Hurricanes are much more likely than other types of disasters to result in heavy costs for debris removal. Expenditures on emergency protective measures are highly associated with flooding accompanied by landslides. Public utilities and public buildings are particularly susceptible to loss in earthquakes in comparison with other types of hazards.

The distribution of losses among different types of infrastructure have two policy implications. First, since over half of all public sector losses are to highways and streets, these data suggest that the imposition of more stringent design standards for new road investments and retrofitting of existing highway facilities may be a prudent course of action. Second, these data also indicate that insurance has a limited ability to reduce federal disaster assistance costs. Insurance coverage is widely available only for public buildings and public utilities. Those categories of loss, however, account for less than 10 percent of total losses from all types of disasters. Thus, even if all of those losses were shifted from relief to insurance, the effect on federal disaster relief costs would be minor.

TABLE 2.3
Losses to State and Local Governments in Presidentially
Declared Natural Disasters, 1980 - 1987, by Type of
Loss Incurred

Type of Loss	Total Losses Amount (millions)	%	Losses by Type of Hazard (%)				
			Floods[a]			Hurri-canes	Earth-quakes
			A	B	C		
Highways, Roads, and Streets	$ 925.0	52%	62%	45%	82%	22%	25%
Debris Removal	263.9	15	6	15	2	49	21
Emergency Protective Measures	199.0	11	9	18	2	6	3
Water Control Facilities	134.8	8	7	11	2	4	*
Public Utilities	122.3	7	7	6	9	6	31
Public Buildings and Equipment	45.7	2	3	1	1	5	19
Parks and Recreational Facilities	7.9	*	1	*	*	1	*
Other Facilities	88.6	5	5	4	2	7	1
Total Losses Percent	---		100%	100%	100%	100%	100%	100%
Amount (millions)	$1,787.2	---	$838	$579	$113	$253	$ 5

Source: Unpublished records of the Federal Emergency
Management Agency and U.S. Department of
Transportation.

*Less than 0.5 percent.

[a]Flood Type A — Flooding from severe storm without
landslides/mudslides or tornadoes.

Flood Type B — Flooding from severe storms with
landslides/mudslides.

Flood Type C — Flooding from severe storms with
tornadoes.

Clearly, if insurance is to play a larger role in reducing the federal costs of disasters, then it needs to be made available for a much larger proportion of public property at risk in natural disasters.

Types of Governments with Losses

Public losses experienced at the state and local level are shared by four types of governmental units: state agencies, counties (including parishes), cities (including towns, villages, townships), and special districts. Of those four, state agencies experienced the greatest losses between 1980 and mid-1987 in Presidentially declared natural disasters—47 percent of all losses to state and local government. Over 60 percent of losses experienced by the states resulted from damages to the federal-aid highway system.

Cities and towns absorbed 25 percent of public losses over the period studied; counties, 15 percent; and special districts (excluding school districts), 13 percent.

Petak and Atkisson (1982: 246) analyzed federal liabilities arising from natural disasters in 1970 and assumed Presidentially declared disasters accounted for about 25 percent of all losses to state and local governments as a result of natural hazards. Using that figure, we can draw on our 1980–1987 disaster loss data to estimate total average annual losses to state and local governments from natural hazards and average losses per governmental unit.

We estimate that state and local governments experience almost $1 billion in losses from natural disasters (both Presidentially declared disasters and less serious events that do not receive a Presidential declaration) each year.[4] (See Table 2.4.) Average annual losses per year for each state government are $8.99 million. For substate governmental units, costs tend to be lower, however. We estimate, for example, that the average annual loss for each of the 3,041 counties in the U.S. is $48,300, while average annual losses per city (including townships) and special districts are under $10,000 each. That low average annual exposure to loss helps account for local governments' reported lack of attention to policies for dealing with the threat of natural disasters.

Losses to different types of public facilities are not spread evenly across different types of governmental units, reflecting variation in governmental responsibilities in the U.S. federal system. (See Table 2.5.)

Sixty-nine percent of losses to **highways, roads, and streets,** for example, are borne by state governments and 20 percent by county governments. Cities and special districts experienced relatively minor losses to roads and streets.

TABLE 2.4
Estimated Average Annual Losses to State and Local
Governments from Natural Hazards

Type of Govern- mental Unit	Losses/Year (millions)[a]			Number of Govern- mental Units in U.S.[d]	Average Annual Losses Per Unit
	Presiden- tially Declared Disaster[b]	Other Hazard Events[c]	Total Losses		
States	$112.4	$337.2	$449.6	50	$8,992,000
Counties	36.7	110.1	146.8	3,041	48,300
Cities and Town- ships	58.2	174.6	232.8	35,810	6,500
Special Districts	31.0	93.0	124.0	25,962	4,800
Total	$238.3	$714.9	$953.2	------	------

[a]Includes damages from coastal storms, earthquakes, floods, hurricanes, and landslides in the following categories: debris removal; emergency protection; roads and streets (including federal aid highways); water control facilities; public buildings; public utilities; and parks. Does not include losses to educational facilities.

[b]Source: Unpublished records of the Federal Emergency Management Agency and U.S. Department of Transportation.

[c]Based on assumption that Presidentially declared disasters account for one fourth of all losses to state and local agencies from natural hazards. See Petak and Atkisson (1983: 244).

[d]Number of governments in 1982. See U.S. Bureau of the Census, *Census of Governments*, Vol. 1, No. 1, Governmental Organization. U.S. Government Printing Office, Washington, 1983.

City governments incur a majority (56 percent) of total **debris removal** costs. Special districts absorbed a quarter of debris removal costs. Debris removal is the single largest source of disaster-related costs for both cities and special districts. Counties and state agencies each shouldered a relatively small portion of debris removal costs.

State (48 percent of all losses) and city governments (25 percent of all losses) bear the lion's share of the costs associated with constructing **emergency protective measures** during natural disasters. Counties and

TABLE 2.5
Distribution of Losses in Presidentially Declared
Natural Disasters, 1980 - 1987, by Type of Loss and
Type of Government

| Type of Loss | Amount of Loss (millions) | | | | |
	County	City	Special District	State Agency	Total
Highways, Roads, Streets					
Amount	$173.6	$ 86.7	$ 29.9	$634.8	$ 925.0
Percent	19%	9%	3%	69%	100%
Debris Removal					
Amount	33.7	148.2	67.0	15.0	263.9
Percent	13%	56%	25%	6%	100%
Emergency Protective Measures					
Amount	29.9	49.6	23.2	96.1	199.0
Percent	15%	25%	12%	48%	100%
Water Control Facilities					
Amount	11.8	25.7	54.2	43.1	134.8
Percent	9%	19%	40%	32%	100%
Public Utilities					
Amount	4.2	72.5	37.9	7.7	122.3
Percent	4%	59%	31%	6%	100%
Public Buildings/ Equipment					
Amount	7.1	14.3	11.1	13.2	45.7
Percent	15%	32%	24%	29%	100%
Parks/Recreation Facilities					
Amount	1.1	3.4	2.0	1.4	7.9
Percent	14%	43%	25%	18%	100%
Other Facilities					
Amount	13.6	35.8	7.4	31.8	88.6
Percent	15%	40%	9%	36%	100%
TOTAL	$274.9	$436.2	$232.7	$843.3	$1,787.2
Per Year	36.7	58.2	31.0	112.4	238.3
Percent	15%	24%	13%	47%	100%

Source: Unpublished records of the Federal Emergency
Management Agency and U.S. Department of
Transportation.

special districts together bear only a little more than a quarter of those costs. Emergency protective measures, however, account for only a small amount of the total losses experienced by states, counties, cities, and special districts.

Special districts absorbed 54 percent of the losses to **water control facilities** in natural disasters. That reflects the widespread use of drainage and flood control districts to provide water control facilities in many states. Losses to water control facilities accounted for just under a quarter of all losses experienced by special districts as a group and, after debris clearance, was the second leading source of losses to those governments. State governments absorbed just under a third of total losses to water control facilities, while cities and counties each experienced lower proportions of total losses. Losses to water control facilities accounted for only about 5 percent of the total disaster-related losses experienced by state and local governments.

Public utility losses were concentrated in city governments (59 percent of total utility losses) and special districts (31 percent of utility losses). County and state governments together absorbed only 10 percent of the damages experienced by utility systems in natural disasters. Among cities, losses to public utilities accounted for 17 percent of all losses experienced in natural disasters, ranking it third behind debris removal and losses to roads and streets among the sources of losses they experienced.

Damages to **public buildings** were fairly evenly distributed across types of governmental units. Cities absorbed the greatest portion (32 percent) of building damages, followed by state agencies (29 percent). Losses to public buildings were a small portion (2 percent to 3 percent) of the total losses experienced by each of the four types of governments, however.

Cities (43 percent) and special districts (25 percent) experienced over two-thirds of the losses to **parks and recreational facilities;** but, as with public buildings, those losses accounted for a minute portion (1 percent or less) of the total losses experienced by each type of governmental unit.

Data on the distribution of losses have clear implications for establishing loss-reduction priorities among governmental units and for targeting technical assistance. States, for example, should be most concerned about losses to highways and other public roads and for the expenses they incur for various emergency protective measures. County losses are concentrated in damages to roads. Cities need to be concerned about losses to city streets, which are substantial, but also with reducing the costs of debris removal and losses to public utilities and public buildings.

TABLE 2.6
Methods Used by Local Governments to Finance the
Reconstruction of Public Facilities Damaged in
Presidentially Declared Natural Disasters

Methods of Financing Reconstruction of Public Facilities	Percent of Governments That Rated Method as "Very Important" in Financing Reconstruction
Transfer the Loss	
Federal disaster assistance grants	51%
State disaster assistance grants	43
Insurance	14
Insurance pools	2
Assume the Loss	
Local contingency funds	21%
Reserves for capital facilities	9
Federal disaster assistance loans	8
State disaster assistance loans	8
Emergency taxes or user fees	6
General obligation bonds	3

Source: Survey of finance directors and risk managers
in 159 local governments that experienced a
Presidentially declared natural disaster between
January 1, 1980 and December 31, 1985.

Special districts incur large costs for debris removal and, of course, for repairing the facilities they operate.

How Losses Are Financed

Local governments' financial liability from natural disasters that receive a Presidential disaster declaration is considerably reduced by federal disaster assistance. In dealing with the local share of losses, localities can attempt to transfer the loss, either by seeking state grants-in-aid or by prior purchase of insurance, or they can assume the loss using either funds on hand or borrowing. We asked city and county finance directors and risk managers in disaster-stricken governments to rate the importance of the various means of paying for the reconstruction of damaged infrastructure. Their responses are summarized in Table 2.6.

Clearly, the predominant way local governments are dealing with losses they incur in natural disasters is to transfer the burden to higher levels of government. For the proportion of the loss burden that is assumed locally, contingency funds provide the most important source of financing. Very few local governments reported that borrowing was an important source of funds to finance disaster losses and fewer still viewed emergency taxes or user fees as important. That latter finding is important, because it shows that at this time local governments are doing little to transfer the costs of disasters backward to the beneficiaries of hazardous locations.

One disadvantage of transferring the loss burden to higher levels of government is the delay localities often experience in obtaining funds. Repairs to put government facilities back into service need to be made quickly, but two thirds of the local governments we queried indicated it took over four months to receive funds from federal and state agencies (and over 40 percent reported funds were not received for over six months after the disaster). Thus, even when losses are transferred, localities must come up with short-term financing of reconstruction on their own. The most frequently used sources of that financing were funds on hand (used by 70 percent of the city and county governments we queried), followed by delayed payment of bills (9 percent) and borrowing (6 percent).

In addition to transferring losses or assuming them, local governments have a third option in dealing with the threats posed by natural hazards: they can attempt to reduce the risk of future losses by investing in various loss prevention measures. Earlier we noted that because of the relatively high proportion of losses concentrated in communities with repetitive losses, retrofitting infrastructure so that it would be more resistant to loss should be receiving attention in any community that has experienced losses in a natural disaster. Although we deal with loss prevention in great detail in Chapters 4, 5 and 6, we note here that loss prevention is not widely practiced among local governments. Thus when we asked public works directors in disaster-stricken communities what they had done to reduce the risk of loss to facilities that had been damaged, less than 40 percent reported they had incurred extra expenses in reconstructing those facilities so that they would be less vulnerable to damage in the future, and only 20 percent had undertaken a systematic vulnerability analysis of the facilities their governments owned and operated.

In summary, at this time disaster assistance from the federal government and to a lesser extent state government are the two principal means localities use to recover from natural disasters that receive Presidential disaster declarations. Insurance, which is highly touted by federal officials as a loss recovery mechanism, has not played an important role in aiding recovery, mainly, we suspect, because damages to insurable property such as public buildings are a low proportion of total local government losses in natural disasters. Finally, loss prevention is not practiced widely by local governments. Whether that is due to the availability of federal and state disaster assistance or to other causes is explored later in this book in Chapters 6 and 9.

Inequities in Disaster Relief

Federal disaster assistance policy is inequitable for two reasons. First, the definition of what constitutes a disaster for local governments is flawed. As a result, thousands of governments that do not really need federal assistance receive aid while some governments that suffer large losses, but do not receive a federal disaster declaration, do not receive aid. Second, on a per capita basis local governments serving small jurisdictions suffer much more serious losses than those serving large jurisdictions, but both small and large jurisdictions receive equivalent amounts of federal aid. Here we provide evidence to support our assertion that disaster assistance is inequitable.

The definition of what constitutes a disastrous event has occupied social scientists (e.g., Drabek 1986; Dynes et al. 1972; Fritz 1961) and policy makers (e.g., see chapter 1) alike for a number of years. According to Nigg and Perry (1988), the following definition of a disaster first formulated by Fritz in 1961 is still widely used. According to Fritz, a disaster is:

> an event, concentrated in time and space, in which a society, or a relatively self-sufficient subdivision of a society, undergoes severe danger and incurs such losses to its members and physical appurtenances that the social structure is disrupted and the fulfillment of all or some of the essential functions of the society is prevented.

That broad definition is helpful, but it leads to a practical question: At what level of loss is social structure disrupted and the fulfillment of essential functions prevented? The Federal Emergency Management Agency attempted to answer that question to provide a basis for determining when a Presidential disaster declaration should be issued, but as we reported in Chapter 1, Congress rejected the formulas FEMA put forward.

Although controversial, the issue of what constitutes a disaster is not trivial, since the answer will determine, in part, the degree to which federal disaster assistance is equitably administered. Few would argue, for example, that it would be equitable for U.S. taxpayers to subsidize recovery in localities that have suffered less than disastrous losses, since literally thousands of small losses occur every year and are not paid by federal taxpayers.

To shed some light on this issue, we asked a sample of 481 local officials:

> "What level of damages to public buildings would be a disastrous loss to your jurisdiction in a single year? By "disastrous" we mean a dollar loss that would generally be above and beyond your normal financial means for covering unexpected damages, such as budgeted contingency funds."

Their responses, summarized in Table 2.7, indicate that local officials believe they can handle losses far larger than those defined by FEMA as constituting a disaster. FEMA, for example, proposed using local government losses of $2.50 per capita as a threshold value for defining whether a local government should be eligible for aid. Our data indicate, however, that for 87 percent of the local governments we queried, that level of loss would be manageable using already budgeted contingency funds and would not be considered a disaster. FEMA further proposed that losses of $10 per capita or more should entitle local governments to federal reimbursement of 90 percent of their losses; our data indicate that only 41 percent of U.S. local governments would rate that level of loss as a disaster.

In fact, the median level of loss defined as a disaster by the 481 local governments we queried was $14 per capita, far above the thresholds FEMA proposed for defining the occurrence of a disaster (and that Congress rejected). Furthermore, our data indicate that with the currently used eligibility criteria, which make all local governments within counties defined as disaster areas eligible for aid, about two thirds of the local governments that received federal disaster assistance during the period we studied suffered losses that they could cover with available budgeted contingency funds (and thus were loses below their own definition of what would constitute a disaster). At the same time, a small percentage of local governments really do suffer from catastrophes; 10 percent of the governments denied federal disaster assistance, for example, incurred losses that were seven times the level they could cope with using already budgeted contingency funds.

In addition to providing aid where it is not needed (and sometimes insufficient aid where it is needed), federal disaster relief policy also ignores the fact that losses, on a per capita basis, fall unequally on small jurisdictions. Table 2.8 summarizes mean and median per capita losses experienced by cities and counties of various sizes. In the case

TABLE 2.7
Local Officials' Definition of Disastrous Loss and
Local Governments' Loss Experience in Terms of Their
Self-Defined Definition of a Disastrous Loss

Disaster Definition/ Experience	Data	

Size of Loss that Would
Be Beyond Normal Financial
Means for Covering
Unexpected Damages

Total Losses

Mean: $ 1,207,546
Median: 148,500

Per Capita Losses

10 percentile:	1.65	
13 percentile:	2.50	(FEMA Proposal)
25 percentile:	5.32	
41 percentile:	10.00	(FEMA Proposal)
50 percentile: (median):	14.29	
75 percentile:	49.50	
90 percentile:	139.08	

Ratio of Actual Losses to Losses Defined as Disastrous	Presidential Disaster Declared[a]	Presidential Disaster Denied[b]
Mean:[c]	4.90	2.29[d]
10 percentile:	.02	.02
25 percentile:	.09	.06
50 percentile: (median)	.39	.28
68 percentile:	1.00	.65
75 percentile:	1.98	.98
90 percentile:	5.17	7.70

Source: Survey of 481 local officials, Summer 1988.

[a]N - 178 city and county governments.
[b]N - 133 city and county governments.
[c]A difference of means test indicates that the
differences between the two groups (jurisdictions
that did and did not obtain a Presidential disaster
declaration) in the ratio of actual losses to losses
that local officials said would constitute a disaster
are not statistically significant (.05 level).
[d]Note that these loss data include total losses
estimated by state and local officials, while data for
Presidential disasters include only losses rated
eligible for federal assistance.

TABLE 2.8
Per Capita Losses to Cities and Counties, by Size and
Wealth of Local Jurisdictions Where Losses Occurred,
1980 - 1987

Size/Income	--------Per Capita Losses--------			
	Cities[a]		Counties[b]	
of Jurisdiction	Mean	Median	Mean	Median
1980 Population				
Under 5,000	$16.31	$ 4.57	$54.09	$23.28
5,000 - 9,999	10.44	3.68	28.31	15.92
10,000 - 24,999	5.96	3.23	13.68	7.18
25,000 - 49,999	4.93	1.92	6.74	3.58
50,000 - 99,999	4.92	1.87	4.50	2.27
100,000 or more	4.99	1.63	2.42	0.93
1980 Per Capita Income				
Under $6,000	$11.58	$3.62	$12.34	$ 5.11
$ 6,000 - $ 9,999	12.11	3.44	14.69	5.72
$10,000 - $13,999	7.10	3.06	6.46	1.63
$14,000 - $17,999	8.76	3.77	c	c
$18,000 or more	9.69	3.63	c	c

Source: Unpublished records of the Federal Emergency
Management Agency.

[a]Data are for cities of 2,500 or more population. The
number of cities in each size class are: under 5,000
(n=600); 5,000-9,999 (n=544); 10,000-24,999 (n=557);
25,000-49,999 (n=299); 50,000-99,999 (n=166); 100,000
or more (n=106). The number of cities in each per
capita income class are: under $6,000 (n=46); $6,000-
$9999 (n=833); $10000-$13999 (n=880); $14000-$17999
(n=306); $18000 or more (n=207).

[b]Data are for all counties. The number of counties in
each size class are: under 5,000 (n=48); 5,000-9,999
(n=107); 10,000-24,999 (n=263); 25,000-49,999 (n=167);
50,000-99,999 (n=93); 100,000 or more (n=156). The
number of counties in each per capita income class are:
under $6,000 (n=144); $6000-$9999 (n=547); $10000-
$13999 (n=118); $14000-$17999 (n=22); $18000 or more
(n=3).

[c]Insufficient number of cases (n of less than 25).

of cities, median per capita losses in the smallest cities (under 5,000 population) were almost three times larger than those in the largest cities (over 100,000 population); in the case of counties, they were over twenty-five times larger in the smaller jurisdictions. Since federal aid formulas do not recognize those differences, citizens living in small jurisdictions bear a larger share of losses in natural disasters than do those living in larger jurisdictions. The data assembled indicate, however, that federal relief policy does not discriminate against poorer or richer jurisdictions. As shown in Table 2.8, there is no clear pattern of per capita losses to cities and counties by the per capita income of those jurisdictions.

Inefficiencies in Disaster Relief

The final question we want to address here concerns another consequence of the federal policy of extending aid to all local governments within counties named as disaster areas. As demonstrated above, that policy results in a number of governments receiving aid they really do not need. It also results in an inefficient use of federal resources. As the data in Table 2.1 indicate, a significant number and proportion of governmental units (1,875 governmental units; 22 percent of those receiving aid) received federal checks for losses of less than $5,000. Those small losses do not account for a very large proportion of total losses (in fact, losses under $50,000 in the aggregate accounted for less than 5 percent of total losses between 1980 and mid-1987), and that may account for Congresses' failure to adopt more reasonable loss thresholds for receiving federal aid (i.e., the political costs of denying aid may not be viewed as worth the small gains to the federal Treasury). But, each of those claims required considerable manpower in making loss estimates and processing paperwork. It seems likely to us that those resources might better be devoted to helping out governments that really do experience disastrous losses. We address that issue further in Chapter 8 and Chapter 11.

We should note here, however, FEMA's rationale for providing aid to help localities recover from small losses. In interviews with FEMA staff members in 1987, they reported that the costs per applicant of processing small claims is not large (they did not have exact figures on those costs, however). The small claims result in part from both the technical problems and the politics of Presidential aid. The county-by-county designation of disaster areas allows underlying cities, towns, and special districts to "ride along on the coattails." However, it is not a simple matter to judge immediately after a disaster the geographic extent of damages. If it is

not obvious that damage is concentrated in a few areas, then an entire
county is declared eligible for relief.

Conclusions

Every year we estimate state and local governments incur almost $1
billion in losses to public property and in cleanup and emergency
response costs as a result of five natural hazards—coastal storms,
earthquakes, floods, hurricanes and landslides. The nature of those
losses—their distribution across governmental units and types of infrastructure damaged—have a number of implications for financing disaster
recovery and reconstruction.

First, although average annual losses are enormous, they represent
only a small portion—about one half of one percent—of the $2 trillion
capital stock of state and local governments in the United States. As
such, they fall far below the level of normal repair and replacement
costs associated with the ongoing depreciation of public infrastructure.
In short, losses to infrastructure as a result of natural hazards do not
pose the staggering financial burdens discussed with regard to the
infrastructure crisis in the United States (see National Infrastructure
Advisory Committee to the Joint Economic Committee of Congress 1984).
That has two implications. On the one hand, public losses should be
manageable financially through appropriate policy. On the other hand,
public losses may not be large enough to attract the attention of policy
makers or to stimulate serious consideration of alternatives to the current
approach to dealing with them.

Second, losses from natural hazards are not shared equally among
governmental units, but instead they are highly skewed. Almost 7,000
state and local governmental units experienced the effects of a large,
Presidentially declared natural disaster between 1980 and mid-1987, but
a relatively small proportion—an estimated 32 percent—experienced
losses beyond those they could cover using already budgeted contingency
funds. While for many governments disasters are, in fact, manageable
financially, a few governments—about one in ten of those with losses—
experience truly catastrophic damages to public property and those losses
account for the lion's share of federal disaster relief costs. Thus, while
only a small proportion of publicly owned capital stock is at risk from
natural hazards, losses can be truly catastrophic for a small number of
governments at the center of large natural disasters. Any scheme designed
to deal with the financial impacts of public losses from natural hazards
must be designed to deal with those rare, but very large, loss occurrences.

Third, since two-thirds of the state and local governmental units that
experienced damages in disasters large enough to merit a Presidential

declaration suffered relatively minor losses of less than $50,000, there is a strong potential for state and local governments to cope with them through adequate financial and physical planning without recourse to federal assistance.

Fourth, examination of the types of losses incurred by state and local governmental units indicates that transfer of the loss burden to the private sector through commercial property insurance, at least as currently available, does not provide a satisfactory alternative to federal relief programs. Property insurance is often (but not always) available for losses to buildings, bridges and public utilities from most natural hazards. Losses to buildings and other structures (including public utilities), however, account for less than 10 percent of the total losses experienced by state and local governments. Major categories of loss, such as highways, debris removal, emergency protective measures, and water control facilities, are not regularly insured by in the private market. Thus, if an insurance mechanism is to provide an alternative to disaster relief as a means of financing losses to state and local governments, it may need to be developed by the public sector, although it could be administered through a public-private partnership similar to the National Flood Insurance Program.

Fifth, because local governments are able to transfer loss burdens to higher governmental levels, they may not be paying adequate attention to financial and physical planning measures to cope with losses from natural hazards which they could undertake on their own. Closely related to that point is the interaction between public and private investment in hazardous areas. If local governments assumed more of the risks of losses to public facilities from natural hazards, they might begin considering how they allocate those costs among their constituents. For example, should those who develop private property in hazardous areas— and demand public facilities and services—be required to pay the costs of managing the risk to those facilities?

Sixth, current federal disaster relief policy appears to be both inequitable and inefficient. It is inequitable because the distribution of aid bears little resemblance to the need for assistance and small governments bear a larger burden, per capita, than do large governments; it is inefficient because, without realistic loss thresholds, federal manpower and resources are devoted to distributing trivial amounts of money to thousands of local governments that do not truly need that federal help. Thus, there clearly is need for reform in federal policy.

Two courses of action seem plausible. The first is to explore alternative policies for coping with losses to infrastructure damaged in natural disasters. Clearly, one policy alternative is to reform, but to essentially continue current programs based on federal assistance to states and localities in the event of large disasters and partial federal insurance coverage of public property. Other policy alternatives merit attention, however. They include increased assumption of losses by local governments, which our data suggests is highly feasible, and the formulation of new insurance mechanisms, such as insurance pools or expansion of federal insurance programs, to spread the risk of loss horizontally across governmental units, vertically between levels of government, and/or between the public and private sectors. The second course of action is to reduce losses to infrastructure through increased adoption of loss prevention measures. Both of those courses of action are explored in later chapters of this book.

Notes

1. Disasters that occurred over this six-year period appear to be typical of disaster experience in the United States; however, the data do not include losses caused by an exceptionally large, billion dollar-plus event such as Hurricane Agnes in 1972. Thus, they understate losses to some degree.

2. Those losses also include damages to federal-aid highways in natural disasters declared by the Secretary of Transportation.

3. The Federal Emergency Management Agency's practice of attributing losses to multiple hazards results in some uncertainty about exactly which hazard agent produced damages in those disasters involving more than one agent, such as disasters with floods and tornadoes or floods and landslides.

4. In calculating this estimate, we did not adjust for inflation. Had we done so, our estimate of average annual losses in, say 1985 dollars, would have been slightly larger.

3

The Special Case
of Earthquake Disasters

In this chapter we look more closely at the consequences of earthquakes for local governments. The Whittier Narrows earthquake of October 1, 1987, one of the most destructive to hit a large urban area in the United States in the last fifty years, serves as a case study for this analysis. Although dwarfed by the Loma Prieta earthquake of 1989, the relatively small (5.9 Richter magnitude) Whittier Narrows event caused considerable property damage near the epicenter in eastern Los Angeles County. In examining public losses, we uncovered additional problems—from the local government perspective—with federal disaster relief mechanisms. In addition, we show that in the case of moderate earthquakes, much of the damage to public property is insurable. Thus, in comparison with losses from floods, hurricanes and landslides, which produce large losses to property that cannot be insured, even if local governments thought that was necessary, earthquakes present a different policy problem. Namely, how can a higher proportion of earthquake-prone local governments be persuaded to insure their property at risk?

The Federal and State Policy Context

Before discussing the consequences of the Whittier Narrows earthquake, a brief review of the policy context surrounding natural disasters in California is in order. In the case of federal policy, it is important to emphasize that a number of disaster-related expenses are not eligible for federal reimbursement. Ineligible costs include individual items that are less than $250, damage to ornamental facilities, and, except for overtime expenses, the costs of police, fire and other municipal personnel who are assigned to work on disaster response and recovery. As we will see shortly, those costs accounted for a large portion of the losses local governments experienced in the Whittier Narrows disaster, and they were not covered by federal disaster relief.

In Chapter 2 we reported that during the 1980s California was far and away the most disaster-prone state in the nation, accounting for fully a third of losses to the public sector nationally. Given that fact, it should not be particularly surprising that California is somewhat unique among the fifty states in the way it handles natural disasters. In May 1974, the California legislature adopted the Natural Disaster Assistance Act (NDAA), which gave the director of the state Office of Emergency Services authority to provide assistance to state and local agencies that sustained damages from fires, floods, earthquakes, and other hazards. State aid can be used for restoration or replacement of public facilities, but before receiving such aid, localities have to obtain the maximum amount of federal aid available for those purposes.

In response to the Whittier Narrows earthquake, the California legislature passed Senate Bill 6 on November 16, 1987. The bill appropriated $64.6 million to an account within the NDAF to be dispersed to local and state agencies. Senate Bill 6 was the fourth appropriation for a natural disaster under the NDAA since 1983. Previous legislation allocated funds to help local agencies recover from the Coalinga Earthquake (1983), the Morgan Hill Earthquake (1984), and storm and flood damage to levees in various locations (1986). In an attempt to streamline the appropriation procedure, a new bill, SB 1910, was introduced into the state legislature in 1989 to establish an account, the Special Fund for Economic Uncertainties, into which funds would be appropriated continuously for disaster relief. Thus, California is pursuing a path parallel to that of the federal government, with individual appropriations for disasters giving way to an institutionalized disaster relief program. In the process, it may further remove local governments from responsibility for loss prevention, and thus may further exacerbate losses from natural disasters.

The Whittier Narrows Case Study

To conduct the Whittier Narrows case study we collected information from three sources. First, we assembled a database from Federal Emergency Management Agency damage survey reports (DSRs) and analyzed that information to determine local government losses that would be covered by federal relief. Second, we supplemented the FEMA DSRs with data supplied by the California Office of Emergency Services (OES) on additional losses that would be covered by state aid. Third, we conducted personal interviews with financial and public works personnel in six jurisdictions to validate the secondary data we obtained from federal and state sources and to identify the funding mechanisms local governments were using to reconstruct and replace damaged public property.

We obtained the federal damage data from FEMA Region IX. All of the Whittier Narrows earthquake damage survey reports filed by Los Angeles County and city and special district governments as of June 15, 1988, were sorted, cleaned and analyzed. Although the federal damage survey data are useful, they present only a partial picture of overall losses. Local governments generally know what types of damage are eligible for federal reimbursement, and they do not submit claims for costs that are clearly ineligible. In interviews with city officials, they suggested that federal claims would account for from 10 percent to 50 percent of their true costs of recovering from the earthquake. Thus, we found it necessary to obtain data from the California Office of Emergency Services (which did not apply rigorous eligibility criteria as a condition for receiving state assistance) to derive a more complete picture of the distribution of losses.

Based on a preliminary analysis of damage survey data, we selected six jurisdictions for more intensive data collection. Those jurisdictions include Los Angeles County and the cities of Alhambra, Los Angeles, Monterey Park, Pasadena, and Whittier. Each had more than $200,000 in losses from the earthquake. We examined the DSRs from those jurisdictions closely, and we conducted lengthy interviews with managers and financial personnel to determine how they handled the reconstruction process.

Overview of Losses

We estimate the Whittier Narrows earthquake resulted in public sector losses of $17,684,608, based on damage survey reports filed and processed through June 15, 1988. (See Table 3.1.) Fifty-six percent of those losses ($9,992,687) were incurred by cities and counties, 6 percent ($1,032,282) by special districts, and the remainder ($6,729,639) by state agencies and nonprofit organizations. Specific loss claims ranged from a low of $6 to a high of $515,751 (for damages to the California State University system).

Almost all (98 percent) of the claims for damages submitted to FEMA by state agencies were deemed eligible for aid. In contrast, a much lower proportion (68 percent) of cities' and counties' requests for federal disaster assistance passed muster, primarily because FEMA disallowed over half of local governments' claims for expenses in providing emergency and protective services. If we add to those claims damages reported to the California Office of Emergency Services but not to FEMA, it appears

TABLE 3.1
Public Sector Losses in the Whittier Narrows Earthquake,
October 1, 1987

Type of Government Experiencing Loss	Losses Eligible for Federal Disaster Relief	Residual Losses Eligible for CA OES Relief	Total Losses Eligible for Reimbursement
State/Nonprofit Agencies	$ 6,729,639	$ ---	$ 6,729,639
Cities and Counties	4,985,010	4,937,677	9,992,687
Special Districts	607,494	424,788	1,032,282
Total Losses Eligible for Reimbursement from State or Federal Sources	$12,322,143	$5,362,465	$17,684,608

Source: Damage survey reports filed with the Federal
Emergency Management Agency and California Office of
Emergency Services as of June 15, 1988.

that less than half ($4,985,010 of $9,992,687) of total city and county
losses were eligible for federal disaster relief. After cost-sharing, federal
disaster relief covered $3,738,758 of cities' and counties' losses. That is
about 37 percent of the total losses for which they filed claims with
federal and state disaster assistance agencies.

Cities' and counties' losses resulted primarily from damages to public
buildings (46 percent) and utilities (24 percent) and expenses they incurred
in providing emergency and protective measures (15 percent) and debris
removal and demolition (9 percent). (See Table 3.2.) Special districts'
losses came mainly from damages to buildings (37 percent) and in
providing emergency and protective services (50 percent).

The types of losses that resulted from the Whittier earthquake are
strikingly different than the national disaster loss experience reported

TABLE 3.2
Types of Losses Local Governments Incurred in the
Whittier Narrows Earthquake

Type of Loss	Amount of Loss	Percent of Loss
Highways, Roads and Streets		
Roads	$ 156,930	
Bridges	16,016	
	172,946	2%
Debris Removal/Demolition	923,623	9
Emergency Protective Measures	1,507,929	15
Water Control Facilities	32,062	*
Public Utilities		
Electric lines/equipment	1,028,956	
Water wells/storage	957,100	
Water pump stations	156,475	
Water lines	155,253	
Sewer lines	41,358	
Gas lines	154	
	2,339,296	24
Public Buildings and Equipment	4,534,510	46
Other Facilities	412,321	4
Total	9,922,687	100

Source: Damage survey reports filed with the Federal
Emergency Management Agency and California Office of
Emergency Services as of June 15, 1988.

*Less than 0.5 percent.

in Chapter 2, which included losses from only two (much less serious) earthquakes. In particular, losses to public buildings owned by cities and counties are trivial (less than 5 percent of total losses) when one looks at the national loss experience during the 1980s, but damages to buildings and their contents accounted for 46 percent of the losses localities experienced in the Whittier Narrows earthquake. In comparison with the national loss data, however, communities suffering damages in the Whittier earthquake did not experience heavy expenses in repairing streets and bridges or in debris removal and demolition. Nationally, those account for over half of the losses to cities and counties, but in the Whittier earthquake, they accounted for just over 10 percent of total losses.

In reviewing these loss data, readers need to keep in mind that failure thresholds for various types of public facilities vary with the magnitude of the event. Thus, this Richter 5.9 earthquake did not cause extensive damages to road networks, while the Loma Prieta earthquake of October 17, 1989, which measured 7.1 on the Richter scale, caused severe damage on the Nimitz Freeway portion of Interstate 880, failure of a 30-foot section of the Bay Bridge, collapse of two roadway overpass bridges in Santa Cruz, and damage to U.S. 101 and California Highway 17. (Forsythe and Harriman 1989) Thus, it is clear that damages from one earthquake cannot be generalized to events of lesser or greater magnitude.

Six Hard-Hit Governments

Six local governments—four medium-sized municipalities with populations between 60,000 and 125,000 and two of the largest local jurisdictions in the country with millions of residents—suffered heavy losses in the Whittier Narrows earthquake. The impact of those losses can be better understood by viewing them relative to the population and area of each jurisdiction. As shown in Table 3.3, on either a per capita or per square mile basis, Whittier suffered by far the largest losses, followed by Monterey Park and Pasadena. Los Angeles and Los Angeles County suffered losses in the millions of dollars, but on a per capita basis their losses were relatively minor. In this section, we first summarize the overall loss and recovery experience of those six governments, and then we look in more detail at each case.

All six jurisdictions had contingency funds budgeted for unexpected events. Those reserves averaged about 10 percent of the annual budgets of the three smaller communities. The percentage of the budget held in reserve was lower in Los Angeles, where contingency funds had been diverted to a war on street gangs, and in Los Angeles County. Thus,

TABLE 3.3
Losses Experienced by Six Hard-Hit Jurisdictions in
the Whittier Narrows Earthquake of October 1, 1987

Juris-diction	Population in 1988	Land Area (sq.mi.)	Total Losses	Losses per Capita	Losses per Sq. Mile
Whittier	70,117	13	1,567,461	22.35	125,397
Monterey Park	60,200	8	730,686	12.14	94,894
Alhambra	71,301	8	485,225	6.81	63,845
Pasadena	125,063	23	426,353	3.41	18,377
Los Angeles County	7,441,300	4,083	$2,474,322	$ 0.33	$ 606
Los Angeles	3,046,969	467	$3,139,565	1.03	6,719

Source: Damage survey reports filed with the Federal
Emergency Management Agency and California Office of
Emergency Services as of June 15, 1988.

it is ironic that the two largest places reported the greatest difficulties financing reconstruction from the earthquake.

Each jurisdiction also carried earthquake insurance on structures that had been financed with bond proceeds. Whittier, however, was the only one of these six governments that carried earthquake insurance on other structures. Of the five jurisdictions that did not carry earthquake insurance, except for bond requirements, three indicated they would continue to rely on self-insurance, since federal and state disaster relief met their needs; one said it would henceforth purchase earthquake insurance for all of its public buildings; and one said it would be willing to join an insurance pool for earthquake protection, if it was available. Several of these cities, in fact, were already members of insurance pools that covered workmen's compensation or liability risks, but the pools did not cover losses from natural hazards. Given the lack of insurance coverage, when we asked financial managers how they would cover losses that were not eligible for federal or state aid and that were in excess of available contingency funds, each said his government would turn to the bond market for financing.

Whittier

Whittier was located closest to the epicenter of the earthquake and it experienced the most serious damages to public property of the six cities studied. Losses included building damages of $925,204 ($800,000 of which was covered by insurance), $598,692 to water and sewerage systems, and $76,446 to city streets and bridges. It also had the highest costs for debris removal and demolition ($431,859), due to the large number of private buildings damaged. With total losses of almost $2.4 million (including those reimbursed by insurance), Whittier expected to cover from $500,000 to $600,000 from its own resources, with the balance paid by federal disaster relief, state aid, and insurance.

Whittier, however, was well prepared for the earthquake. It had a large budget surplus that had built up over the years, it carried earthquake insurance for all of its public buildings, and it had reserve funds for capital improvements to its water system that also helped finance repairs. That was fortunate, because the city expected to lose as much as $500,000 per year in property and sales tax revenues due to severe damages to a number of commercial buildings in the downtown.

Monterey Park

The pattern of damages in Monterey Park was unique among the six cities studied. Infrastructure, rather than buildings and emergency and protective services, accounted for most of the city's losses. In fact, one item—$339,300 in damages to a water storage reservoir—accounted for almost half of the total losses of $730,686. Public buildings experienced little damage ($20,972) in Monterey Park, even though the city is located close to the epicenter of the earthquake. Local officials expect federal disaster relief to cover three quarters of the costs of the earthquake, with state aid covering much of the rest. As of June 1988, however, funds from federal and state sources had not been received.

Monterey Park officials told us the city would absorb about $100,000 in incidental costs of recovery. They expected little difficulty in absorbing those losses, however, since the city had the largest general fund reserve (nearly 20 percent) of the six jurisdictions we studied. That fund balance was used to pay for initial clean-up costs, emergency and protective services, and emergency repairs. Monterey Park purchased earthquake insurance coverage after the earthquake. Officials also seemed interested in adding earthquake risks to those covered by the municipal liability pool to which the city belonged.

Alhambra

Alhambra claimed just under half a million dollars ($485,225) in losses from the earthquake. The costs of emergency and protective services accounted for almost half of that amount and damages to public buildings (principally damages to two fire stations) about a third. However, the city was in the midst of an argument with FEMA about losses to the fire stations. According to Alhambra officials, the stations needed to be replaced at a cost of over $800,000, while FEMA believed they could be repaired. Thus, depending on the outcome of that dispute, losses in Alhambra could increase sharply.

Because emergency and protective service costs, other than overtime pay, generally are not eligible for federal disaster relief, Alhambra was relying on the State of California to provide assistance to pay over 60 percent of its losses. As of June 1988, the city had expended over $200,000 from its general fund on earthquake recovery and had received $46,000 in reimbursement from FEMA. The shortfall was made up with already budgeted contingency funds. Losses to public buildings in Alhambra were not covered by earthquake insurance, but the city said it planned to carry insurance in the future. When asked why the city did not carry earthquake insurance in the past, officials cited the availability of state, not federal, disaster assistance as the primary reason.

Pasadena

Pasadena's relatively small (125,053) population is misleading in terms of its exposure to damages from natural hazards. The city has a large downtown with considerable public investment there, and it owns a number of special-purpose facilities, such as the Rose Bowl and Pasadena Convention Center. The city claimed losses with FEMA and OES of $426,353, with most of those due to damages to public buildings ($264,485) and expenses for emergency and protective services ($111,032). About half of its losses were deemed eligible for federal disaster relief, and the state assumed responsibility for the other half. As of June 1988, nine months after the earthquake struck, however, Pasadena city officials had received neither federal nor state reimbursement for earthquake-related expenses and were relying on previously budgeted emergency reserves to fund repairs.

Pasadena was largely self-insured. It did not carry earthquake insurance on its public buildings and was not a member of a municipal insurance pool. City officials told us earthquake insurance offered little benefit given the generous nature of federal and state disaster relief policies.

City of Los Angeles

Los Angeles filed eligible claims with FEMA and the state Office of Emergency Services for over $3 million in losses, and city officials estimated total claims could run as high as $8.5 million depending upon the resolution of disputes with federal and state officials over whether additional damages were cosmetic or structural. The city's electrical distribution system (with over $800,000 in damages) and public buildings (with damages of $1.1 million) accounted for much of the city's losses. FEMA rated two thirds of the losses claimed by city officials as ineligible for federal disaster relief, but the state came to the city's aid, providing over $2 million in earthquake recovery assistance.

Although losses per capita were small ($1.03), city officials reported great difficulty financing recovery. Previously budgeted funds had been diverted to its war on street gangs, and general fund reserves were virtually nonexistent. Because the city had been postponing capital improvements, capital reserves also were not available for earthquake recovery. Furthermore, Los Angeles was largely self-insured for property, liability, and workmen's compensation risks and could not turn to insurers to provide the ready cash needed for recovery.

Los Angeles County

Los Angeles County experienced approximately $2.5 million in losses, principally in damages to public buildings (82 percent of total losses). Interviews with local officials revealed that the county and FEMA were in the midst of a major dispute over the damages to two buildings: a health services center and a warehouse. FEMA contended the buildings suffered only minor damage, while the county argued they had to be replaced entirely. With other losses in dispute as well, the total costs of the disaster to the county could have risen to as high as $22 million. County officials were not particularly interested in earthquake insurance, however, even though they were responsible for the safety of over 4,000 public buildings, because they felt it might not be cost effective.

Conclusions

Comparison of losses from the Whittier Narrows earthquake with the national loss data presented in Chapter 2 indicates that public buildings and water systems are more vulnerable to damages from earthquakes than from floods and hurricanes, while roads and streets and water control facilities are less vulnerable. That suggests the most appropriate loss recovery funding mechanisms may be different for earthquakes than for other types of natural disasters.

Since more than half of the damages to the public sector in the Whittier Narrows earthquake was to buildings, much of the loss incurred was insurable at the time of the event. As demonstrated by the case of Whittier, where $800,000 in damages to buildings that otherwise would have been covered by federal and state disaster relief were paid by the city's insurance companies, insurance has definite advantages for federal and state tax payers. Insurance also provides benefits to local governments, since they have more certainty as to losses that will be covered than is true of federal and state disaster relief programs, where disputes over what is and is not eligible for assistance are common. Finally, insurance payments are received shortly after a loss is incurred; relief payments can take a number of months, which requires localities to find interim sources of funding to pay for reconstruction.

Considering the lag time between when losses are incurred and relief payments arrive, local governments at risk from natural hazards need to have adequate contingency funds in reserve. Those moneys do not have to be earmarked for disaster recovery to be useful. The experience of local governments in the Whittier Narrows earthquake indicates that the rule of thumb of setting aside 5 percent of operating budgets for contingencies provides adequate reserves to meet most emergency expenses.

The six case studies suggest that federal and state disaster relief provide a significant disincentive for localities to purchase earthquake insurance or to earmark contingency and other reserve funds specifically for disaster recovery. In light of federal relief policies and those of the State of California, which stood ready to fund most losses that the federal government would not cover plus all of the required state/local match, jurisdictions felt that earthquake insurance was not worth the expense, even though it was widely available. As a result, earthquake risk and the cost of recovery largely have been transferred from the local level to higher levels of government.

PART 2

How to Control Losses

4

Financial Planning Strategies

The fiscal environment of state and local governments has changed markedly over the past decade. Periods of continued growth in revenues that sustained an ever-expanding service pie came to an abrupt halt in the late 1970s. As state and local governments have become more aware of resource limits, their financial planning strategies have undergone a profound change. Risk management is no longer viewed as a passive activity involving little more than the purchase of commercial insurance. Instead local government financial planners are becoming more aggressive in designing and implementing strategies that limit government exposure to resource losses. That trend offers an opportunity to integrate consideration of natural hazards into local financial planning. In this chapter, we describe a set of procedures for doing that.

Risk management is an important element of the financial planning processes of local governments. Its objective is to conserve governmental resources from accidental loss. All resources—including human, financial, physical and natural—are exposed to risks that may result in losses. A successful risk management program protects government assets, assures a safe environment for government employees and the general public, minimizes the interruption of essential public services, and reduces the financial impact of losses. The components of a risk management strategy are identification of potential loss situations; application of reasonable and effective loss-control measures; and evaluation of the effectiveness of the risk management program.

We begin this chapter by reviewing the elements of a risk management program and current risk management practices in state and local governments. We then apply that model to the particular category of losses of concern here—those to the public sector from natural hazards. We pay particular attention to the recent developments in risk management of self insurance and risk pooling and their potential as tools state and local governments can use to deal with the threats posed by disasters.

We then conclude by suggesting key elements that will comprise a financial planning strategy for natural hazards.

Identifying Exposure to Risk

The first step in managing risk is to identify the exposure of governmental resources to potential risks. State and local governments experience four basic types of risk: damage to real and personal property; loss of property; loss of income or increased costs that ensue from property losses; and liability to others resulting from injury to persons or property. Those risks may be further classified according to whether the risk results in direct or indirect losses to the governmental entity. Direct losses, which reduce a government's stock of human, physical and natural resources, include the damage to or loss of real and personal property and the risk of liability claims arising from injuries to persons and/or damage to their property. Losses in income, earnings or cash flow reflect indirect losses. Examples include reduced tax revenues resulting from the loss of taxable or revenue-generating property (e.g. a municipal utility), or additional expenses incurred in purchasing public services from other agencies, renting other buildings, or repairing damaged facilities. Risks are often interrelated, both among direct losses (e.g. damage to real property resulting in liability risks) and between direct and indirect losses (e.g. damage to the municipal sewage treatment plant resulting in lost revenues and increased costs of service delivery).

Once potential risks are identified, the governmental entity must then assess the likelihood that a risk will occur, or *frequency*, and the size of the loss that might result, or *severity*. The severity of the loss has two dimensions: the value of each individual resource at risk and the number of resources likely to be affected by the risk. The degree of loss, which depends on those two elements, may be characterized as: low frequency/low severity, high freqency/low severity, low frequency/ high severity, and high frequency/high severity. Losses would be least for low frequency/low severity events and greatest for high frequency/ high severity events.

In order to estimate the probable exposure to risk acurately, governments must maintain complete inventories of property, its replacement cost, and a historical log of past incidences of loss. Because it may be necessary to replace property after a loss, estimates of replacement costs should be adjusted periodically to account for inflation. A benchmark of a three-to-five-year history of losses from high frequency events is generally required to adequately predict a government's exposure to risk from that source of loss. For real or personal property, those data are often readily accessible, while the valuation of other resources (e.g.

human or natural resources) is often more difficult. In assessing risk from low frequency events, governments may distinguish between maximum foreseeable loss (i.e. the worst case scenario) and maximum probable loss (i.e. the worst loss to be expected under "average" conditions).

State and local governments ultimately should be interested in ways to protect their resource base and hence with ways to control the potential risks they face. The objective of risk control is the elimination, reduction, assumption or transfer of risk and its attendant losses. The manner in which risks are controlled is often determined by the severity and frequency of the loss.

Elimination of Risk

The total elimination of risk would obviously be the most desirable control mechanism for any government. Because of the adverse effects of severe losses on resources, risk management experts recommend that governments eliminate high severity risks of all frequencies whenever feasible. Risk may be eliminated by changing the way something is done (e.g. by using safety equipment) or by discontinuing risk-prone activities. Although certain to eliminate risk, as a general rule, discontinuing activities is viable only with nonessential services.

Reduction of Risk

All losses cannot be prevented; but, the frequency of their occurrence can be controlled, and the severity of the loss can be reduced to the extent that it is no longer a significant drain on resources. In pursuing a risk management strategy, governments should reduce exposure to all risks while paying particular attention to reducing those risks with the greatest severity. Exposure to loss can be reduced by changing work methods or equipment, developing and enforcing safety programs, or mitigation efforts. Risk reduction strategies are most effective when dealing with losses to property (e.g. fire, windstorm, flood, collapse, machinery breakdown) and preventing casualty losses (e.g. workers' compensation, general liability, product liability, fleet automotive, professional errors and omissions).

After taking all feasible steps to eliminate or lessen the possibility of loss, governments must determine whether they should assume or transfer the financial burden of risks that remain. Because of their lower cost or predictable nature, low severity risks are often assumed; because they are impossible to predict and have potentially devastating effects, high severity/low frequency risks are often transferred.

Assumption of Risk

Governments may assume the financial burden of loss unexpectedly, because of unintended circumstances, or on a planned basis. Unexpected assumption of risk may arise due to a lack of understanding of risk management processes (e.g., a failure to understand the terms of commercial insurance) or unsatisfactory risk identification and control. Once a governmental unit has a reasonable idea of what risks it faces, and has eliminated or reduced those risks to the greatest possible extent, it may choose to process and pay for all remaining losses or a portion of losses from its own financial resources. The planned assumption of low-frequency risks, such as through the deductible portion of commercial insurance coverage, is usually justified on cost effectiveness grounds and may take the form of expensing the loss to a departmental budget or charging the loss to a funded reserve.

Non-Funded ("No-insurance") Loss Control

Low-severity losses are often treated as an operating expense and charged to departmental budgets. That practice is sometimes referred to as a "non-funded" or "no-insurance" means of loss control. The size of the departmental budget and the competition from alternative uses of funds will determine the usefulness of this strategy as a means of assuming losses. Obviously, non-funded loss control is more feasible with larger departmental budgets and more slack resources.

Reserve Funds

State and local governments have historically relied upon reserve and contingency funds as a financial management tool for dealing with unexpected events. Reserve funds may be used as a general source of financing, or they may be targeted for particular purposes. Governments may accumulate general cash reserves for precautionary reasons such as a natural catastrophe (e.g. a hurricane or flood), as protection against fluctuations in business cycles, or because of cash flow problems associated with variation in the timing of revenues and expenditures. Financial analysts have traditionally accepted a 5 percent ratio of unobligated balances to expenditures as a reasonable level of general reserves. (National Governors' Association 1985: 18) Those general purpose reserves have recently become more prominent tools of financial management. Gold suggests that the increasing use of contingency funds by states reflects attempts to reduce uncertainty in the budgeting process; by 1985, twenty-nine states had established stabilization or "Rainy Day" funds. (ACIR 1986: 160)

Governments also may target reserve funds more narrowly in managing risk. Self insurance programs are structured and funded so that sums of money are appropriated annually for the purpose of paying for losses. Self insurance is often used for workers' compensation, employee benefit programs (e.g., medical, hospitalization, accident and sickness) and to a lesser degree, for property, group life and short-term liability. A general guideline is that governments should be willing to accept from 0.1 percent to 0.5 percent of their operating budgets in uninsured losses arising out of a single occurrence, and up to 1 percent of their operating budgets as the aggregate of all such self-insured losses in a single fiscal year. (Cragg and Kloman 1985: 16)

The feasibility of self insurance as a risk management tool is largely determined by the financial resources of a jurisdiction, its ability to reasonably predict future losses, and the cost effectiveness of pursuing such a program.

A funded reserve is like a bond sinking fund, where the total size of the fund is decided in advance for a given number of years, and annuity calculations are used to arrive at the required annual deposit needed to reach the desired fund size. The size of the fund is determined by the average loss experience of the governmental unit over the past three to five years. Unlike a bond fund, though, the value of resources may increase with inflation, and hence the size of the reserve fund needed may also increase. The advantages of self insurance are more promptly realized if sufficient reserves exist to set up the plan immediately, because of the income earnings of the reserve.

When large amounts are required to establish the reserve fund, it may be infeasible to set up the full reserves out of available cash. In that situation, a government could begin the self insurance program with a moderate retention of risk and set aside the insurance premiums saved thereby for the creation of the reserve. As the reserve grows, additional exposure can be retained on the same basis and the plan expanded to its full scope over a period of years.

Another way to capitalize the reserve fund is risk financing through capital markets. When capital markets are used, governments (often special districts with the power to incur debt) issue long-term debt to finance the reserve fund. Advantages of the capital market approach include a larger reserve up front which provides higher levels of risk coverage and yields greater investment income, greater stability and predictability of annual contributions due to the fixed nature of debt service payments, and the potential to encumber the loss reserve fund so that its resources are unavailable for other uses. Because this is a relatively new and untested means of risk financing, however, all of the legal, financial and tax implications are not fully understood. The disadvantages of this approach arise primarily from the costs and implied obligations of issuing debt. Since most local governments face limits on the amount of debt they may issue, this use of debt may preclude long-term borrowing for other purposes. And in some cases, the debt service payments may extend beyond the years of losses funded.

Handling Catastrophic Events When Reserve Funds Are Used. Because the viability of self insurance as a means of risk control depends on the government's ability to accurately predict its future losses, special provisions should be made for catastrophic events (high severity risks) and recurrent events (high frequency risks). Protection from catastrophic events may be provided by purchasing excess coverage insurance from commercial insurers. It will be easier to obtain excess coverage insurance if a government has retained a high level of risk through self insurance. Governments may provide funds for recurrent events through "post-loss funding," whereby the entity arranges for a standby letter (or line) of credit from a commercial financial institution. That arrangement allows the government to borrow funds at an agreed upon rate in the event a loss occurs.

Cost-Effectiveness of Reserve Funds. Self insurance tends to promote better loss control because governments are acutely aware of the cost of losses. In addition, self insurance improves the processing of claims, and perhaps most importantly, saves money. Comparable-coverage commercial insurance is more expensive because it includes the overhead costs and profits of the insuring firm, which in some cases may be as much as 40 percent of a typical premium. (Rakich no date)

The assumption of risk by relying on funded reserves is not problem-free, however. The viability of this option hinges on the legal authority to carry over balances from year to year or the legal authority to incur debt to fund the reserve. Even with that legal authority, public officials may be inclined to raid a reserve fund for other purposes unless the funds are strictly encumbered for loss reimbursement purposes. Finally, as a result of the unpredictability of potential losses, the reserve may be underfunded and less than adequate as a means of financial support.

Transfer of Risk

A final means of providing financial resources to deal with losses is to transfer risk to another party. Local governments may transfer risk to the private sector, to higher levels of government, or, through insurance pools, to other local units of government. In most cases of risk transfer, governments assume a portion of the risk and then transfer the residual to another party.

Transfer to the Private Sector

Governments may transfer risk to the private sector by contracting out for the risk-prone activities or by purchasing commercial insurance. When contracting is used as a means of transfer, the contractor assumes the responsibility for service delivery and hence assumes the potential risk. The more common form of transfer to the private sector, however, is through the purchase of commercial insurance.

When purchasing commercial insurance, a government pays a premium to the insurance agent in return for the receipt of revenues in the event that losses occur to the government's resources. The amount of the premium depends upon the expected severity and frequency of loss and the cost of administering the insurance policy. Governments often assume a portion of the loss through the use of deductible clauses, and they may purchase coinsurance, where a stipulated share of the insurable value of an asset must be carried at the face value of insurance if the government wishes to be fully reimbursed for partial losses. Or, excess coverage insurance (or reinsurance), which offers an additional umbrella of protection, may be purchased. Commercial insurance is frequently carried by governments for damage to real and personal property.

Transfer to State and Federal Governments

Governments may rely on the financial resources of higher levels of government to provide resources to deal with losses. The federal government underwrites flood insurance protection through the National Flood Insurance Program and offers emergency loans and grants for losses incurred as a result of Presidentially-declared disasters (federal disaster relief programs are described in Appendix A). In establishing those programs, Congress intended to provide financial assistance (or insurance, in the case of the flood insurance program) to supplement the financial efforts of state and local governments. As a result, the national government expects state and local governments to assume a portion of the financial losses stemming from natural disasters. State governments also provide grants and loans to local governments for use in meeting catastrophic losses, as illustrated by the Whittier Narrows earthquake described in Chapter 3.

Transfer to Insurance Pools

Self insurance may be a solution for larger local governments, but most small governmental units do not have the financial capacity to assume large risks. Smaller governments can increase their ability to manage risk, however, by pooling their funds with other governments.

Insurance pooling, a relatively recent development in risk management, is now undertaken on local, state, regional and inter-state bases. The first public sector insurance pool arose from dissatisfaction with the services of commercial insurers and was implemented in 1974 by the Texas Municipal League for workers' compensation claims for its member cities. By 1986, municipal leagues in twenty-two states sponsored insurance pools. (See Table 4.1.) The first interstate insurance pool in the nation, the Housing Authorities Risk Retention Group, was chartered in 1987 by a group of housing authorities (including those of New York, Chicago and San Francisco). The dissemination of pooling throughout local governments is expected to continue; insurance analysts have noted the possibility that ". . . by 1995, more than one half of all governmental risk funding will be carried out through government sponsored pools and excess insurance companies." (Cragg and Kloman 1985: 16)

Insurance pooling is commonly used for workers' compensation and health insurance because of the predictability of payments from these plans, although pooling for liability purposes became common in 1984 at the height of the insurance liability crisis. Participants in insurance pools include cities, counties, school districts, utility districts, and water districts.

Forming a Pool. Insurance pooling entails the coordination of several governmental entities together to handle the risks of accidental loss on a group basis. The group may be structured along geographic or functional lines. This coordination sufficiently enlarges the base of exposure to make losses more predictable, thereby reducing the costs of dealing with those risks; the more participants in the pool, the greater the spreading of risks and the lower are the pro-rata share of costs for each participant.

In order to form a pool, enabling legislation, interlocal cooperation or joint powers acts must exist that authorize pooling. Local government pools are often organized under a joint powers agreement or an interlocal agreement that spells out the terms and conditions of pool membership. These agreements often contain information concerning the means of governance of the pool, powers of the pool to conduct financial transactions, fiscal year of the pool, sources of funds, assessment of costs, disposition of assets upon termination of the pool, accounts and records of the pool, the pool's functions and responsibilities, constituent governments' responsibilities, requirements for the initial formation of the pool, and any other information germane to the pool agreements.

Funding the Pool. Once the structure of the pool has been established, the next concern is how the pool will be funded. The establishment of the insurance pool is very similar to the establishment of reserve funds, except that funds are contributed by each of the constituent governments and the magnitude of the pool is likely to be considerably larger since

TABLE 4.1
Group Self Insurance Pools
Sponsored by State Municipal Leagues

State	Health and Accident	Workers Compensation	Type of Pool — Liability	Unemployment Compensation	Property
Alabama		X			
Arkansas	X	X	X		X
Connecticut		X	X[a]		X[a]
Florida	X	X	X		
Georgia	X				
Illinois		X	X		X
Iowa		X			
Kentucky		X		X	
Louisiana		X	X		
Maine	X	X	X[a]	X	
Massachusetts		X			
Michigan		X	X	X	X
Minnesota	X	X	X		X
New Hampshire	X			X	
New Mexico		X			
North Carolina	X	X	X[a]		
Oklahoma	X	X	X		
South Carolina	X	X			
Tennessee	X	X	X		
Texas		X	X		
Utah	X	X	X		X
Vermont		X[a]	X[a]	X	
Virginia		X			

Source: Based on information from National League of
Cities, April 1986.

[a]Pool being developed as of 1/86.

the scope of risk coverage extends across many governments. Insurance pools are often structured according to a protective pyramid with self insurance at the base, pooling in the middle, and excess coverage (or catastrophe insurance) at the apex. Together those three tools can combine to provide sufficient protection for governmental units.

For high-frequency/low-severity losses, governmental units generally self insure to keep the financial claims against the insurance pool to a minimum. That self insurance feature permits premiums to be held at a reasonable level, while encouraging loss control activities by constituent governments.

For moderate-frequency/moderate-severity losses, governments rely on the financial resources of the pool; in order to maintain the financial viability of the pool, pools often set an upper limit on the amount the pool will pay to an individual government.

For low-frequency/high-severity losses (i.e. catastrophes), excess coverage insurance is generally purchased by the pool or by the pool's individual member governments.

Advantages and Disadvantages of Pools. Insurance pools provide many advantages to governmental units. Primary among these advantages are: lower and more stable costs; greater control over insurance services, since the pool represents the interests of governmental units; and access to professional management services. The costs of insurance pools tend to be lower than self insurance or commercial coverage due to the economies of scale of providing a large scope of coverage and the incentive provided for improved loss prevention and control by member governments. Because a well-capitalized insurance pool provides a broad measure of coverage, the pool may have access to excess coverage insurance that would not be available to an individual governmental unit.

The disadvantages associated with insurance pooling stem from the relinquishment of control by individual governmental units to a broader organization. Inequities may occur due to disparities in size (e.g. when larger governmental units have a disproportionate say in establishing the policies of the pool) or exposure to risk (e.g. when certain governmental units control losses less effectively than others). An additional problem arises from the notion of joint and several liability—the situation where an individual governmental unit is responsible for losses of another governmental unit. Membership in an insurance pool may obligate governments to the pool on a long-term basis. By the terms of some joint powers agreements, for example, pool members may be assessed for payments to the pool even if they have withdrawn their membership. In the case of withdrawal, governments may also sacrifice their claims to any assets of the pool.

Evaluating Risk Management Programs

The final step in a risk management strategy is the continual evaluation of the risk management program. Because the successful management of risk is an ongoing process, it is important for governments to make certain that risk management policies and processes are followed, that risk management goals are being achieved, and that this evaluation is complemented by periodic independent audits of the risk management program. That procedure assures risks are identified correctly and controlled to the maximum extent, such that the government's resources are shielded from losses.

Using Risk Management Concepts
to Cope with Disasters

The previous section delineated the elements of a risk management strategy, namely the identification of risk, the control of risk, and the evaluation of risk management programs. This section applies those tools to the specific consideration of how state and local governments might better control the almost $1 billion they experience in average annual losses from natural hazards. This extension is a straightforward application of the risk management model to certain classes of property (namely public infrastructure) that represent valuable resources of state and local governments that are subject to loss.

Identifying Exposure to Losses from Natural Hazards

The first step in a viable risk management strategy is to identify the exposure to risk, as determined by the frequency and severity of losses to public facilities. The assessment of the frequency and severity of losses is referred to as vulnerability analysis. Though applicable in theory and advocated by the Federal Emergency Management Agency, which has produced guides to vulnerability analysis, this step is generally more difficult when assessing losses resulting from natural disasters than for other types of risks that governmental entities face. Many governmental units have poor data on or lack an inventory of facilities and find it difficult to estimate the liklihood of many natural disasters (the difficulties of risk assessment are discussed further in Chapter 7).

The identification of facilities at risk is difficult because many state and local governments do not keep detailed records of the value of their entire inventory of public facilities. Certain classes of property, such as buildings and public utilities, may be measured regularly and accurately for insurance purposes, while other classes of property which are less likely to be insured, such as bridges and sewer lines, may be measured infrequently and valued poorly. Capital budgeting and planning reforms, the movement toward compliance with Generally Accepted Accounting Practices (GAAP), and the establishment of General Fixed Asset Account Groups (GFAAG), may provide the needed inventory data in the future, however.

Because extreme natural events that result in disaster occur infrequently and in varying degrees of severity, it is highly unlikely that a jurisdiction will have an adequate history of past losses, although data may be available for certain types of disasters, such as flooding. Without a past history as a base of information, governments may rely on national average occurrences of natural disasters as a means of predicting vulnerability. The problem here, though, is that the severity and frequency of natural disasters is highly variable (see Table 2.1); in fact, more than one-quarter of the dollar value of all losses experienced between 1980 and mid-1987 was absorbed by less than one percent of the 6,816 state and local governments affected by the disasters we studied. Although the identification and assessment of risk is difficult, it is not an insurmountable task, as discussed in Chapter 7.

Controlling the Risk to Public Facilities from Natural Hazards

Our discussion focuses on controlling the risk to public facilities from natural disasters. As mentioned previously, governments have four basic avenues of risk control: the elimination of risk, the reduction of risk, the assumption of risk, and the transfer of risk to another party. The choice of which risk control mechanism is adopted depends in part on the frequency and severity of the losses that result from natural hazards.

Eliminating Losses from Natural Hazards. The losses of greatest concern here are those of the highest severity. Governments may eliminate those losses by discontinuing the service that is at risk or by moving facilities to an area that is less risk prone. For many of the public facilities considered here, however, governments cannot discontinue the provision of the services they provide, since they are often essential and not amenable to private provision. The movement of at-risk facilities is also problematic given the scope and durability of large fixed investments. Hence the elimination of risks to public facilities from natural hazards is a limited risk management tool for governmental entities.

Reducing Losses from Natural Hazards. Governments may reduce losses by limiting the severity or frequency of exposure to risk. Opportunities for reducing the occurrence of natural disasters through technological means such as flood control are diminishing and, in the case of other hazards, such as hurricanes and earthquakes, that is not possible. Governments can reduce losses from natural disasters by limiting the susceptibility of facilities to damage through various hazard mitigation measures, such as retrofitting facilities and adopting appropriate land use regulations. A comprehensive approach for doing that is discussed in the following chapter.

Assuming Losses from Natural Hazards. Governments may assume the financial burden of dealing with losses from natural disasters on an unexpected or planned basis. An unexpected assumption of these losses might be treated as an operating expense and charged to a departmental budget. That may be a viable strategy for many local governments, since we found earlier that two-thirds of governmental entities that reported losses in Presidentially declared natural disasters between 1980 and mid-1987 experienced losses of less than $50,000 (see Table 2.1), and a quarter experienced losses of less than $5,000. The ability to absorb losses as an operating expense depends on the amount of funds available to the government and the frequency and severity of the loss. If currently available funds were insufficient to meet low-severity/low-frequency losses, then a government might resort to the imposition of emergency taxes or surcharges on a one-time basis, or it might turn to the capital markets and issue debt to finance the losses, which is what governments that experienced losses in the Whittier Narrows earthquake told us they would do.

For losses from natural disasters of low-severity/high-frequency or of low-to-medium severity (i.e. between $50,000 and $5,000,000), governments might be best advised to assume those losses through the use of contingency or reserve funds, provided that the funds have adequate levels of resources.

A high-severity loss would be virtually impossible for most governments to adsorb through contingency funds or emergency charges. Few local governments could finance a $5 million catastrophic loss from funds on hand, or from the imposition of a one-time charge or fee. Borrowing may present an alternative source of funding for those catastrophic losses, although a catastrophic loss may have eliminated resources to such an extent that the borrowing capacity of the governmental entity is severely constrained.

Because these actions present a noticeable drain on the resources of a government, assumption of risk may encourage governments to eliminate or reduce risks more effectively in the future, however.

Transferring Losses from Natural Hazards. Governments may obtain financial resources for losses from natural disasters by transferring the loss, or a portion of the loss, to the private sector, higher levels of government, or other governmental units.

The full transferral of losses to another party lies at the opposite end of the continuum from full assumption of losses. It is unlikely that governments would be able to fully transfer losses from natural disasters to commercial insurance companies, since such insurance is generally contingent upon the assumption of a portion of the losses through a deductible provision. The intent of the deductible provision is to encourage governments to eliminate and/or reduce their exposure to loss as much as possible, which then reduces the exposure of the insurance company.

Losses could be fully transferred to higher levels of government in the form of federal and state disaster assistance grants. Because of the greater financial capacity of states and the federal government, they are better able to finance losses from natural disasters than local governments. The primary shortcoming of grant-in-aid financing is that it may discourage the elimination or reduction of risks since benefitted governments have no incentive to limit their exposure to loss. Without these first important steps of a risk management strategy, federal and state disaster relief will not conserve scarce financial resources.

A partial transfer of risk is a more likely policy option. Governments currently transfer a portion of risk to commercial insurance companies through deductible provisions and the purchase of excess coverage insurance. But, that transfer scheme has limited applicability with regard to losses from natural disasters. As we demonstrated in Chapter 2, commercial insurance coverage is not available for many types of property damaged in natural disasters, so the deductible provision would not apply in those situations. Simulations of the effects of extremely large disaster events ($7 billion catastrophic losses to property) have noted the difficulty the domestic insurance industry would have in providing coverage for such events. (All-Industry Research Advisory Council 1986) Without sufficient reserves to cover large catastrophic losses, commercial insurance alone is not a viable risk management tool for coping with natural disasters.

Higher levels of government could operate as reinsurers for governmental entities providing self insurance against losses from natural disasters of high severity, with the necessary precondition that lower levels of government eliminate and/or reduce their exposure to losses from natural hazards to the maximum possible extent. It is unlikely that an individual state would have sufficient financial resources to deal with catastrophic losses of the highest magnitude, although the federal government's resources would be sufficient to cover such losses.

Insurance pools offer a final means to transfer a portion of the risk of loss from natural disasters to other governmental entities. The three key elements of a successful insurance pool are the retention of a portion of risk by each governmental entity, the pooling of resources across a large group for losses of a greater magnitude, and the use of excess coverage or reinsurance to maintain the financial viability of the pool in the event of catastrophic losses. Governmental entities would be required to assume low severity losses from natural hazards in order to encourage the reduction and elimination of losses to the maximum possible extent. Because the large losses from natural disasters that would require the resources of the pool tend to be concentrated in a few geographic areas, a successful insurance pool would require federal or state oversight to assure that adverse selection does not affect the participants in the pool. Adverse selection occurs when only those governmental entities most likely to suffer large losses are interested in joining the insurance pool. The success of an insurance pool depends on a large distribution of risk, so that the probability of loss at any one time is relatively small. With adverse selection, each participant faces a high probability of loss, and the resources of the pool would be exhausted very quickly. Federal or state participation would also be required as a provider of excess coverage insurance.

Conclusions

In conclusion, it seems clear that a successful risk management strategy for dealing with public sector losses from natural disasters would encourage loss elimination and loss reduction strategies and would involve higher levels of government. The two most promising policy options for dealing with potential catastrophic losses from natural disasters appear to be self insurance with higher levels of government operating as reinsurers, and greater use of insurance mechanisms. In the event of catastrophic losses of the greatest magnitude, the federal government would play the dominant role through the provision of relief.

5

Physical Planning Strategies

Many local governments engage in community physical planning, which we propose is both a familiar and a suitable approach to manage risk from natural hazards. Four common elements of community planning—comprehensive planning or master planning, community facility planning, capital improvement programming, and growth management—provide a ready-made framework for managing risks to the public sector from natural hazards. Those elements of community planning provide vehicles for balancing risk management objectives with other fundamental community objectives, such as economic development, environmental quality, equity, and choice. Those elements of community planning also can address three of the five aspects of risk management identified in Chapter 4: identification of government's exposure to risks, risk elimination, and risk reduction. The fact that comprehensive planning, community facility planning, capital improvement programming, and growth management are already undertaken by many local governments and are relatively well understood and accepted by local officials and citizens makes them particularly appropriate. In this chapter, we describe how community physical planning can both incorporate risk management considerations and be used as a tool in analyzing risk and formulating risk management policy.

Comprehensive Planning

Many if not most local governments in the U.S. undertake comprehensive planning and have a comprehensive plan. That fact, in combination with the ready availability of data needed for risk analysis from the Federal Emergency Management Agency (e.g., floodplain mapping), U.S. Geological Survey (e.g., flood, earthquake, and landslide hazard-zone delineation) as well as from other sources, such as state geological offices, and the innate suitability of comprehensive planning for risk analysis and risk management policy (more on that below), all combine to provide a basis for including risk identification, risk elimination, and risk reduction in comprehensive plans.

Characteristics and Functions
of the Comprehensive Plan

The comprehensive plan is an official statement of a city or county legislative body and planning board that sets forth important policies concerning the future development of the community. It is long range (ten to twenty-five years). And it is comprehensive in the sense that it: (1) encompasses all geographic areas of the community, including areas outside present city limits but expected to be developed within the time span of the plan; (2) includes all functional elements that bear on development (land use, infrastructure, environment); (3) pursues multiple governmental objectives; and (4) contains policies for private and public development, including public facilities and infrastructure. Thus it generally specifies the location of future private and public land uses, community facilities, open space, transportation, and redevelopment areas.

The comprehensive plan generally serves three functions for local government. First, it is a vehicle for determining policy. That is, it provides a process by which the legislative body, advisory boards, staff and citizens consider and agree on a coherent set of policies to guide future decisions about the development and redevelopment of the community. Second, the comprehensive plan communicates policy to the development industry, future legislators, neighborhood and other interest groups, citizens, and planning board members and other appointed officials. Beyond being informative about policy, the plan can be educational—arousing interest, identifying trends, clarifying issues, awakening people to possibilities for the future. Third, the plan can help implement policy. It does that when legislative bodies use it as a guide to decisions on specific legislation and development matters that come up weekly or monthly. What we propose is that information and policy about natural hazards, their associated risks, and strategies to control those risks be included in comprehensive planning, and that in turn comprehensive plans serve as a mechanism through which risk management policy is determined, communicated, and effectuated.

The comprehensive plan usually devotes sections to goals and objectives, analyses of conditions and trends, and policies in the form of guidelines for whole classes of decisions (such as where development will be encouraged or discouraged and under what conditions utilities will be extended). It almost always has elements on land use, circulation, housing, community facilities, and, if a city rather than a county, on redevelopment. Sometimes it will have sections on economic development, specific districts (such as the downtown area or a historic neighborhood), environmental protection and open space, and perhaps less frequently it has a section on hazardous areas or seismic safety. The state of California, for example, requires municipalities and counties to have a safety element (floods, fires and geologic hazards such as earthquake faults if relevant) and encourages individual governments to incorporate earthquake hazards into a required open space element if the state geologist delineates an earthquake study zone in the community. (Office of Planning and Research, State of California 1987: 128, 146–153, 252–254)

Role of the Comprehensive Plan
in Risk Management

There are seven reasons why the comprehensive plan is particularly well suited for risk management. First, risk management objectives must at some point be balanced against other important governmental objectives such as efficiency of governmental operations, economic development, environmental quality, equity and choice. Being long range, comprehensive in the scope of governmental and private-sector activities addressed, and already concerned with balancing multiple objectives, the comprehensive plan is an excellent place to begin balancing risk management with other objectives.

Second, the comprehensive plan almost always has a strong spatial dimension to it, including conditions and trends as well as policies. Since most natural hazards have a spatial pattern of likely occurrence and severity and the inventory of infrastructure has a spatial dimension of location and relative vulnerability, the comprehensive planning process is a suitable place to begin identifying spatial aspects of exposure to risk and formulating locational strategies for controlling risk.

Third, comprehensive planning is based on a broad foundation of information, analysis, and projection about soils, topography, hydrology, geology, structures, infrastructure, population, land value, and economic activity, all of which relate to risk from natural hazards. In other words, the comprehensive planning process is often the best information source available to local government.

Fourth, comprehensive planning already has a tradition of incorporating hazard information and other spatially differentiated environmental and land use data into analyses of the landscape (called suitability assessments or urban capacity assessments). Those suitability analyses are the primary bases for allocating urban development, including community facilities, to sites best suited in the sense of long-run efficiency. Suitability analyses suggest which locations should be avoided, which are usable if certain mitigation standards are met in site design and construction, and which are highly desirable for reasons that may tend to outweigh the risks from natural hazards. Suitability assessment can, and already often does, include indicators of vulnerability to natural hazards such as flooding, storm surge, landslide, subsidence, earthquake fault and soil liquefaction. Suitability analyses add accessibility, amenities, quality of community services, and ease of providing future services to the judgment about where urban development should occur.

Fifth, the comprehensive plan is where the scale and location of public investments begin to be coordinated with the scale and location of private investment, which in turn determines the pattern of demand for public services and infrastructure. Thus, considerations of risks from natural hazards can enter into the determination of suitable location for private development that will in turn create demand for public infrastructure. Indirectly then, comprehensive planning can reduce the demand for public investment in hazardous areas.

Sixth, because of the features mentioned above, the comprehensive plan is a good framework for beginning to sort out which locations and which public facilities are best addressed by which risk control strategies— elimination, reduction, assumption or transfer. It does that within a comprehensive framework of other community values, such as economic development.

Seventh and finally, the comprehensive plan and the analyses behind it form an important part of the legal justification for regulations and other risk management devices, such as acquisition of land and buildings in hazard zones, taxing to recover the costs of hazard mitigation, and pricing of services to recover hazard mitigation costs.

Community Facility Planning

While the comprehensive plan includes both private and public development, community facility planning focuses on just the public sector. That is precisely what makes it valuable as a complementary niche of the community planning system for incorporating risk control considerations.

Characteristics of Community Facility Plans

Community facility plans normally include a facility inventory and an analysis of current and projected needs for public facilities. In theory and usually but not always in practice, they include a proposed list of new facilities, with locations and specifications, and also improvements to existing facilities. The plan's content varies from community to community, depending of course on what services the municipality or county is responsible for providing. Usually the community facility plan includes the total range of public buildings (e.g., city hall, fire and police stations, public works maintenance buildings, libraries) and parks and recreation facilities. Normally it does not include schools, water and sewer lines or other utilities, or roads. Those are the subjects of separate plans—school facility plans, water and sewer plans, and thoroughfare plans. For our purposes, however, we regard those as part of over-all community facility planning, though they may be prepared by different local agencies (e.g., school districts and utility districts). For risk management purposes, coordination would be critical.

Role of Community Facility Plans in Risk Management

There are two reasons why community facility plans, school facility plans, thoroughfare plans, and utility plans are good sources of information for risk control planning and management and good vehicles for planning a risk management strategy. First, such plans are the best, initial, comprehensive source of information on the size, capacity, condition, and location of the above-ground physical plant. By comparing maps of natural hazard zones with maps of community facilities, analysts can get an initial handle on exposure to risk.

Second, the facility plan is an ideal second step, after the comprehensive plan, to balance risk control objectives against other important community goals, to balance risk elimination against risk reduction (mitigation), and to weigh alternative risk assumption and transfer strategies for specific existing and proposed community facilities. That is, community facility planning is an early point in the capital investment planning process at which to consider arguments for and against abandoning existing and planned facilities or moving or retrofitting them and comparing those strategies to the strategies of assuming the risk or transferring it.

But, as mentioned above, the community facility plan, per se, is not likely to help much with school facilities or so called "lifeline" infrastructure such as water and sewer lines, gas and electric lines, stormwater drainage lines and retention or detention structures, or the roads, bridges, tunnels, and transit rights of way of the transportation system. Those tend to be addressed in separate analyses and plans, often by separate agencies. For purposes of risk management planning, however, they address infrastructure at the same level of detail for geographic, financial, site design, and structural specification.

Capital Improvement Programming

The capital improvement program (CIP) is a proposed schedule of capital improvements over the next five years or so. It is more detailed than the community facility plan about the location, size, design, and structure of proposed capital improvements. More importantly, it includes a financial dimension—costs and sources of proposed financing. Thus, ideally the CIP gives due consideration to the comprehensive plan and community facilities plan, while specifying financial aspects and providing greater detail on proposed capital improvements.

A community can use the capital improvement program to consider the costs and benefits of hazard reduction (site design, building design, and structural mitigation measures) for facilities in hazardous areas, compared to (1) the hazard elimination strategy of building on non-hazardous but perhaps more expensive or less well located sites and (2) risk assumption or risk transfer for the facilities on the hazardous site. Including the latter alternatives requires consideration of annual (operating) costs of risk management in addition to the lumpy capital investments implied in the capital investment decision.

The capital improvement program is also a good place to consider funding alternatives. Capital improvement financing is a part of the CIP and can include funding for risk reduction and for risk transfer (e.g., hazards insurance premiums). Tax increases, borrowing (revenue and general obligation bonds), grants-in-aid, user fees, impact fees, and creation of special districts are possible sources of proposed revenue for consideration in a CIP.

Capital improvement programming and budgeting can help generate support for hazard mitigation efforts that require capital expenditures. Plans to retrofit buildings and other structures or make them more resistant to damage from natural hazards, or to relocate existing facilities from hazard zones, or to divert proposed new public facilities to safer sites—all of those options—can be analyzed and highlighted with the help of community facility plans and capital improvement programs.

Growth Management

Growth management is the fourth component of a community planning program appropriate for devising risk management strategies for public facilities. While the previous three components dealt with analysis, goal setting, and proposals for solutions (policy making), growth management adds implementation measures to influence decisions in the private sector.

Growth management includes regulations (such as zoning, subdivision regulations, and special regulations for hazardous areas), acquisition of open space and other property to prevent development from locating in harm's way, construction of public facilities to service people and property and to control the hazard, and taxes, user fees, impact fees, and special assessments and districts (which both discourage development of hazardous areas and allocate the costs of risk management to those who directly benefit from the hazardous location).

There is ample precedent for using development regulations and related growth management tools to divert some or all development from the most hazardous areas of a community, to require development that is allowed in the hazardous area to meet special standards of site design and building construction, and to shift the costs of controlling the hazard or incorporating mitigation measures to those who create the need for the loss control expenses and who benefit from them.

The principle and practice of requiring the development industry to provide or pay for public facilities needed to serve their development is well established. (Kaiser and Burby 1988; Lamont 1979; Merriam and Andrew 1988; Frank, Lines and Downing 1987) Yet, there is a wider range of potentially useful devices than those that now are commonly used, and they should be identified and evaluated more systematically in both risk management planning and growth management planning. Table 5.1 lists growth management devices that are suitable for incorporating risk reduction measures. Those items with asterisks are particularly well suited for pursuing risk reduction policies with respect to community facilities and infrastructure. Readers interested in additional information about the application of those measures to cope with specific hazards should consult various guidebooks and other references that have been prepared over the past decade. For flood hazards, those include works by Kusler and Lee (1972), Kusler (1976), Leopold (1968), and Owen and Wall (1981); for earthquake hazards, see Blair and Spangle (1979), Davis et al. (1982a, 1982b); Jaffe (1981), Kockelman (1975; 1976; 1979), Nichols and Buchanan-Banks (1974), and Petak (1973); for hurricane hazards, see Conservation Foundation (1980) Godschalk, Brower and Beatley (1989), and White and his associates (1976); and for landslide hazards, see Griggs and Gilchrist (1977) and Kockelman (1975, 1976, 1979).

Sound implementation strategy should allow for flexibility in applying risk elimination, risk reduction, risk assumption, and risk transfer strategies. Thus, for example, a developer might be able to make the case that on a specific site, with better information on hand than was available when the zone was designated, he be granted a special use permit to build what would otherwise be a prohibited structure. The special use permit, of course, should specify standards for the adequate protection

TABLE 5.1
Physical Planning Hazard Loss Reduction Measures
(Measures marked by asterisks are particularly well
suited for reduction of risk to infrastructure)

Informational Measures

    Real estate disclosure requirements
        Posting the boundaries of hazard areas
        Educational/awareness programs

Police Power Measures (Regulatory)

    Moratoriums (for limited time, with clear
        reasons, with variances)
    Zoning ordinance
        Downzoning hazard zones to lower intensity,
            less vulnerable uses
        *Hazard overlay zone (special mitigation design
            standards required for public capital
            improvements in the hazard zone)
        Density transfer to less hazardous portions of
            site
    Transfer of development rights from hazard zone to
        development zones elsewhere in the jurisdiction
    Subdivision regulations
        *Required mitigation measures for infrastructure
        *Stormwater control requirements
        Open space dedication requirements
    *Building Code, special standards for structures in
        hazard zones
    *Impact fee for new development to reflect costs of
        mitigation measures for infrastructure required
        in hazardous areas
    *Separate hazardous area (e.g., floodplain) develop-
        ment regulations

Acquisition

    Fee-simple acquisition of hazardous land for open
        space use
    Purchase of development rights in hazardous areas
    Land dedication and donation programs

TABLE 5.1 (Continued)

Capital Improvements

> *Avoidance of hazardous zones where net benefit
>   fails to justify the risk or cost of mitigation
> *Special standards for structures and infrastructure
>   in hazardous areas

Taxation

> *Impact tax on new development to reflect costs of
>   mitigation measures for infrastructure required
>   in hazardous areas
> *Taxes or assessments in special districts to cover
>   costs of structural hazard control measures or
>   mitigation design of infrastructure
> *Special supplements to user fees in hazardous areas
>   to cover costs of mitigation measures for infra-
>   structure to bring the service
> Preferential taxation in hazardous areas to encourage
>   agricultural and other open space uses
> City-wide and special district assessments to fund
>   a self-insurance fund

State and Federal Legislation

> *Requirements for hazard zone avoidance and/or
>   mitigation measures
> *Requirements for risk assumption or risk funding
>   to protect against financial losses
> *Requirements for incorporation of risk manage-
>   ment principles into comprehensive planning,
>   community facility planning, and capital improve-
>   ment programming.

---

of public facilities associated with the project and protection of public health, safety, and welfare.

Devices in Table 5.1 can be combined into coordinated risk and growth management systems to provide more sophisticated control. None of the devices is sufficient by itself; they must be combined into effective packages. Further, there must be an institutional element built into the system. For example, unless financing is city-wide or county-wide, there must be an authority, district, or utility created to administer financial aspects of a system that depends on financing in part by owners of vulnerable properties.

Conclusions

Comprehensive risk management incorporates a five-pronged approach—risk information, risk elimination, risk reduction, risk assumption, and risk transfer—for coping with losses to infrastructure from natural hazards, as noted in Chapter 4. Community physical planning is an available and particularly suitable approach for planning and implementing the first three of those five strategies—risk information, risk elimination, and risk reduction.

In risk elimination, physical planning policy would divert public investment from areas where the risks of a natural hazard are particularly concentrated, where and when suitable alternative sites exist, for infrastructure and community facilities that are most vulnerable to the hazard. Risk elimination is the preferred tactic for types of development and locations where it is clearly less costly to avoid the hazard than to either mitigate it through site design and building adjustments, assume the risk, or transfer it by purchasing insurance. An example would be to prohibit development in the floodway portion of the floodplain.

Risk reduction policy would require special site and structure design and engineering standards be met for development that is not diverted from the hazard area through risk elimination policy. Ideally, local governments would apply that layer of risk management to those investment situations where the marginal cost of mitigation is clearly less than the expected loss prevented, but where it is not clear that the least cost solution would be to leave the site undeveloped. An example would be to require that roads and other infrastructure be elevated in the floodway fringe portion of the floodplain.

Four components of community planning, in particular, lend themselves to integration with a comprehensive risk management program in local government. They are comprehensive planning, community facility planning, capital improvement programming, and growth management (sometimes called land use planning or land use management).

Long range comprehensive planning is a suitable context in which to balance risk management objectives against other community objectives, roughly balance risk management approaches, specify the spatial pattern of the risk elimination and risk reduction strategies, and provide an information base to support policy development and implementation. It is also a mechanism for communicating and implementing risk management strategies.

Community facility planning is the place to introduce risk analysis into locational analyses (i.e., susceptibility of specific sites to hazards) for both new facilities and modifications to existing public facilities. Community facility plans are also a source of and place for inventorying existing facilities and assessing their vulnerability to natural hazards.

Capital improvement programming is a good place to consider in more detail the costs of alternative siting and mitigation measures and to assess alternative financing methods for paying the costs of risk reduction, assumption, and transfer. This is the place to introduce the analysis of the vulnerability of particular materials and facility designs. And, this is the place to be sure to specify the location, hazard mitigation, revenue sources, and cost sharing for specific facilities, because the CIP is much closer to actual construction than the comprehensive plan or community facilities plan.

Finally, growth management measures are good candidates as vehicles for imposing mitigation requirements on the private sector where appropriate and for diverting development from hazardous areas. They can also allocate some of the costs of mitigation, risk assumption and risk transfer to the private sector. Potentially useful growth management measures include not only land use and building regulations, but also acquisition, taxation and other pricing devices, informational programs, and state and federal legislation.

Community physical planners would do well to incorporate risk management more systematically into comprehensive planning, community facility planning, capital improvement programming, and growth management than is now the case in most communities. At the same time, local financial planners and risk managers would do well to use the information, analyses, plans, and implementation devices already available and politically acceptable in community planning.

6

Theory Versus Practice

In the previous two chapters we identified a number of financial and physical planning measures local governments can use to cope successfully with the threat of large losses from natural hazards. Here we look at the actual state of practice in the United States. Our aim is twofold. One goal is simply to describe the degree to which local governments are taking steps to protect themselves from catastrophic losses. A second is to explain why local governments vary in their attention to natural hazards. Both goals are important for public policy.

Our documentation of the state of practice provides vivid, scientific evidence of the degree to which local governments are ignoring the potential for catastrophic losses in natural disasters. Those results emphasize the urgent need for programs to strengthen local capacity for dealing with hazards. Evaluation of how federal and state policy is already affecting local practices is equally important. In chapter 1 we suggested that federal assumption of risks associated with natural hazards could result in inefficient local behavior, with local governments ignoring cost-effective loss prevention measures on the assumption that federal disaster relief would take care of their needs. (We found in Chapter 3 that such an assumption would be faulty in many cases, since disaster relief may in fact cover a much lower proportion of losses than a naive local government might assume.) We also reported in Chapter 1, however, that federal policy was attempting to counteract the potential for relief to foster inefficient local policy and to limit the federal costs of disasters. Thus, the 1974 disaster relief law conditioned federal aid on state adoption of hazard mitigation plans, FEMA initiated programs such as the Interagency Hazard Mitigation Task Forces to stimulate attention to loss prevention, and Congress took steps to limit aid where insurance could have covered a loss. Here we assess the net impact of those federal policies.

We show that federal efforts to promote loss prevention are having an effect; but, that effect is not even across all hazards or all governments.

Federal policy, for example, is resulting in greater attention to loss prevention among governments that have experienced a Presidentially declared disaster than among governments that have not experienced a disaster and among governments threatened by flood hazards than among governments threatened by earthquake hazards. The use of disasters as a loss-prevention lever is logical, in the sense that repetitive losses account for a majority of damages from natural hazards, but it leaves unprepared thousands of governments that have not experienced a disaster (but most certainly will in the future). The focus on flood-loss prevention is also logical, in the sense that floods account for the largest percentage of disaster losses, but it also leaves unprepared thousands of governments threatened by potentially staggering damages from a Richter 7.9 or larger earthquake along several faults in California and the New Madrid fault in mid-America. In sum, while disaster relief policy is not the disaster it has been painted—it does not seem to foster inefficient local policy to the extent suggested in the literature—it also does not foster the amount of loss prevention effort among local governments that is needed if federal disaster relief costs are to be curbed.

Some Lessons from Previous Research

In examining the state of practice, we add to a growing body of literature that explores local governments' efforts to limit exposure to losses in natural disasters. Before turning to our study methods and findings, we discuss briefly what we already know from previous work and what gaps in the literature remain to be filled.

Financial and Physical Planning

To our knowledge no one has yet examined the attention local governments give to financial planning to minimize risk from natural hazards. Numerous studies, however, have produced evidence that local governments ignore physical planning adjustments to earthquake, hurricane, and flood hazards, except where they are required to take action by federal and state mandates. (Burby and French et al. 1985; Drabek 1986; May and Williams 1986; Nilson and Nilson 1981; Rossi, Wright and Weber-Burdin 1982; Turner et al. 1980)

In the case of earthquakes, for example, research by Berke and Wilhite (1988) revealed that outside of California (where land use planning and a safety element of the plan are mandated by state law), only 11 percent of local governments in areas subject to earthquake hazards have attended to seismic safety in their comprehensive physical planning.

In the case of hurricanes, a national survey of hurricane-prone local governments by Godschalk, Brower and Beatley (1989) revealed that only 20 percent had adopted hazard mitigation elements of their comprehensive plans.

In the case of floods, Murphy (1958) surveyed national experience in the mid-1950s and could find only about 35 communities with floodplain planning and land use regulations; a decade later, another study found less than 500 cities and counties with floodplain regulations in place (see Kusler 1982b). After federal incentives for floodplain regulation were adopted with the Flood Insurance Act of 1968, only about one in five communities with identified flood hazards chose to participate, which led Congress to enact severe penalties for nonparticipation with the Flood Disaster Protection Act of 1973. Those sanctions led to widespread adoption of development management measures to reduce flood losses, but much less attention to land use planning for hazardous areas, which was not required by the federal mandate. (Burby and French et al. 1985)

Loss Reduction Measures

The adoption of loss reduction measures specified by plans also may be problematic, particularly in the cases of the seismic safety elements of comprehensive plans (Mader et al. 1980), plans calling for redevelopment or retrofitting of existing structures or neighborhoods (Dalton 1989), and plans for areas with high development potential or located in communities undergoing rapid growth. (Burby et al. 1988) Potential implementation problems pointed out in the literature include a lack of adequately trained personnel in local government (Petak 1984; Mushkatel and Weschler 1985) and the complexity of loss reduction strategies that involve a variety of types of policies (regulatory, distributive, redistributive). (See Dalton 1989.) Equally fundamental, however, could be the political difficulties of taking actions that might slow local economic development or run counter to the interests of economic elites (e.g., see Forester 1982) and the lack of a clearly defined local constituency for hazard mitigation. (Petak 1984; Wyner 1984) (In that regard, Federal Insurance Administrator George Bernstein [1978] observed, "It is naive and perhaps ingenuous to depend on the common sense and good will of elected authorities . . . to voluntarily restrain local growth in the face of real hazards and experienced losses.")

Studies actually documenting implementation failures are rare, however, and those that have been conducted have reached conflicting conclusions. On the one hand, Wyner and Mann (1983; also see Wyner 1984) studied the implementation of the mandated seismic safety element of the general plans of thirteen California jurisdictions. They concluded:

Resource allocation for implementation of seismic safety policy has been virtually nonexistent. Most jurisdictions have chosen not to allocate monetary or non-monetary resources in a manner that would permit fulfillment of the adopted goals; most jurisdictions have made only slight movement toward goal accomplishment. Whatever level of risk was accepted in the adoption of the SSE, very little has been done to make it a reality through policy implementation. (Wyner and Mann 1983: 321–22)

On the other hand, Mintier and Stromberg (1983) studied seven California local governments' implementation of the seismic safety element of their general plans and found that "All had adopted policies regarding existing hazardous buildings," and "Most had adopted extensive policies with regard to critical facilities."

A Policy Determinants Theory

Although we know something about what local governments are doing (or, more accurately, not doing) to cope with threats posed by natural hazards, we know much less about why they do or do not adopt the various financial and physical planning strategies that are available. To make sense of the growing body of case studies and other research on local policy toward natural hazards, we developed a theory of local policy determination. Our theory, which draws on the literatures dealing with human systems responses to disasters, policy determination, and policy implementation, focuses on three broad determinants of local hazards policy: characteristics of the environment that either result in demands for policy to resolve hazards problems or provide resources governments can use in meeting those demands; characteristics of governmental organizations that affect their ability to solve hazards problems; and characteristics of hazards policy itself that affect the choice of policy instruments.

Environmental determinants include the variable of most interest to us here—federal disaster relief and hazard mitigation policies—as well as other factors that either stimulate policy outputs (e.g., policy catalysts such as the occurrence of a disaster) or provide resources that enable governments to react to policy demands. Governmental determinants include officials' attitudes toward natural hazards and the availability of personnel and other resources needed to pursue physical planning adjustments. Policy characteristics include costs of implementation and the degree to which particular policies involve regulation, distribution of benefits, or redistribution. Together we believe those factors can account for a significant proportion of the variation that exists in local hazards policy.

Our review of previous research uncovered a number of policy determinants (we list them in Table 6A-1 in the appendix to this chapter) that have been found to be associated with the adoption of physical planning measures to cope with the threat of disasters. In most cases those variables have not been tested thoroughly (i.e., they have emerged from studies of a few cases in a single state or from cross-sectional mail surveys in which only single questionnaire items were used as a measure of the concept). Nevertheless, they provided us with an inventory of empirically based hypotheses with some theoretical grounding that we could draw upon in exploring the impacts of federal policy on local governments.

Answering Questions About the State of Practice

We gathered information on the state of practice through a mail survey of local officials responsible for risk management decision making in 800 local governments. After a post card reminder and two follow-up letters with replacement questionnaires, we obtained a response rate of 60 percent, which resulted in data on 481 local governments. The sampling strategy for this survey is reported in Chapter 2.

We used both bivariate and multiple regression analysis to measure the relative effect of federal disaster relief on local policy while controlling for other factors our policy determinants theory suggests might also affect policy outcomes. The measurements we formulated for the various elements of the theory, using data from the mail survey and records of the Federal Emergency Management Agency, are summarized in Table 6.1. Although we were able to measure the most important variables suggested by our theory, readers will note that we were not able to measure all of the variables listed in the appendix (Table 6A-1). Possibly important variables we did not measure include: an objective measure of the risk of loss; population growth; characteristics of the political environment; the priority government officials attach to natural hazards in relation to other problems; efficacy officials attach to financial and physical planning measures; presence of a hazards policy advocate; and the costs of adopting various measures. Their omission limits our ability to explain fully variation in local governments policies' toward natural hazards; however, we do not believe that compromises seriously our ability to estimate the effects of federal disaster relief policy on local government behavior.

In Table 6.2 we summarize characteristics of the three groups of communities we studied. The effect of federal disaster relief policy is clearly evident: the jurisdictions that received aid to recover from a disaster were much more likely than those whose requests for aid were

TABLE 6.1
List of Variables and Measures

Variable	Measurement

Status of Financial/Physical Planning

Variable	Measurement
Information about Hazard	Evaluation of adequacy of information available about potential losses from floods and potential losses from earthquakes on 5-point scale.
Vulnerability Analysis	Yes/No
Loss Reduction Measures for Existing Facilities	Floods: Additive scale based on adoption of facility retrofitting, facility relocation, flood control works, shoreline protection works, and flood hazard mitigation plan. Earthquakes: Additive scale based on adoption of building retrofitting, facility relocation, and seismic safety plan
Loss Reduction Measures for New Facilities	Floods: Additive scale based on adoption of damage resistant design standards, flood control works, shoreline protection works, zoning, subdivision regulations, land acquisition, and flood hazard mitigation plan Earthquakes: Additive scale based on adoption of damage resistant design standards, zoning, subdivision regulations, land acquisition, and seismic safety plan
Loss Reserve Fund	Yes/No

TABLE 6.1 (Continued)

Variable	Measurement
Insurance	Floods: all, some or no buildings insured against flood losses
	Earthquakes: all, some or no buildings insured against earthquake losses
Overall Preparedness	Flood: standardized index of above measures
	Earthquake: standardized index of above measures

Characteristics of the Environment

Availability of federal aid	Aid received for disaster (from FEMA records) (yes/no and dollar amount received)
	Perceived chance of receiving aid in the event of a future loss in excess of available contingency funds (5-point scale)
State mandates (earthquake only)	California locality (yes/no)

Policy catalysts:

Experience with hazards	Total dollar losses in disasters, 1980-1987 (from FEMA records)
	Recent losses (1987/1988) (Yes/No)
	Ratio of total losses to losses rated as disastrous

Community resources:

Urbanization	Population in 1980

TABLE 6.1 (Continued)

Variable	Measurement
Ability to absorb losses	Size of loss (dollars) to public buildings that could be handled with available contingency funds

Governmental Characteristics

Variable	Measurement
Recognition of hazard	Perceived odds (1/200, 1/100, 1/50, 1/20 or 1/10 of disastrous loss in any given year)
Active risk manager	Additive scale based on participation in the following activities: hazard management committee, emergency preparedness exercise, informal discussions among departments, developing emergency operation plan
Risk management experience	Additive scale based on adoption of the following risk management measures: comprehensive liability insurance, retention of funds for self-insurance, employee safety training, preventive maintenance, participation in insurance pool

denied or those that did not experience a disaster to believe that future losses would be covered by federal disaster relief. Among the other characteristics we examined, the two groups of disaster-stricken communities differed in a number of respects from communities that had not experienced a disaster, but not from each other. For example, in comparing jurisdictions that did and did not receive aid we found no significant differences in total losses experienced, the ratio of losses experienced to losses rated as disastrous, percentage of governments with recent losses in either 1987 or 1988, size of loss that officials believed would constitute a disaster, recognition of hazards, risk management experience, or employment of an active risk manager. In

TABLE 6.2
Characteristics of Communities Studies

Characteristics	Sample Stratum		
	Disaster 1980-1986 No Federal Aid	Disaster 1980-1986 Aid Received	No Disaster 1980-1986
Federal Aid			
Aid received (mean)	$ 0	$ 256,107	NA
Perceived odds of aid (1 – low to 5 = high)	2.6*	3.3*	2.8*
Experience with Disasters			
Losses, 1980-1986 (mean)	$ 205,366	$ 316,545	$ NA
Losses in 1987/88 (percent)	2	1	1
Ratio of losses experienced to loss rated as disastrous	2.3	4.9	NA
Community Resources			
Population, 1980	53,392*	39,828*	24,808*

TABLE 6.2 (Continued)

Characteristics	Sample Stratum		
	Disaster 1980-1986 No Federal Aid	Disaster 1980-1986 Aid Received	No Disaster 1980-1986
Loss that could be handled with contingency funds			
Total (mean)	$1,008,728	$ 1,557,164	$ 988,329
Per capita (mean)	$ 75	$ 128	68
Governmental Characteristics			
Recognition of hazard (1-low to 5-high) (mean)	1.8*	1.9*	1.6*
Active risk manager (0-low to 5-high)	1.7*	1.8*	1.2*
Risk management experience (0-low to 5-high)	2.7	2.9	2.6

Source: Survey of 481 local officials, summer 1988.

*Difference among groups is statistically significant at .05 level (analysis of variance test).

comparison to the communities that had not experienced a disaster, however, the two groups of governments with disaster experience were more likely to recognize risks from natural hazards and to employ an active risk manager. Finally, all three groups of communities differed somewhat in the average size of their population, which ranged from a low of 24,808 among the communities that had not had a disaster to a high of 53,392 among those with a disaster and no federal aid.

Many Governments Do Not Know the Risks They Face

The first step in integrating consideration of natural hazards into local financial and physical planning is to obtain information about the nature of the risk. Very few risk managers (less than one in five), however, were aware of any studies of natural hazards risks (probability of loss and expected damages) to their governments' infrastructure. (See Table 6.3.) Nevertheless, a significant percentage (between 40 percent and 60 percent) felt they had adequate information about potential losses. Thus, many risk managers seem content with information that constrains them to highly subjective estimates of natural hazards risks.

Experience with a natural disaster and receipt of federal disaster assistance had no effect on whether local officials had or had not conducted vulnerability analyses and no effect on their assessments of the adequacy of the hazards information that was available to them for risk management decision making.

Many Governments Are Not Reducing Vulnerability to Loss

After securing information about risks, the next step in the risk management strategy we proposed in Chapters 4 and 5 is to reduce potential losses to facilities at risk, where that is feasible. We found that in California a number of local governments are taking steps to reduce their vulnerability to seismic losses: about half of the 40 jurisdictions we queried there had formulated hazard mitigation plans for public facilities (the state mandate for seismic safety planning and relative frequency of earthquakes account for that we think), and between 30 and 45 percent had retrofitted public facilities. (See Table 6.4.) Outside of California, however, very few local governments in areas subject to seismic risks either plan for or take actual steps to reduce potential losses from earthquakes. (For similar findings from other research, see Beavers 1985 and Berke; Beatley and Wilhite 1988.)

TABLE 6.3
Acquisition of Information and Conduct of
Vulnerability Analyses

Practice	Sample Stratum		
	Disaster 1980-1986 No Federal Aid	Disaster 1980-1986 Aid Received	No Disaster 1980-1986
Vulnerability Analyses Conducted			
For any hazard	14%	18%	14%
Information about Hazard Rated Adequate			
Flood hazards	49	55	60
Earthquake hazards			
California	--	61	50
Other states	42	32	46

Source: 1988 survey of local officials.

[a]Difference between disaster stricken communities
that did and did not receive aid is statistically
significant at .05 level on the basis of chi square
or difference of means test.

[b]Difference between disaster stricken communities
and communities that did not experience a disaster
between 1980 and 1987 is statistically significant
at .05 level on the basis of chi square or difference
of means test.

TABLE 6.4
Adoption of Measures to Reduce Losses to Existing
Facilities

	Sample Stratum		
Practice	Disaster 1980-1986 No Federal Aid	Disaster 1980-1986 Aid Received	No Disaster 1980-1986

Flood Loss Reduction:

Hazard mitigation plan	18%	23%	10%
Flood control	26[b]	35[b]	18[b]
Shoreline protection	12[b]	21[b]	7[b]
Flood/windproofing	7[a]	14[a]	6
Relocation of facilities	5	5	6
Loss reduction index (mean)	0.7[a,b]	1.0[a,b]	0.5[b]

Earthquake Loss Reduction:[c]

Seismic safety plan			
California	--	50	56
Other states	7	5	0
Quakeproofing			
California	--	32	44
Other states	6	7	0
Relocation of facilities			
California	--	4	0
Other states	0	5	3
Loss reduction index (mean)			
California	--	0.9	1.0
Other states	0.1	0.1	0.1

TABLE 6.4 (Continued)

Source: 1988 survey of local officials.

[a]Difference between disaster stricken communities that did and did not receive aid is statistically significant at .05 level on the basis of chi square or difference of means test.

[b]Difference between disaster stricken communities and communities that did not experience a disaster between 1980 and 1987 is statistically significant at .05 level on the basis of chi square or difference of means test.

[c]Because previous research has indicated that California local governments are much more concerned about earthquake risks than those in other states, data are presented separately for those two groups of governments. The sample sizes for the California sample strata are: disaster without federal aid, n - 0; disaster with federal aid, n - 31; no disaster, n - 9. The sample sizes for the stratum in other states are: disaster without federal aid, n - 133; disaster with federal aid, n - 148; no disaster, n - 160.

Furthermore, at the same time that California local governments are making progress in dealing with earthquake hazards, they along with local governments in other states are doing very little to reduce losses from flood hazards. Thus, we found that relatively few governments have flood hazard mitigation plans and fewer still have floodproofed or relocated facilities to avoid flood losses. The most frequent way of dealing with flood threats to existing facilities is the construction of flood control and shoreline protection structures, probably because of the ready availability in past years of federal aid for those public works; but, as we noted earlier, federal aid for flood control has diminished sharply, and that approach to risk reduction will be more costly to local governments in the future.

The occurrence of a disaster stimulated flood loss prevention efforts among local governments, but it had no effect on the adoption of earthquake loss prevention measures. None of the governments we studied experienced earthquake losses, however; thus, what these data show is that the loss reduction stimulus provided by a natural disaster is specific to that hazard and does not lead governments to protect themselves against other hazards. That finding is important, since a number of local governments in the United States face threats from more than one type of hazard. Federal policy makers cannot assume that when a government experiences losses from one of those risks, that experience will lead to action to control other risks.

The data in Table 6.4 indicate that federal aid is associated with more rather than less attention to flood risk reduction. That conclusion is affirmed by multiple regression analyses that control for other factors that might affect loss reduction activity in local government. (See Table 6.5.) Thus, for flood hazards the federal efforts to foster mitigation that we outlined in Chapter 1 seem to be paying off. Those policies, however, have had little effect on attention to earthquake hazard reduction. That result reflects, we think, the focus of federal policy on flood losses and the paucity of incentives or assistance for local government seismic safety, particularly outside of the state of California.

Recognition of the hazard, the presence of an active hazard manager, and previous risk management experience all seem to promote adoption of flood loss reduction measures. The presence of an active risk manager and risk management experience also affect the adoption of earthquake hazard reduction measures, but the effect is small, and because of the relatively small number of governments in our sample that are exposed to seismic risks, those factors are not statistically significant at the .05 level. The key variable affecting localities' efforts to reduce seismic risks is location in the state of California. That reflects the greater seismic risk in California and also, we think, the federal government's and State of California's efforts to promote seismic safety among local governments there.

After attending to risks to existing facilities, we recommend that local governments then take steps to reduce the potential for losses to any future facilities they might build. As we discussed in Chapter 5, they can do that by integrating loss reduction considerations into building codes and various physical planning measures, such as the comprehensive plan and growth management regulations, and by using various areawide protective measures, such as flood control works, that provide protection to both existing and future public facilities. We found, however, that there is a large gap between theory and practice. (See Table 6.6.)

The average number of measures adopted to reduce losses to new infrastructure ranged from a low of 1.2 (of a possible seven measures we asked about) among governments that had not experienced a disaster to a high of 2.0 among those that had a disaster and received federal aid. Zoning to reduce the intensity of development in hazard zones and subdivision regulations that incorporate damage-resistant design standards—two effective ways of limiting the susceptibility to loss for new

TABLE 6.5
Factors Associated with Adoption of Measures to
Reduce Losses to Existing Facilities

Factor	Index of Flood Loss Reduction Measures		Index of Earthquake Loss Reduction Measures	
	Std. B	Significance	Std. B	Significance
Environmental Characteristics				
Federal Aid:				
Aid received for past disaster	.14	.01	-.01	.87
Perceived odds of aid in future	.09	.07	.05	.43
Previous Losses:				
Total losses, 1980-87	.09	.09	-.06	.52
Recent loss, 1987/88	.02	.68	.25	.00
Ratio of total losses to loss rated as disastrous	-.03	.48	.07	.41
Resources:				
Population, 1980	.09	.06	.00	.96
Ability to absorb loss	.04	.46	.12	.10

TABLE 6.5 (Continued)

Factor	Index of Flood Loss Reduction Measures		Index of Earthquake Loss Reduction Measures	
	Std. B	Signifi-cance	Std. B	Signifi-cance
Governmental Characteristics				
Recognition of Hazard:	.16	.00	.06	.34
Active Risk Manager:	.21	.00	.05	.51
Risk Management Experience:	.10	.03	.09	.25
City Jurisdiction:	.05	.28	-.07	.37
California Jurisdiction:	--	--	.50	.00
Adjusted R^2	.20		.45	
F-Value	9.70		9.85	
Degrees of Freedom	11/369		12/118	
Significance	.0001		.0001	

Source: Survey of 481 local officials, summer 1988.

facilities—are being used by less than half of the governments we studied.

The efforts of the State of California to promote seismic safety are again apparent. Officials serving two-thirds of the California jurisdictions we surveyed told us that they had adopted damage-resistant design standards for new infrastructure; outside of California less than one of every six earthquake-prone jurisdictions had done that, and the adoption of other measures to deal with earthquake threats to new facilities is much lower. In fact, of the five measures they could use to reduce

TABLE 6.6
Adoption of Measures to Reduce Losses to New Facilities

	Sample Stratum		
Practice	Disaster 1980-1986 No Federal Aid	Disaster 1980-1986 Aid Received	No Disaster 1980-1986

Flood Loss Reduction

Hazard mitigation plan	18%	23%	10%
Zoning which limits development of hazardous areas	37[a]	52[a]	41
Subdivision regulations require floodproofing	32	35	26
Flood control	26[b]	35[b]	18[b]
Land acquisition to prevent hazard area development	17	13	13
Damage-resistant design standards	12[a]	23[a]	13
Shoreline protection	12[b]	21[b]	7[b]
Loss reduction index (mean)	1.6[a,b]	2.0[a,b]	1.2[b]

Earthquake Loss Reduction[c]

Seismic safety plan California	--	50	56
Other states	7	5	0
Damage-resistant design standards California	--	68	67
Other states	29	14	15

TABLE 6.6 (Continued)

| Practice | Sample Stratum | | |
	Disaster 1980-1986 No Federal Aid	Disaster 1980-1986 Aid Received	No Disaster 1980-1986
Subdivision regulations require quakeproofing			
California	--	36	33
Other states	10	7	3
Zoning which limits development of hazardous areas			
California	--	18	11
Other states	3	7	3
Land acquisition to prevent hazard area development			
California	--	0	0
Other states	0	5	3
Loss reduction index (mean)			
California	--	1.7	1.7
Other states	0.5	0.4	0.3

Source: 1988 survey of local officials.

[a]Difference between disaster stricken communities that did and did not receive aid is statistically significant at .05 level on the basis of chi square or difference of means test.

[b]Difference between disaster stricken communities and communities that did not experience a disaster between 1980 and 1987 is statistically significant at .05 level on the basis of chi square or difference of means test.

[c]Because previous research has indicated that California local governments are much more concerned about earthquake risks than those in other states, data are presented separately for those two groups of governments. The sample sizes for the California sample strata are: disaster without federal aid, n = 0; disaster with federal aid, n = 31; no disaster, n = 9. The sample sizes for the stratum in other states are: disaster without federal aid, n = 133; disaster with federal aid, n = 148; no disaster, n = 160.

seismic losses to new facilities, the average number in use in jurisdictions outside California ranged from 0.3 to 0.5 among the three groups of governments we studied. Adoption rates were four to five times higher in California, but even so the average jurisdiction there is using less than half of the measures available to it.

The effects of federal disaster relief policy are evident in the data summarized in Table 6.6 and the regression models presented in Table 6.7. Federal disaster relief, as with local governments efforts' to reduce losses to existing facilities, is having a positive effect on flood loss reduction but not earthquake loss reduction. Beyond that, we found that recognition of the hazard by risk managers, having an active risk manager, and prior risk management experience all tend to promote the adoption of flood hazard mitigation measures and, for the latter two factors, earthquake hazard mitigation measures as well (although with the smaller number of earthquake-prone jurisdictions in our sample, those effects are not statistically significant). Recognition of the hazard is not a statistically significant factor in earthquake hazard mitigation, but it seems likely that the effect of risk perception is being captured by the California location variable (risk managers in California are much more aware of potential losses from earthquakes than risk managers in other states).

Many Governments Are Not Purchasing Insurance or Setting Aside Contingency Funds

Transferring risk through the purchase of insurance and setting aside contingency funds—two additional means governments can adopt to cushion the effects of a disaster—are also being ignored by many local governments. Fewer than half of the governments we queried, for example, had purchased either flood or earthquake insurance and even fewer had set aside contingency funds specifically for losses in natural disasters. (See Table 6.8.)

Provisions of the Disaster Relief Act of 1974 allowed local governments to receive federal aid for losses to uninsured facilities, but the act stipulated that subsequent losses that could have been insured would not be aided. Congress saw that as an incentive for localities to acquire hazards insurance, but our data indicate it is not having that intended effect. Thus, we found no statistically significant differences in insurance coverage between localities that did and did not receive federal disaster assistance. That finding raises questions about provisions of the Stafford Act that tried to increase the incentive localities had for purchasing insurance by taking away the "one free bite." In other words, if experiencing a disaster and knowing that future uninsured losses would

TABLE 6.7
Factors Associated with Adoption of Measures to Reduce
Losses to Future Facilities

Factor	Index of Flood Loss Reduction Measures		Index of Earthquake Loss Reduction Measures	
	Std. B	Signifi-cance	Std. B	Signifi-cance
Environmental Characteristics				
Federal Disaster Aid:				
Aid received for past disaster	.09	.09	-.03	.69
Perceived odds of aid in future	.12	.02	.07	.33
Previous Losses:				
Total losses, 1980-87	.09	.08	-.08	.46
Recent loss, 1987/88	-.01	.83	.15	.04
Ratio of total losses to loss rated as disastrous	.05	.30	.15	.08
Community Resources:				
Population, 1980	.07	.17	-.05	.56
Ability to absorb loss	.03	.52	.21	.01

TABLE 6.7 (Continued)

Factor	Index of Flood Loss Reduction Measures		Index of Earthquake Loss Reduction Measures	
	Std. B	Signifi-cance	Std. B	Signifi-cance
Governmental Characteristics				
Recognition of Hazard:	.08	.11	-.01	.94
Active Risk Manager:	.25	.00	.15	.06
Risk Management Experience:	.16	.00	.09	.22
City Jurisdiction:	.07	.16	-.04	.55
California Jurisdiction:	--	--	.47	.00
Adjusted R^2	.21		.43	
F-Value	10.09		9.13	
Degrees of Freedom	11/369		12/118	
Significance	.0001		.0001	

Source: Survey of 481 local officials, summer 1988.

not be covered by relief does not affect localities' insurance purchase decisions, it seems to us very unlikely that localities that have not experienced losses will now be persuaded to insure themselves. Kunreuther's and Slovic's research on individuals' willingness to purchase insurance led them to similar conclusions; the availability of disaster relief does not affect decisions about insurance because just do not think about the issue at all. (See Kunreuther et al. 1978; Slovic, Fischoff and Lichtenstein 1987.)

TABLE 6.8
Purchase of Insurance/Contingency Funds Budgeted for
Hazard Damages

Characteristics	Sample Stratum		
	Disaster 1980-1986 No Federal Aid	Disaster 1980-1986 Aid Received	No Disaster 1980-1986
Purchase of Insurance			
Flood Insurance	39%	49%	44%
Earthquake Insurance[c]			
California	--	53	33
Other states	21	25	27
Contingency Funds for Damages from Hazards			
Fund for damages to public buildings	3[a]	11[a]	6
Fund for damages to sewage and water treatment plants and mains	3[a]	11[a]	8
Fund for damages to streets, roads and bridges	5[a]	14[a]	5
Fund for any public facility	8[a]	20[a]	11

TABLE 6.8 (Continued)

Source: 1988 survey of local officials.

[a]Difference between disaster stricken communities that did and did not receive aid is statistically significant at .05 level on the basis of chi square or difference of means test.

[b]Difference between disaster stricken communities and communities that did not experience a disaster between 1980 and 1987 is statistically significant at .05 level on the basis of chi square or difference of means test.

[c]Because previous research has indicated that California local governments are much more concerned about earthquake risks than those in other states, data are presented separately for those two groups of governments. The sample sizes for the California sample strata are: disaster without federal aid, n - 0; disaster with federal aid, n - 31; no disaster, n - 9. The sample sizes for the stratum in other states are: disaster without federal aid, n - 133; disaster with federal aid, n - 148; no disaster, n - 160.

When we examined local governments' purchase of insurance and use of contingency funds in relation to our policy determinants model, we found few factors that are highly associated with either action. In fact, the risk manager's assessment of the probability of experiencing a loss is the only variable that is associated with the purchase of both flood and earthquake insurance. That, of course, is logical and consistent with our findings reported earlier regarding local governments' actions to reduce loss exposures for existing facilities. But, as we will show in Chapter 9, risk managers tend to underestimate the probability of experiencing a loss from natural hazards.

Our finding that actual loss experience is not associated with the purchase of insurance is important, because it differs sharply from what one would expect from previous research findings. Thus, unlike individuals, where experience with a disaster rather than perception of risk leads people to insure their property (see Kunreuther 1978; Britton, Kearney, and Britton 1983; Burby et al. 1988), for local governments perception rather than experience seems to be key. That difference is probably due to the fact of turnover among local government personnel. The person making insurance purchase decisions today may not even be aware of the losses his or her government experienced in a natural disaster some years earlier. Our data also suggest, however, that provision of information is not sufficient by itself to stimulate the purchase of insurance. We found virtually no correlation between the conduct of vulnerability assessments and either recognition of hazards or purchase of insurance and virtually no correlation between the perceived adequacy of hazards information and either recognition of the hazard or purchase of insurance. Thus, if policy makers want to persuade a higher proportion of risk managers to acquire insurance against flooding and earthquakes, information needs to be more compelling than that presently available to them.

Overall, Governments Are Not Prepared for Disasters

When we looked at the overall preparedness of local governments to cope with the threat of a natural disaster, we found most local governments to be unprepared. We measured overall preparedness by standardizing on a scale of 0 to 100 each of the six risk management strategies we recommend (conducting vulnerability analyses, securing adequate information about hazards, reducing the vulnerability of existing facilities, reducing the vulnerability of future facilities, setting up a loss reserve fund, and purchasing insurance) and then adding the scores achieved on each of those indexes.

A government that used each of those risk management techniques to the maximum extent possible would score 600 on this overall index, while a government that used none of them would receive a score of 0. Average scores for flood disaster preparedness ranged from 168 to 218 among the three sample strata and for earthquake hazard preparedness from 124 to 293. (See Table 6.9.)

Local governments that had experienced losses and obtained federal disaster relief tended to be most prepared for flood hazards, while those that experienced losses but did not obtain disaster relief were least prepared. Thus, as we pointed out earlier, in the case of flood threats, federal relief policy is not fostering inefficient local behavior; in fact, just the opposite tends to be true. Disaster relief (more accurately, the conditions attached to relief) stimulates the adoption of disaster preparedness measures among flood-stricken local governments, so that the potential for disruption from future losses is reduced. That effect, however, does not carry over to preparedness for earthquake disasters. Earthquake preparedness is highly dependent on location: California jurisdictions are much better prepared for an earthquake disaster than earthquake-prone local governments located in other states.

TABLE 6.9
Overall Disaster Preparedness[a]

Characteristics	Sample Stratum		
	Disaster 1980-1986 No Federal Aid	Disaster 1980-1986 Aid Received	No Disaster 1980-1986
Overall Preparedness for Flood Hazards (mean)	168[b]	218[b]	181
Overall Preparedness for Earthquake Hazards (mean)			
All jurisdictions	191[c]	203[c]	140[c]
California jurisdictions[d]	---	293	214
NonCalifornia jurisdictions[d]	191	138	124

Source: 1988 survey of local officials.

[a]The overall preparedness index, which has a possible range of 0 - 600, is the sum of six indexes, each scaled from 0 to 100, of jurisdictions' adoption of the following six sets of measures: (1) adequate information on hazards; (2) vulnerability analyses conducted for specific facilities; (3) mitigation measures adopted to protect existing facilities; (4) mitigation measures adopted to protect future facilities; (5) contingency funds budgeted for potential damages from natural hazards; and (6) flood or earthquake insurance purchased for one or more facilities at risk.

TABLE 6.9 (Continued)

[b]Difference between disaster stricken communities that did and did not receive aid is statistically significant at .05 level on the basis of difference of means test.

[c]Difference between disaster stricken communities and communities that did not experience a disaster between 1980 and 1987 is statistically significant at .05 level on the basis of difference of means test.

[d]Because previous research has indicated that California local governments are much more concerned about earthquake risks than those in other states, data are presented separately for those two groups of governments. The sample sizes for the California sample strata are: disaster without federal aid, n - 0; disaster with federal aid, n - 31; no disaster, n - 9. The sample sizes for the stratum in other states are: disaster without federal aid, n - 133; disaster with federal aid, n - 148; no disaster, n - 160.

The results of multivariate analyses of flood and earthquake preparedness are summarized in Table 6.10. Those findings tend to reiterate key points we made earlier as we reviewed the state of practice in relation to each component of our recommended risk management strategy. Thus, using standardized regression coefficients as the criterion, we found four variables that have a significant effect on flood hazard preparedness: an active risk manager; perceived likelihood of obtaining federal aid in future disasters; population size (an indicator of community resources); and recognition of the hazard by the risk manager. Two of those factors—an active risk manager and population size—are also among the key factors associated with overall earthquake hazard preparedness. Other factors with a statistically significant effect on earthquake hazard preparedness include location in the state of California, prior risk management experience, and an ability to absorb large losses.

Our ability to explain variation in local government preparedness, although low, is similar to that achieved by other studies of this type (e.g., Godschalk, Brower and Beatley 1989; Burby et al. 1985). Nevertheless, there is a clear need to test more fully specified models of local government policy.

In comparing our findings with those of previous research (see the appendix to this chapter), there are notable differences and similarities. The most important differences are these three. First, using a much more

TABLE 6.10
Factors Associated with Overall Preparedness

Factor	Index of Preparedness for Flood Hazards		Index of Preparedness for Earthquake Hazards	
	Std. B	Signifi- cance	Std. B	Signifi- cance
Environmental Characteristics				
Federal Disaster Aid:				
Aid received for past disaster	.08	.15	-.03	.68
Perceived odds of aid in future	.13	.02	.05	.49
Previous Losses:				
Total losses, 1980-87	.05	.37	-.09	.44
Recent loss, 1987/88	.03	.61	.13	.08
Ratio of total losses to loss rated as disastrous	-.02	.72	.13	.15
Community Resources:				
Population, 1980	.13	.02	.19	.05
Ability to absorb loss	.05	.34	.26	.00
Governmental Characteristics				
Recognition of Hazard:	.10	.05	.10	.18

TABLE 6.10 (Continued)

Factor	Index of Preparedness for Flood Hazards		Index of Preparedness for Earthquake Hazards	
	Std. B	Significance	Std. B	Significance
Active Risk Manager:	.26	.00	.19	.02
Risk Management Experience:	.03	.59	.22	.01
City Jurisdiction:	.07	.23	-.11	.21
California Jurisdiction:	---	---	.28	.00
Adjusted R^2	.19		.46	
F-Value	7.72		9.10	
Degrees of Freedom	11/310		12/101	
Significance	.0001		.0001	

<u>Source</u>: Survey of 481 local officials, summer 1988.

sophisticated research design than previous studies, we show rather convincingly that federal disaster relief is not inducing local governments to ignore the potential for losses from natural hazards. We attribute that difference to federal efforts to stimulate the adoption of flood loss prevention measures. Second, we found that experience with losses is not a good predictor of overall preparedness. We attribute that difference to the lack of institutional memory in local government. That is, governments, not individuals, experience public sector financial losses, and individuals making decisions about loss prevention may not have been on the scene when their government experienced a disaster. Third, preparedness for earthquake hazards does not seem to be any more intractable than preparedness for flood hazards. We attribute that difference from previous findings to the more sophisticated research design we employed (i.e., we examined preparedness for both earthquake and flood hazards using the same research methods).

Our findings also lend further support to findings reported from previous research. In particular, consistent with previous research we found that urbanization, recognition of the hazard, and state policy mandates all tend to stimulate preparedness. Two of those—recognition of the hazard and state policy mandates—are likely targets for federal policy.

Conclusions

The findings of this chapter have a number of important implications for public policy. We review those very briefly here. After looking at ways of overcoming various barriers to local governmental action in the four chapters of Part 3 that follow, in Chapter 11 we offer more complete prescriptions for action to improve local capacity to cope with natural disasters.

In chapters 4 and 5 we described a number of financial and physical planning measures that local governments can employ to reduce the adverse fiscal effects of natural disasters. In this chapter, we demonstrated that most local governments are not taking adequate steps to implement those measures. There are a number of reasons for that, but federal disaster relief policy is not one of them. Instead, the principal causes for the lack of preparedness appear to be inadequate appreciation of the potential for catastrophic losses, inadequately developed risk management capacity, and insufficient resources for loss prevention.

Federal policy is already addressing some of those factors, but in this chapter we showed that the current approach has an important limitation. It tends to be skewed toward flood-loss prevention and does not treat all hazards equally. That occurs because of past federal support for flood-hazard mitigation measures through appropriations for flood control works and the National Flood Insurance Program and because federal policy is linked to disaster assistance. Since floods are the most frequent disasters by far, flood threats receive more attention than other hazards. The lack of balance in federal policy has been corrected in California, where state mandates have forced local governments to pay attention to measures to cope with earthquake hazards. Elsewhere, however, states have not filled the vacuum created by federal policy and local governments are even more unprepared for a catastrophic earthquake than they are for catastrophic flooding.

TABLE 6A-1
Inventory of Research Findings on the Determinants of
Local Hazards Policy

I. Characteristics of the Environment

A. Federal and State Policy

1. Availability of federal aid/federal mandates:

a. Federal disaster assistance diminishes
interest in physical planning measures to
reduce losses, due to the availability of
aid to cover local costs. (Godschalk,
Brower and Beatley 1989: 91)

b. Federal hazard mitigation mandates increase
attention to physical planning measures by
forcing mitigation on to the local
political agenda. (Drabek, Mushkatel, and
Kilijanik 1983)

c. Federal financial assistance fosters
adoption of physical planning measures.
(Mushkatel and Weschler 1985)

2. State mandates: State mandates increase
adoption of physical planning measures to
mitigate hazards. (Berke and Hinojosa 1987;
Berke and Wilhite 1988; Burby and French et al.
1985; Burby and French 1981; May and Williams
1986; Wyner 1984) But, state mandates do not
guarantee implementation. (Mittler 1989; Wyner
1984)

B. Policy Catalysts

1. Experience with hazardous events: Recent
losses increase the adoption of physical

TABLE 6A-1 (Continued)

planning adjustments. (Alesch and Petak 1986;
Godschalk, Brower and Beatley 1989; Luloff and
Wilkinson 1979; May and Williams 1986; Wyner
1984) Other studies, however, have found no
association between recent losses and physical
planning adjustments. (Berke, Beatley and
Wilhite 1988; Rubin 1981)

2. Risk of hazardous events:

   a. Higher risk stimulates adoption of physical
      planning adjustments. (Berke and Hinojosa
      1987; Mushkatel and Nigg 1987) Other
      studies, however, have found that risk per
      se has little association with adoption of
      such adjustments (Godschalk, Brower and
      Beatley 1989) or on local elites' support
      or opposition to physical planning
      measures. (Mitler 1989)

   b. Uncertain risks stimulate policy adoption
      (Graham 1982), but another study suggests
      that uncertainty leads to fatalism and
      failure to adopt adjustments. (Wyner 1984)

3. Population growth: High growth rates stimulate
   adoption of physical planning adjustments.
   (Burby and French et al. 1985)

4. Percent of community located in hazard
   area/more intensive development of hazardous
   areas: Intensive development of hazardous
   areas stimulates adoption of physical planning
   adjustments. (Burby and French 1981; Burby and
   French et al. 1985)

C. Tractability of the Hazard

   1. Earthquake hazard: Technical difficulties
      identifying faults; the large size of the

TABLE 6A-1 (Continued)

population whose behavior needs to be affected; diversity of behaviors to be changed; and high costs imposed on a narrow group make earthquake hazards less amenable to physical planning adjustments than other hazards. (Wyner 1984)

2. Flood hazard: Ease of identifying potential victims makes flood hazards more amenable to physical planning adjustments than hazards, such as earthquakes, where victims are more spatially diffuse. (Graham 1982)

D. Political Environment

1. Political culture: Conservative political culture and opposition to government interference with private property rights decreases adoption of physical planning adjustments. (Beatley and Berke 1989; Godschalk, Brower and Beatley 1989; Hutton, et al. 1979; Mittler 1989; Rubin 1981)

2. Local political constituency/interest groups:

   a. Absence of a political constituency for physical planning adjustments and presence of active opposition by economic development and real estate interests diminishes the adoption of such measures. (Drabek 1986; Godschalk, Brower and Beatley 1989; Rubin 1981; Wyner 1984)

   b. Varying values and perceptions among stakeholders makes it difficult, if not impossible, to reach consensus about appropriate physical planning policy. (Alesch and Petak 1986; Petak 1984)

   c. The more nonhazardous sites available for development, the more likely communities are to have adopted physical planning

TABLE 6A-1 (Continued)

adjustments to natural hazards, since those measures will not constrain the real estate and development industry. (Burby and French 1981; Burby, French et al. 1985; Godschalk, Brower and Beatley 1989)

3. Mass political support: Mass political support has not been a critical factor in adoption of physical planning adjustments, except possibly in the wake of a disaster. (Wyner 1984)

4. Power structure: Communities with centralized power structures are less likely to adopt physical planning adjustments to natural hazards than communities with pluralistic power structures. (Hutton, et al. 1979)

E. Community Resources

1. Urbanization/Population: Larger jurisdictions are more likely to adopt physical planning adjustments than smaller jurisdictions (Burby and French 1981; Burby and French et al. 1985; Godschalk, Brower and Beatley 1989; Hutton, et al. 1979); other studies have not found any effect of population size. (Berke and Hinojosa 1987; Rubin 1981)

2. Affluence/median home value/wealth of community: Higher median home values/community wealth increase local attention to physical planning adjustments to hazards. (Burby and French 1981; Burby and French et al. 1985; Godschalk, Brower and Beatley 1989; Hutton, et al. 1979; Nilson and Nilson 1981; Wyner 1984)

TABLE 6A-1 (Continued)

II. Characteristics of the Governmental Unit

A. Perceptions of and Attitudes Toward Natural Hazards

1. Recognition of hazards: Greater recognition of hazards and the probabilities of loss leads communities to adopt physical planning adjustments. (Alesch and Petak 1986; Burby and French et al. 1985; Drabek, Mushkatel and Kilijanek 1983; French and Harmon 1982; Mushkatel and Weschler 1985)

2. Priority of hazards problems: Where hazards problems have higher priority communities give more attention to physical planning adjustments. (Burby and French 1981; Burby and French et al. 1985; Dalton 1989; Godschalk, Brower, and Beatley 1989; Wyner 1984) Priority of natural hazards relative to other problems, however, is irrelevant to support or opposition of nonstructural hazard mitigation among state and local elites. (Mitler 1989)

3. Degree of individual control possible: Where hazards are viewed as controllable by individuals, communities are less likely to adopt physical planning adjustments. (Graham 1982)

4. Perceived efficacy of physical planning adjustments:

a. The availability of a policy option that is viewed as practical and efficacious is an important factor in the adoption of physical planning adjustments. (Alesch and Petak 1986; May and Williams 1986). Efficacy of physical planning adjustments may vary by hazard, however. Wyner (1984), for example, notes that seismic safety policy is imbued with a strong dose of fatalism, since unlike flood hazards,

TABLE 6A-1 (Continued)

        policies are not available to prevent
earthquakes from occurring and reasonable
predictions about where, when and with what
magnitude earthquakes will occur are not
available.

    b. Ignorance is a major contributor to
opposition to physical planning
adjustments. (Drabek 1986)

  5. Policy advocates: Strong advocates who have
access to policy makers and a high degree of
legitimacy, political power, or the prospects
of longevity in office promote adoption of
physical planning measures. (Alesch and Petak
1986; Beatley and Berke 1989; Drabek, Mushkatel
and Kilijanek 1983; May and Williams 1986;
Wyner 1984)

B. Capacity to Adopt and Implement Physical Planning
Measures

  1. Personnel resources:

    a. Lack of trained personnel diminishes local
attention to physical planning adjustments.
(Godschalk, Brower and Beatley 1989; French
and Harmon 1982; Mushkatel and Weschler
1985; Petak 1984; Wyner 1984)

    b. Staff professionalism increases attention
to physical planning adjustments. (Hutton,
et al. 1979)

  2. Land use management experience: Experience
with land use management stimulates the use
physical planning adjustments. (Burby and
French 1981; Burby and French et al. 1985)

  3. Participation in professional meetings:
Communities whose personnel participate more

TABLE 6A-1 (Continued)

> frequently in professional meetings (where physical planning adjustments to hazards are discussed) are more likely to adopt such measures than communities where such participation is low. (Alesch and Petak 1986)

4. **Type of government**: Reformed (i.e., city manager) governments are more likely than others to adopt physical planning adjustments to natural hazards. (Hutton, et al. 1979)

5. **Size of government**: Larger governments are more likely to adopt physical planning adjustments to natural hazards. (Hutton, et al. 1979)

6. **Source of revenue**: Governments which depend on property taxes for revenue are less likely to adopt physical planning adjustments than governments that rely on other revenue sources. (Hutton, et al. 1979)

III. Type of Policy/Policy Options

A. **Type of Policy**

1. **Type of policy**: Each type of policy (distributive, redistributive, regulatory) may be more or less likely to be adopted, depending upon characteristics of local political arenas (participatory, specialist, pluralist, elitist). (Dalton 1989; Drabek 1986; May and Bolton 1986; Olson and Nilson 1982)

2. **Regulatory policy**: Regulatory policies open the way for agency capture and failure to implement policies proposed by physical plans. (Dalton 1989)

3. **Structural solutions**: Where flood control and other areawide structural solutions are

TABLE 6A-1 (Continued)

available (i.e., a distributive or
redistributive solution), communities will look
toward them before pursuing land use (i.e.,
regulatory) adjustments to hazards. (Burby, et
al. 1988; Burby and French et al., 1985)

B. Costs of Adjustment

    1. Costs of adjustment: The more visible the
costs of the adjustment, the less likely it is
to be adopted. (Graham 1982)

C. Links to Other Policies

    1. Links to other policies: Hazards adjustments
can be furthered to the extent they are linked
to other policies with greater political
salience. (Beatley and Godschalk 1985; Berke
and Hinojosa 1987; Berke and Wilhite 1988;
Berke, Beatley and Wilhite 1988; Burby and
French et al. 1985; Drabek, Mushkatel and
Kilijanek 1983)

PART 3

Four Issues in Sharing Environmental Risks

7

The Technical Feasibility
of Risk Analysis

In Chapter 4 we described five strategies available to policy makers for dealing with risks from natural hazards: risk identification, risk elimination, risk reduction, risk assumption and risk transfer. The first of those, risk identification, is in fact a necessary condition for pursuing any of the other strategies efficiently. In this chapter we explore the technical feasibility of assessing natural hazard risks and the methods that are available to do so.

Risk identification requires more than simply noting the types of hazards that threaten a particular infrastructure system. To employ most of the available risk mitigation strategies, the type of risk must not only be identified, but the degree of risk also must somehow be quantified. Modern decision making strategies require quantification of risk so that investments in hazard mitigation can be evaluated and compared with other possible uses of public funds. The degree and nature of risk also must be understood to make efficient choices among alternative mitigation strategies.

This chapter evaluates technical issues that affect the feasibility of identifying and quantifying the degree of risk present in a particular situation. After a brief discussion of some of the salient characteristics of risk, we describe a generalized risk analysis methodology. We then look at three risk analysis approaches that can be used in conjunction with various mitigation strategies. The chapter concludes with an assessment local governments' ability to implement those methods.

It is important to realize at the outset that mitigation strategies vary in the type and amount of information they require before they can be employed effectively. Risk transfer strategies, for example, may only require an aggregate estimate of annual expected losses, while many risk reduction strategies require very detailed information to determine the system components that should be strengthened to reduce their susceptibility to damage. Thus, the scope of risk analysis depends on the purpose it will serve.

Before proceeding we need to clarify the distinction between "hazards" and "risks." Hazards are natural phenomena that result in physical effects (e.g., flooding) that can cause property damage and other losses. The insurance industry often uses the term peril to denote this causative mechanism. (See, for example, Denenberg et al. 1964.) Here we are concerned with four natural hazards: floods, hurricanes, landslides and earthquakes. Risks are threats to life or property that can result from the action of a hazard upon a structure, system, or person. Thus, risk implies the potential for loss and requires both a hazard and some item or items of human value that may be damaged by the hazard.

The Nature of Risk

The concept of risk implies the possibility of suffering a loss. The size and occurrence of the loss, however, is uncertain. The inclusion of uncertainly is central to the notion of risk. If a loss is certain to occur, many would argue that no risk exists. (See for example, Elliot and Vaughn 1972.)

Dealing with uncertainty is one of the primary technical issues to be confronted in assessing risk. That fact was noted by the National Research Council's Panel on Earthquake Loss Estimation Methodology (1989):

> No loss estimate prepared today, or in the foreseeable future, can be completely accurate. There are major gaps in our knowledge, both as to the time of occurrence, magnitude, and location of future earthquakes and as to the manner in which the ground and structures will respond to earthquakes. Any loss estimation inherently involves uncertainties. Despite their limitations, loss studies that are properly conducted and used with an understanding of the method's limitations can be of great value.

The observations made by the panel with respect to earthquakes are more or less true for the entire range of hazards that can affect public property.

The insurance literature draws an important distinction between two types of risk: particular risks and fundamental risks. Particular risks are wholly independent events that affect individuals or small numbers of people. The death of an individual, a residential fire, or a property theft are examples of particular risks. While large numbers of people face these risks, the consequences of a particular occurrence are limited and independent from other occurrences. A fundamental risk is broader in extent and has a large catastrophic potential. A single occurrence of a fundamental risk can affect large numbers of individuals. Floods, hurricanes and earthquakes are all fundamental risks.

As a rule, private insurers avoid writing coverage for fundamental risks because resulting claims would not be independent, and as a result companies could be exposed to catastrophic losses. Instead, insuring fundamental risks has been deferred to the public sector, principally to the federal government. The National Flood Insurance Program is one example of such a program. (For a detailed discussion of the National Flood Insurance Program and associated local regulations see Burby and French et al. 1985.) Thus, the extent and comprehensiveness of risks posed by natural hazards are important factors in considering which risk management strategies are most appropriate in a particular setting.

Losses can take many forms. Typically, damage to urban infrastructure systems from natural hazards results in four types of losses:

1. Financial, either direct (e.g., damage to public facilities/emergency response and cleanup costs) or indirect (e.g., loss of tax base).
2. Injury and loss of life.
3. Disruption of service and subsequent business interruption.
4. Inability to cope with secondary hazards (e.g., fire following an earthquake).

Here we are concerned primarily with direct financial losses associated with repair and replacement of damaged facilities. The risk associated with losses to facilities is borne by local governments and through disaster assistance and other aid programs, by the states and federal government. Risk associated with other types of loss (e.g. disruption of service or loss of life), however, are still borne by private firms and individuals.

In addition to the form of loss, the frequency of loss is also important for risk analysis. Frequency is generally inversely related to severity. Typically, when we consider damage to public property from natural hazards we are dealing with relatively low probability events that recur in a particular community once in 25 to once in 500 years; however, as we aggregate losses over larger geographic areas, the probability of experiencing significant losses every year becomes more likely.

For shorthand purposes, the distribution of potential losses is often reduced to an expected value by summing the various losses times their associated probabilities (or by integrating a continuous loss-frequency function). The expected value of losses is useful for insurance purposes because the premium charged must be sufficient to recover that amount plus administrative costs. (See Singer 1986 for an application of this technique to setting flood insurance premiums.) The expected value does not, however, convey all of the information about risk that is provided by a full loss-frequency distribution. For example, suppose there are two hazards, one with a .1 probability of a $100 loss and another with .01 probability of a $1000 loss. Both hazards produce expected losses of $10, but the one with a higher loss is a much less frequent event. Insurance companies are often unwilling to write coverage for low probability events with the potential for catastrophic losses. Thus, a full characterization of the loss frequency distribution provides a clearer picture of a hazardous situation than does a single measure such as expected value.

We have also found it useful to distinguish perceived risk and objective risk because each has a different effect on people's choices of hazard mitigation strategies. Kunrenther et al. (1978), for example, reported that participants in a number of risk experiments consistently preferred to insure against hazards that were relatively frequent and resulted in small amounts of damage. Insurance was not bought for low probability hazards with potentially catastrophic losses. Therefore, it is important to understand the loss-frequency pattern of risk that a particular hazard poses for different kinds of infrastructure and how that compares to other hazards and types of infrastructure.

A General Approach to Risk Analysis

As we have seen, risk depends on the interaction between a causative mechanism (e.g., one of the natural hazards) and something of value (e.g., public facilities). Risk analysis is a procedure for combining those two factors to produce an estimate of potential losses.

A number of risk analysis methods have been developed and implemented over the past twenty years. (For a comparative list of some thirty-seven earthquake damage estimation models applicable to risk analysis, see Reitherman 1985.) The scope and sophistication of those methods varies considerably, but most include three basic components: (1) information about the hazard itself (e.g., the probability and intensity of likely events); (2) an inventory of property at risk from the hazard; and (3) estimates of the response of various classes of property to different levels of hazard. Existing methods range in scale from those that aggregate data to the state level (e.g. Petak and Atkisson 1982) to those that focus on the behavior of a particular structure. While detailed methods provide greater accuracy, they require substantially greater amounts of data on both the hazard and the characteristics of the property at risk. As a result, they are often too expensive for application to large areas.

There are two main classes of damage models used in risk analysis: deterministic and probabilistic. Deterministic models postulate an event of a given magnitude and estimate the resultant damage that can be expected to occur. That type of analysis can be useful if a fairly plausible hazard scenario is chosen. The probabilistic approach takes account of the whole range of likely events by assigning probabilities to each event (or range of events) and estimating the damage that could be expected. The expected value of the weighted damage distribution can then be used to characterize the degree of risk. For financial decision making and insurance rate setting, the more complex probabilistic approach is definitely preferred, but its cost and complexity often forces analysts to rely on a deterministic approach.

Risk analysis typically involves three distinct steps:

1. Define the hazard.
2. Inventory property at risk.
3. Apply vulnerability functions to estimate probable damage.

(See Scawthorn 1986, Reitherman 1985, or French and Issaacson 1984 for discussions of this methodology.) To provide a sense of the technical issues involved in conducting a risk analysis, we review each steps in turn.

Defining the Hazard

Most risk analysis methods focus on a single type of hazard and are performed by specialists trained in a particular discipline. As a result, risk analysis most often is not undertaken within a multi-hazard framework. Regardless of whether a method focuses on one hazard or many, however, the intensity and location of each hazard threatening a locality must be defined. The parameters that are used to quantify the intensity of each type of hazard are quite different, yet all are reflections of the magnitude of the hazard event. Table 7.1 outlines some of the typical parameters that might be used to describe various hazards.

There are a number of ways in which to characterize the degree of hazard present at a given hazardous location. Most methods use a probability statement to describe the likelihood or frequency of occurrence of the hazard. There are two ways in which probabilities can be used: single probabilities can be used for hazards employed in evaluating a loss scenario or the whole probability distribution can be examined.

Most simply, a probability can be assigned to an event of a given severity, such as the 100-year flood: the flood event has a 1 percent probability of occurring in any given year. Other examples of single

TABLE 7.1
Hazard Parameters

Hazard	Measure of Intensity
Flood	Area Flooded, Water Depth, Water Velocity
Hurricane	Area Flooded, Water Depth, Water Velocity, Wind Velocity
Landslide	Area of Ground Failure
Earthquake	Peak Acceleration, Area of Ground Failure, Fault Displacement

probability characterizations of risk are found in engineering design where a structural member is designed to perform with a known probability of failure. Such characterizations of risk are useful and provide more information than simple ordinal rankings, but they do not give a sense of the entire range of events that can occur.

Alternatively, the probabilities of events over a whole range of severities can be used to characterize the hazard. That provides a more thorough way to characterize the hazard and its effects. A probability distribution $p(I)$ which describes the likelihood of attaining (or more often the probability of not exceeding) a given level of intensity for each parameter is used to characterize the physical intensity of the hazard. Figure 7.1 shows a typical probability distribution of hazard intensities. As might be expected, the probabilities of extreme events is lower than for less severe hazard intensities. A similar curve could be drawn for floods, hurricanes, earthquakes or landslides. These probability distributions are usually based on historical data for relatively frequent events. Adequate historical data do not exist for extremely rare events, and probabilities must be estimated using models which simulate the physical mechanism of the hazard.

Furthermore, if the risk analysis is being conducted over a fairly large area (e.g., an entire city), the level of hazard will vary with location, and that spatial variation should be calculated. Hazards such as floods,

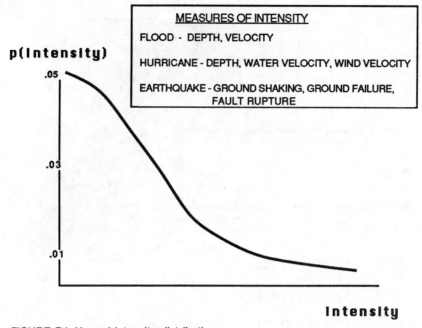

FIGURE 7.1 Hazard intensity distribution

landslides and hurricanes tend to be more localized in nature. Figure 7.2 demonstrates conceptually how the hazard can vary within a particular community. Some aspects of the earthquake hazard are more regional in nature (i.e., the level of ground motion may be fairly constant over a large area). Some aspects of the earthquake hazard, such as landslide, liquefaction, and fault rupture, however, are localized in space. Those areas face greater hazard intensity than surrounding areas. (The Marina District in San Francisco with its unstable geology provides a graphic example of such a localized hazard; the district experienced extensive damage in the 1989 Loma Prieta earthquake.) To perform an acceptable risk analysis it is necessary to know where the greatest intensity of hazard is likely to occur.

The type and intensity of hazards also varies at a much larger scale. Earthquakes, landslides, and floods, for example, require the attention of hazard analysts in California, while hurricanes are the most important hazard in Florida, and flooding is most important in Missouri. The likely intensity of any one hazard that is likely to be experienced can also vary at this larger scale. Thus, we see that intensity can vary considerably

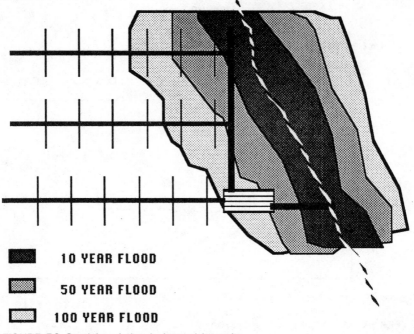

▓▓	**10 YEAR FLOOD**
▒▒	**50 YEAR FLOOD**
░░	**100 YEAR FLOOD**

FIGURE 7.2 Spatial variation in hazard intensity

for any one location, and that it is likely to vary over both large and small scales of analysis.

Inventorying Property at Risk

Since risk is determined by the action of a hazard upon some property of value, risk analysts need to know the type, amount, location and value of the property exposed to the hazard. A typical property inventory classifies structures and utility systems into a finite number of types that are known to experience similar vulnerability to the hazard. Classification schemes range from as few as four classes (French and Isaacson 1984) to more elaborate classifications, such as the thirty-seven building classes used in the Earthquake Engineering Facility Classification (Applied Technology Council 1985). Most classification schemes are based on the construction material, type of framing system, and age of the structure. Other desirable characteristics that can help in estimating the vulnerability of a structure include the number of stories, base elevation, building configuration and information on site characteristics such as localized geology. To estimate the expected dollar value of losses from a hazard event or to make estimates of the life and safety threat, it is also important to know the use of the structure (e.g., residential, retail, office etc.), and its occupancy, value, and size.

Readers might assume that the inventory of property at risk would involve the least uncertainty, since it is simply a matter of counting and classifying the number of structures and components of various types. Indeed, given unlimited resources that is the case. In most cases, however, adequate inventories do not exist and the cost of developing an inventory based on field inspection is prohibitive except for extremely small areas.

At this point, we need to distinguish between public buildings and public infrastructure systems. While the funding and management of both types of property are the responsibility of local governments, the problem of developing an inventory of property at risk is somewhat different for each.

Since they are discrete, identifiable entities, buildings can be treated individually. A city could (and our survey of risk managers shows many do) choose to insure some subset of the buildings at risk. An overall inventory is needed for a local government to accurately assess its level of risk, however, because each structure must be described at the time insurance is purchased. Thus, the problem of developing an asset inventory is relatively easy to handle for structures. Furthermore, since public buildings are inherently similar to commercial buildings, well established commercial insurance inventory and rating techniques can be used to rate their risk to fire, flood and earthquake hazards. These methods require a description of the building, including its size, building material and type of frame (e.g. wood frame, steel frame, unreinforced masonry). In addition, information on the age and other attributes of the structure may also be required by the insurer.

Publicly owned infrastructure systems are more difficult to inventory. These systems include water and sewer facilities, roads and bridges, drainage and flood control facilities, and in some cities electric power generation and distribution facilities. There are three problems that have to be confronted. First, various components of those systems are likely to have different characteristics that determine the kind and amount of damage they are likely to sustain in a hazard event, but parts of the system cannot easily be separated out for insurance coverage the way individual buildings can. Second, infrastructure systems are complex networks consisting of many nodes and links that typically have been constructed in increments over time. The quality and format of inventory information kept by local jurisdictions varies considerably between and even within jurisdictions. Third, since there is no existing commercial counterpart, the list of features that can be used for rate setting is not well understood.

Securing detailed information on the components of infrastructure systems is particularly problematic. Our mail survey of 189 public works departments, conducted in 1987, and our exploratory case studies in five southern California jurisdictions (see Chapter 3) indicate that high quality data on characteristics of infrastructure systems are simply not available in most jurisdictions. Where inventories are available, they are rarely in digital form and would require significant amounts of coding before they could be used for risk analysis. Furthermore, those communities that do have detailed data on the characteristics of their infrastructure systems rarely have information on the replacement costs of system components. Public works departments are moving to automated systems to maintain public facility inventories, however, and as these systems become more widely available, access to digital records of facilities at risk will greatly improve the prospects of getting accurate data for risk analysis.

A complete risk analysis requires not only that the distribution of various types of buildings and facilities be determined, but also that the location of the various types of structures be identified. Location is important because the level of hazard varies spatially. It is, therefore, important to prepare maps that indicate the locations of buildings and other infrastructure systems so that variations in the intensity of the hazard can be accounted for in the risk assessment.

Applying Vulnerability Functions to Estimate Probable Damage

Vulnerability models provide the link between the hazard and its resulting damage. These models describe the level of damage (usually a percent of total value) as a function of hazard intensity. Thus, as in the general model below, damage is a function of the hazard intensity at the particular site:

$$DRi = f(I)$$

where DRi is a damage ratio at intensity i and (I) is the intensity of the hazard. Separate vulnerability models can be developed for different classes of facilities and types of buildings. Many vulnerability models are empirically estimated curves based on past loss experience.

Figure 7.3 shows a typical damage function in which the damage ratio increases with the intensity or severity of the hazard. Since each intensity can be characterized by a probability, we can assign a probability to each level of loss. Based on those probabilities, we can develop a loss-frequency distribution. Such a distribution shows the likelihood of experiencing various levels of damage.

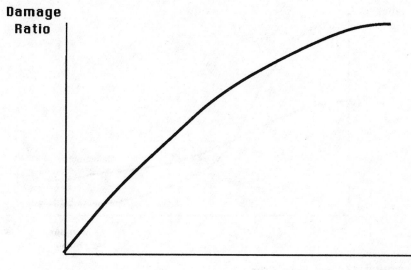

FIGURE 7.3 Typical damage function

Risk may also be characterized as the expected value of losses over the whole range of hazard intensities. The value of the loss at risk at each hazard intensity is simply the damage ratio times the value of property exposed to that hazard intensity. The losses for each intensity can then be weighted by their respective probabilities. This model takes the following general form:

$$\text{Expected Value} = p(DR_{ij})\ (V_{ij})$$

where p is the probability of attaining a given damage ratio, DR is the damage ratio at intensity i for property type j, and V is the value of the property type j which is exposed to intensity i. Such an expected value provides a convenient way to compare the risk across hazards and locations.

For example, in earthquake hazard analysis expected damage is typically estimated by using an empirically determined damage function that relates the level of ground motion at the site, usually expressed as peak ground acceleration or a Modified Mercalli Index (MMI), to a percent damage value for a particular structure type. A separate damage curve is used for each class of structure in the analysis. The damage curves developed by Algermissen, et al. (1978) are typical of those types of functions and are still used frequently.

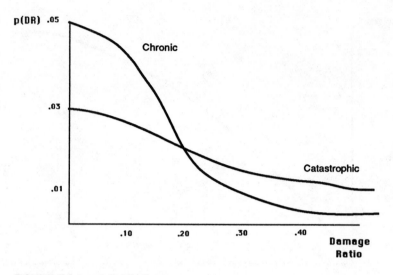

FIGURE 7.4 Loss distributions

The reader should be reminded that there is a some uncertainty regarding the response of various types of structures to different levels of hazard. In the case of extreme events, uncertainty is increased because of the paucity of past experience upon which estimates of future events can be based. Scientific and engineering advances over the past decade have greatly improved our understanding of this aspect of the problem, however.

It is interesting to compare the loss-frequency curves for floods and earthquakes. In any given time period we would expect to see a greater number of damaging floods than earthquakes; however, earthquakes have much greater potential for catastrophic damage. Thus, the overall risk pattern posed by these two hazards is very different even where the expected value of the loss may be the same. Losses from earthquake tend to be catastrophic, while losses from floods tend to be chronic. Clearly, it is sometimes useful to have a risk analysis method that can distinguish the loss-frequency characteristics of the hazard. The most complete characterization of risk is provided by looking at the entire distribution of losses and their associated probabilities. Figure 7.4 shows two loss functions: one for a relatively frequent hazard with chronic losses and the other with a very low probability of occurrence, but with a catastrophic loss potential.

Existing Methods

A number of risk analysis methods have been developed over the last two decades for use in insurance rate setting, emergency planning, and hazard mitigation analysis. Singer (1986) provides a good description of risk analysis techniques applied to flood hazards. Reitherman (1985) and the National Research Council (1989) provide a useful overview of various methods used to estimate earthquake risks.

Methods Used to Estimate Flood Risks

The method used by the National Flood Insurance Program to characterize the hazard provides an interesting example of how hazard intensity parameters are estimated and expected losses are used. The typical flood hazard risk analysis is based on hydrologic modeling of a watershed (typically using the HEC-1 and HEC-2 models developed by the Army Corps of Engineers). First, the historical rainfall record is analyzed to determine a distribution of rainfall duration and intensity. The model generates a flow based on various storm events and levels of rainfall. This flood flow is routed down the drainage course to determine the area inundated by the 100-year and 500-year flood events. These flood flows are then used to develop a Flood Insurance Rate Map (FIRM) that shows the depth of flooding that can be expected from a 100-year flood. The FIRM also identifies a floodway, which is expected to carry high velocity flows, and the area likely to be inundated by the 500-year flood. Flood insurance rates are then set based on the depth of flooding at the location of the structure to be insured and stage-damage curves developed from historical records that relate damage to depth of flooding. Inventory problems are avoided because each building is covered by a separate policy. The application for flood insurance must include only the location and value of the property to be insured.

In the case of floods, then, relatively little information is needed about the property at risk; the key factor is the first floor elevation of a building at risk. The type of structure, its value, the value of its contents, and any floodproofing measures in place are also useful in estimating potential losses. Most flood risk analysis methods do not require detailed information on the structural characteristics of buildings. Stage-damage functions based on historical data are used to estimate damage as a percentage of the value of the structure and its contents as a function of depth of flooding.

The Flood Insurance Rate Map is used to set a premium for an individual structure. The overall risk associated with the 100-year flood can be estimated by summing the likely damage for all the structures in a given floodplain. This deterministic approach would only provide a snapshot of risk for an event of a single probability, however. To get a fuller picture of overall risk, risk managers would have to replicate the analysis for a range of floods of different magnitudes (typically the 10-year, 25-year, 50-year, 250-year and 500-year events). That basically is the approach used by the Corps of Engineers when calculating the benefits of a flood control project.

Methods Used to Estimate Hurricane Risks

Hurricanes are also covered by the National Flood Insurance Program. Hurricane risk analysis is conceptually similar to the flood case in that the first floor elevation of the structure is the single most important factor in determining damage. Structural characteristics of the building also become important due to the effects of storm surge and wind. Flood Insurance Rate Maps for coastal areas denote "V zones" where high velocity storm surge is likely to occur. Flood elevations for other areas are similar to those for the riverine flood situation. Structural characteristics such as the strength of roof tiedowns are important factors to consider with regard to potential wind damage. Again, given the value of individual structures and their location relative to various flood depth and storm surge areas, a reasonable analysis of risk can be performed. As with the flood situation, the analysis should be replicated for a range of storm events to get an overall view of the loss-frequency distribution.

Methods Used to Estimate Earthquake Risks

Earthquake risk analysis procedures are more diverse due to the absence of any national program which prescribes a standard method. Numerous special purpose risk analyses have been undertaken for earthquake risks, usually to estimate the overall amount of damage to structures that is likely to occur in a given area or to support local or regional emergency planning efforts. Earthquake risk analysis differs from flood and hurricane risk analysis in two important ways. First, the level of earthquake hazard is not as closely tied to location as are floods or hurricanes. Second, the structural characteristics of the property at risk tend to be as important as the level of hazard in determining damage. Thus, earthquake risk analysis requires significantly more detailed information about the property at risk.

The earthquake hazard is not limited to just those areas along a fault line. Ground motion radiates from the epicenter of the event and generally attenuates with distance, but it may be intensified by local soil and geologic conditions (e.g. the Mexico City earthquake that was some 140 miles from its epicenter). In addition, since the epicenter can occur anywhere along a fault (or even in areas where faults have not been identified), there is more uncertainty as to what the actual ground motion effects will be at any given site. To deal with that, most earthquake hazard analyses ascribe fairly constant ground motion levels to fairly large areas. The earthquake also generates secondary hazards: landslides and liquefaction (which are associated with specific soil and geologic conditions), fire, and inundation due to dam failure or tsunami. Thus, it is possible to differentiate the level of hazard in space, but the scale of spatial differentiation is much coarser than with floods or hurricanes. (An example of earthquake risk analysis is presented in French and Isaacson 1984.)

The structural characteristics of the property at risk are critical in earthquake risk analysis (the performance of a wood frame building, for example, will differ markedly from that of an unreinforced masonry building subjected to the same ground motion forces). This structural information may be as simple as grouping structures into two or three broad classes (e.g. woodframe, masonry and other), but more elaborate classification schemes have been used that include the type and shape (configuration) of the structure, the age (a proxy for building code requirements) of the structure, and the number of stories, as well as building materials.

Several applications of earthquake risk analysis are of particular interest here: the Building Seismic Safety Council's (1985) recommended provisions for seismic regulations for new buildings, the California Division of Mines and Geology earthquake planning scenarios (Davis et al. 1982a; 1982b), and the Applied Technology Council's (1985) damage estimation method for California. Those studies represent some of the most interesting recent work on how to assess damage from natural hazards.

The Building Seismic Safety Council developed a model ordinance for new construction that incorporates seismic resistant standards. Recognizing that the likely intensity of earthquake ground motion varies considerably across the country, the stringency of regulations for a particular area is determined by the likely acceleration for that area. To aid local governments in knowing what level of regulations apply to their area, the model ordinance includes a county map of effective peak acceleration for all 3,200 counties in the United States.

The California Division of Mines and Geology has produced several studies that are of particular interest because they focus entirely on damage to infrastructure. The Division of Mines and Geology used a USGS model to predict ground shaking intensity for small areas in the

San Francisco and Los Angeles urban areas in the event of an 8.3 magnitude event on the San Andreas Fault. Potential ground failure areas were identified based on soil and water table conditions. Those data on the hazard were then combined with a detailed infrastructure inventory to estimate damage in each area. Infrastructure damage estimates were prepared for highways, airports, railroads, marine facilities, communications, water supply and wastewater facilities, and electric power, natural gas and petroleum facilities. The locations of infrastructure damage were mapped at a scale of approximately 1 inch to 6 miles, and duration of service disruptions for each damage site were estimated. Since the scenarios were intended for emergency preparedness planning, the dollar value of damage to infrastructure systems was not estimated. It is interesting to note how closely the northern California scenario predicted the actual damage experienced in the Loma Prieta earthquake of October 1989.

The Applied Technology Council (1985) has developed a detailed method to estimate the earthquake damage in the urban areas of California. The method employs a variety of existing databases to estimate the number and value of 40 classes of buildings and 38 classes of infrastructure systems at risk. As an example, the Applied Technology Council classification system distinguishes between pipelines that are buried and those that are at grade, but it does not take into account the age or construction material of the pipe. A panel of experts was used to develop damage matrices that relate the intensity (MMI) to damage as a percent of value. These data on the inventory of property at risk were intended for use with hazard intensity data coded at the level of postal Zipcodes. When used with FEMA's FEDLOSS earthquake damage model, the ATC data are intended to produce dollar estimates of losses to buildings and infrastructure as well as losses due to the duration of service disruption. The classification of infrastructure into 38 classes and their associated damage matrices along with the suggested inventory procedures make this an useful method for risk analysis.

Three Approaches to Risk Analysis

Three different levels of risk analysis can be used to support risk elimination, risk reduction, risk assumption and risk transfer strategies for coping with the threat of damages from natural hazards. To do this effectively the risk analysis method must have the following characteristics.

1. It should focus primarily on direct financial damage rather than disruption of service or death and injury.

2. The level of uncertainty in any output estimates should be assessable.
3. The accuracy of the method should be matched to the level of policy analysis that is being undertaken.
4. The cost of employing the method should be low enough so that it can be absorbed within the administrative budget of the program.

The last two requirements of accuracy and low cost tend to be inversely related: generally greater accuracy implies higher cost.

The reason for undertaking a risk analysis can be used to determine how detailed the resolution of the method must be. On the one hand, if the purpose is to set insurance rates at the community scale, relatively coarse methods may be used. If, on the other hand, the intention is to undertake intensive mitigation and pass the costs along to those firms and residents in the most hazardous locations, then the resolution of the method must be considerably greater.

Three different methods for risk analysis can be employed in devising strategies to deal with potential damages to urban infrastructure. The methods are:

1. Community Indicators Method.
2. System Subarea Method.
3. Component Specific Method.

All of these methods follow the standard risk analysis approach of identifying the hazard, inventorying the property at risk and applying a vulnerability model or damage function to the property inventory. They differ in the level of detail at which they implement the general approach. As a result, the accuracy, cost and resolution of the methods vary considerably. Each method is described below along with its input data requirements and potential uses of its output. It is, of course, possible to mix hazards data collected for one scale (e.g., community-level data) with inventory data at another scale (e.g., component-level data), but the overall accuracy of the model will be no better than the least accurate data input.

Community Indicators Method

The community indicators method is the most general. It uses very imprecise hazard information; for example, an indicator that merely sums the number of hazards facing a particular community might be used. Since such an approach is implemented at the community level, only very generalized hazard maps, such as the earthquake zones included

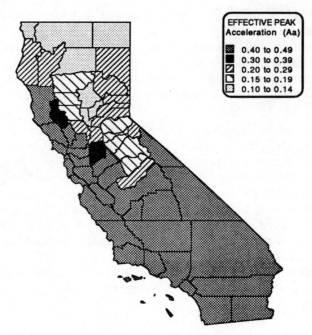

FIGURE 7.5 Earthquake intensity by county

in the Uniform Building Code (ICBO 1985), are used to define hazard intensity. The county-level acceleration maps prepared by the Building Seismic Safety Council (1985) also provide that level of hazard infor-mation. In Figure 7.5, a California county map is used to illustrate the community-indicator level of hazard mapping. While this level of mapping is relatively coarse, it works well in estimating ground motion aspects of the earthquake hazard. More localized hazards would not be as well suited to this level of analysis, however.

The community-indicators method also employs very general indi-cators, such as the population and area of a community, to estimate the value of the inventory at risk. Rough approximations of the value of property at risk can be derived based on secondary data about the jurisdiction. For example, if Census data shows that a given community has 20,000 residential units with an average value of $100,000, we might estimate that the total value of the residential property in the community is $2 billion. We could then use a general rule of thumb that infrastructure is valued at 15 to 25 percent of total residential property value to approximate the value of infrastructure at risk as between $300,000,000 and $500,000,000. Similar techniques could be employed to estimate the infrastructure associated with non-residential land uses.

That type of estimate can be useful in very general analyses conducted for policy decisions at the state or federal level. Petak and Atkisson (1983), for example, use a community-indicator method to analyze federal policy options for dealing with natural hazards. Given the uncertainty associated with the method, however, insurers would be uncomfortable with anything but very minimal coverage based on such gross estimates of risk.

System Subarea Method

The system subarea method uses postal Zipcodes or Census tracts to provide an intermediate level of mapping resolution for the infrastructure and the hazard. Generalized hazard information by Census tract or Zipcode boundary is generally not available from secondary sources, but it is relatively easy to produce. A number of models that estimate ground shaking intensity by Zipcode have been developed. (See, for example, the Insurance/Investment Risk Analysis System (IRAS) developed by Stanford University for the insurance industry.) The degree of flood hazard could also be approximated taking the average flood zone of flood policies issued to addresses in that Zipcode. Figure 7.6 shows the city of San Francisco by Zipcode. While still somewhat crude, it is interesting to note that a particularly hazardous area, such as the Marina District, can be identified at this scale.

The use of Zipcodes or Census tracts for aggregating data by subareas allows estimation of facilities in particular locations by using population and density estimators. A number of methods have been developed to estimate the facilities needed to service a subarea with a given population. For example, the Environmental Protection Agency (1980) and Deb (1982) developed methods for estimating water and wastewater system costs based on population and density.

The system subarea approach divides the infrastructure into a finite number of categories as a basis for the facility inventory. The 40 building and 38 infrastructure classes used for the Applied Technology Council report described earlier provide this useful intermediate degree of detail for a facility inventory. The system subarea method is appealing because it avoids the requirement for a detailed infrastructure inventory database, yet it still recognizes some spatial variation in the hazard and inventory. Accuracy of the damage estimates will of course suffer because the method cannot distinguish between tracts where infrastructure is con-

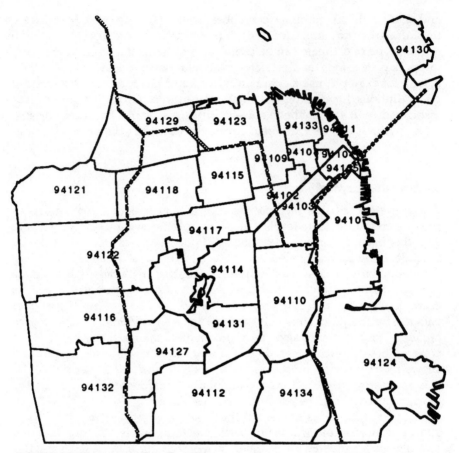

FIGURE 7.6 Zipcodes in San Francisco

centrated in the hazard area from those where local governments have avoided locating facilities in hazardous areas.

Component Specific Method

The component specific method is the most detailed; its resolution is roughly two orders of magnitude greater than the subarea method. It requires a detailed inventory of infrastructure components, small area (microzoned) data about the hazard, and component-specific damage functions. This detailed infrastructure inventory would include the age, capacity, structural characteristics, location and value of all the components that make up each infrastructure system. For example, the water system inventory would include information on distribution lines, pump stations, treatment plants and storage facilities. The component-level inventory must then be combined with detailed hazards information that divides a study area into microzones containing relatively constant levels of each hazard of interest. Such an approach allows the analyst to take into account variation in the level of hazard within a jurisdiction and to account for the differences in response between infrastructure components of different types with different structural characteristics. For example, the response of newer plastic or reinforced concrete water lines is likely to be very different from the response of older cast iron lines. Furthermore, failures are often associated with the joints and connections between sections. A thorough damage modeling approach must be able to associate specific performance criteria with each separate node and link in the system. Therefore, damage modeling for infrastructure systems requires a disaggregate approach that takes account of a complex inventory of components. Clearly, a database management approach is needed to capture the relevant attributes of systems components with a variety of response characteristics.

The fact that infrastructure systems are spatially distributed networks, consisting of nodes and links, makes modeling damage to these systems more difficult than modeling damage to structures that exist at a single site. Infrastructure systems are spread over wide areas and are therefore affected by a variety of site characteristics, and different parts of the system are subjected to very different seismic loadings in the event of an earthquake. (Shah and Benjamin 1977) A traditional database approach is not sufficient to deal with this problem because it does not deal adequately with the distribution of infrastructure components in space and does not provide the capability to associate varied site conditions and shaking intensities with specific components of the systems. The Building Seismic Safety Council (1987: 66–67) recently highlighted this problem and called for development of seismic hazard assessment methods that meet the needs of spatially distributed infrastructure systems. Using a geographic information system allows the network of infrastructure components to be grouped into zones that can be expected to experience relatively similar levels of earthquake hazard.

Given the amount of data involved, a database management system is needed to organize and manipulate the detailed inventory. Since it is necessary to know how much of the infrastructure is exposed to each level of hazard, a simple database of facilities is not, however, adequate. Location is the common field on which the combination of inventory and hazard takes place. A geographic information system (GIS) with database management capabilities provides the most efficient way to combine the spatial variation in the hazard with the spatially distributed components of the infrastructure system. Such a system provides a means to identify the amount, value, and structural characteristics of

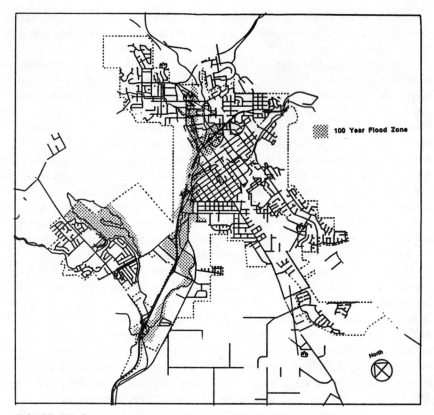

FIGURE 7.7 Component level map of water system and floodplain

infrastructure elements exposed to each level of hazard. This approach allows the proper damage function to be applied to each segment of infrastructure depending on its location with regard to the hazard.

In most areas existing hazard data should be of sufficient scale and accuracy to support the component specific method. The data used to produce Flood Insurance Rate Maps provide an adequate base of hazard mapping in flood- and hurricane-prone communities. Ground shaking, ground failure and fault rupture maps are also available from the USGS and state geologists for most metropolitan areas subject to earthquake hazards, although those maps are not in a standard format. Landslide susceptibility maps are available in many urban areas subject to that hazard.

Figure 7.7 demonstrates the application of geographic information system technology to component level mapping. This small city of San Luis Obispo, California covers roughly six square miles, has a population 40,000, and seven Census tracts. Here we see each of the 1,648 pipe segments that comprise the water system of the city. The flood plain is mapped over the water system. The power of the GIS is that the database of pipe attributes can be queried to extract and analyze the characteristics of those pipes that fall within the 100-year floodplain. Since the associated database contains the length, diameter, age and material of each pipe segment, earthquake risk modelling is also straightforward.

The attraction of the component specific method is that it should produce more accurate damage assessments because it takes account of the spatial variation in the hazard and the different response characteristics of various infrastructure components. For example, two areas may have the exact same inventory of facilities, but if one area is in a particularly hazardous location, the risk is much higher in that area. In addition, characteristics of facilities that affect their performance under hazard conditions improve the accuracy of the damage estimates. For example, an 8-inch PVC sewer pipe will behave very differently than an 8-inch cast iron pipe under identical loads in the same location. A detailed approach is necessary if the different levels of hazard within a community are to be used to finance hazard mitigation through differential tax rates or impact fees.

Most research on infrastructure damage has focused on system reliability parameters rather than economic damage. While it is possible to translate such "breaks per mile" models into economic damage, a damage ratio approach is more straightforward. Further research is needed to explore the statistical relationship between hazard intensities and damage ratios for infrastructure systems, however.

The most serious obstacle in employing the component specific method is cost. Given the paucity of existing data on the inventory of infrastructure in most communities, implementation of this approach would be too costly for most risk management programs or for the insurance industry. As better inventory data become available, however, this method will be the best approach for estimating losses with enough accuracy for setting insurance rates. That is important, because the inability to insure losses to many infrastructure systems is an important limitation on effective risk management.

Governments' Capacity to Analyze Risk

Local governments' ability to implement the three risk assessment methods discussed above is limited by three factors: (1) available data; (2) staff expertise; and (3) available resources. While the techniques of risk analysis are technically feasible, those constraints will hamper their implementation in most places.

It appears that data are widely available for the two more general methods, but data are not available for the more detailed component specific approach. The intensity of the hazards that are the root cause of the risk of natural disasters varies considerably over space, certainly among different communities, and in most cases over different parts of a single community. Relatively good hazard data are available for most localities, largely due to the efforts of federal agencies such as FEMA, USGS, and the Army Corps of Engineers and state water resource and geologic agencies. Flood and hurricane data are particularly good, although they may not be in a form that is readily usable in some types of risk analysis.

The systems at risk, which include water and sewer systems, roads and bridges, park facilities and public buildings, are distributed over wide areas. At the present time the detailed component specific approach may well be too costly in most communities. However, with rapid advances in database management and geographic information systems, most local governments are likely to be able to support this level of analysis within the 1990s. In those cases where detailed inventory and hazard information already exist, the increased accuracy of the component specific approach may warrant the additional costs.

The key problem in applying component level risk analysis to urban infrastructure systems is the poor quality of existing public facility inventories and the rudimentary state of the art of infrastructure damage modeling. Many public agencies do not have detailed public facility inventories that include the value and structural aspects of infrastructure systems by location. To be really useful this information must be in a form (hard copy maps or preferably an automated system) which can be readily combined with maps of hazard intensity. Most local agencies also lack the expertise to conduct such a risk analysis.

Studies by French and others show that most local governments now employ database management technology. (French and Wiggins 1989) Many planning and public works departments indicate that they will be implementing geographic information system technology within the next five years. In the very near future, then, the data and equipment to conduct component level analysis will be relatively widespread. The expertise is also likely to be available if there is adequate incentive to develop it.

State and federal mandates to conduct some level of risk analysis either in the mitigation of new and existing hazards or as a part of the comprehensive planning process are likely to do much to increase governmental capacity. Those mandates, when coupled with the provision of information and technical assistance, can be particularly effective.

More general methods that characterize the facility inventory and the level of hazard by areas such as Census tracts provide an appealing alternative for the present because they recognize some spatial variation in hazard but can be used at much lower costs. Further investigation of the relation between population, population density and the value of infrastructure is needed before such methods can be used with confidence, however. In general, we recommend that local governments use the most detailed method that can be supported by available data and funds.

Conclusions

An adequate technical basis exists to assess and evaluate the risk posed by natural hazards to urban infrastructure. While considerable uncertainty exists in any type of risk analysis, the existing scientific base seems strong enough to support most risk management responses likely to be undertaken by local governments. Each of the three levels of risk analysis described above is suitable for certain types of analysis. They differ significantly in the cost required to implement them and in the accuracy and resolution of their results. Given the availability of existing data, the system subarea method seems most workable for financial mitigation strategies.

It is important to distinguish between buildings and utility systems. Given that buildings can be handled individually the inventory problem is less problematic than for infrastructure systems. Commercial insurance already exists to protect public buildings against losses from floods, hurricanes and earthquakes. The technical basis for rate setting for those hazards, while not flawless, is clearly workable.

Because they are not separable and because data on the inventory of property at risk are not readily available, infrastructure systems present more of a problem. Given that infrastructure networks are integrated systems, risk management must focus on strategies that deal with whole systems rather than incremental parts. A method that uses the damage ratio approach typical of regional assessments of structural damage is well suited to infrastructure system risk analysis at this time.

8

Economic Considerations

Economic efficiency cannot be used as the sole criterion for evaluating policy, but, as discussed in Chapter 1, an economic criterion is undoubtedly an important consideration to many decision makers, and economic efficiency arguments have significantly influenced, and at times dominated, the policy debate on natural hazards. In this chapter we examine the arguments for and against different policy options from an economic or cost-benefit perspective. To begin, we review the economic benefits to an individual of reducing the cost of risks to public infrastructure. We then examine policy choices from the perspective of the federal government, assuming that federal policy should reflect the interests of all members of society, and from the perspective of local governments.

The Individual's Perspective on the Cost of Risk[1]

An individual living in a community effectively "owns" a portion of the community's public infrastructure: its roads, libraries, schools, water system, parks, and other public facilities. His share of this stock of public infrastructure is at risk from natural hazards. If the responsibility for this risk rested upon the members of his local community and if a natural disaster was to occur, the individual would suffer a loss of welfare, either in terms of the increased tax burden necessary to repair the damages or in terms of reduced public services if the damages were not repaired. If the damages were repaired, his loss would be dependent upon his share of the tax burden. If the damages were not repaired, his loss would depend upon the extent to which he valued the public services that used to be provided by the public facilities.

Figure 8.1 illustrates the magnitude of an individual's welfare loss from the risk to public infrastructure from natural hazards. The utility function of a risk-averse individual is depicted by $U(y)$, where y is the individual's income. (See Schoemaker 1982, for a discussion of the

Utility

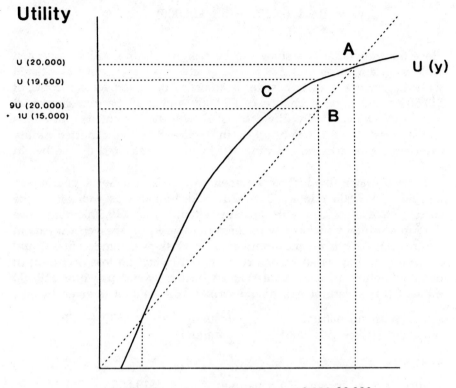

FIGURE 8.1 The cost of risk to a risk-adverse individual facing the possibility of losses to public infrastructure from natural hazards

expected utility model.) We assume that there are two possible states of the world: (1) a natural disaster does not strike the community, and (2) a natural disaster strikes the community. For purposes of illustration, the probability that a natural disaster will occur is assumed to be 10 percent in a given year; there is thus a 90 percent probability that a natural disaster will not occur. If a natural disaster does not occur, we assume the individual receives his normal income level of, say, $20,000. If a natural disaster does strike, assume the individual's share of the losses to the community's public infrastructure is $5,000, and that the community repairs the damages to the public infrastructure in the year in which the natural disaster occurred. The individual's expected income is thus . . .

$$E(y) = 0.9(\$20,000) + 0.1(\$15,000)$$
$$= \$19,500$$

Since the individual is assumed to be risk-averse, the utility associated with a certain income of $19,500 is greater than the utility associated with the current uncertain state of affairs with an expected income of $19,500 (a 90 percent chance of $20,000 and a 10 percent chance of $15,000). The expected utility associated with the current state of affairs is measured by the height of B in Figure 8.1; the expected utility associated with a certain income of $19,500 is measured by the height of A.

Because the individual is assumed to be risk-averse, a guaranteed income of $19,500 minus CB would make him just as well off as the current state of affairs with an expected utility of $19,500: both have the same utility associated with them (measured on the vertical axis in Figure 8.1). What is the maximum amount a risk-averse individual would be willing to pay as an insurance premium (when no loss occurred) in order to obtain an agreement that an insurer would pay him $19,500 minus CB if a natural hazard did strike? This amount is given by . . .

Income if no natural   − Insurance = [$19,500 − CB]
hazard strikes ($20,000)   premium

or . . .

Insurance = Income if no natural   − [$19,500 − CB]
premium   hazard strikes ($20,000)
            = $500 + CB

On average the insurer would have to pay $500, so its expected profit would be CB. Nevertheless, the individual is just as well off as before the purchase of the insurance. By purchasing insurance against natural hazards, the individual has converted the current situation [0.9 chance of $20,000; 0.1 chance of $15,000] into a situtation in which he is certain to receive $19,500 minus CB. The cost of risk, CB, is the difference in value to the individual of the expected value of the uncertain situation and the certain income which yields the same utility as the expected utility of the risky situation without insurance against natural hazards. The more risk-averse the individual, the greater the cost of this risk.

If an individual is risk-averse and if his share of the tax burden (or the value he places on the services available from the public facilities) is large relative to his total income (or wealth), then his welfare can be increased by reducing the cost of the risk to the public infrastructure from natural hazards. Although the probability that a natural disaster will strike the community does not change, the cost of risk can be reduced either by risk-pooling[2] or by risk-spreading[3] mechanisms. By spreading the risks of natural hazards, the welfare of each risk-averse individual in the community can be increased.[4] The maximum economic benefit to a given individual which can be achieved by such risk management strategies would be associated with reducing the cost of risk CB to zero. Considering all the individuals in the community, the total potential benefit from such strategies would be the summation of each individual's corresponding value of CB, minus the cost of administering the insurance scheme.

The next question to ask is whether these total benefits are likely to be large. The answer depends upon (a) whether individuals are, in fact, risk-averse with respect to losses to public infrastructure from natural hazards, and (b) the size of their potential losses relative to their income. With regard to the first question, there are many plausible explanations of how individuals might behave in the face of risks from natural hazards. For example, Tversky and Kahneman (1981) have suggested that people suffer from losses much more than they benefit from corresponding gains—even more than expected utility theory would indicate. In that case the benefits from risk management strategies designed to reduce the cost of risk would be greater than suggested by CB in Figure 8.1. The gambler's fallacy and the availability bias (Tversky and Kahneman 1981) suggest that individuals will underestimate the probability of a natural hazard striking their community, and thus in terms of their ex-ante preferences, the benefits of reducing the cost of risk would be less.

The empirical evidence with respect to individuals' preferences toward the risks from natural hazards suggests that people are generally reluctant to insure against most natural hazards. It is difficult, however, to judge the policy significance of such evidence, in part because the existing policy environment has created the expectation that the community at risk is ultimately not wholly responsible for possible damages to its infrastructure. If people expect the federal government to provide disaster assistance in the event of even relatively minor losses, then it is quite rational from the individual's perspective not to desire the elected representatives of his community to independently insure against such risks. It is also rational from the community's point of view to place more of its public facilities in hazard-prone areas than is prudent because the risks from such behavior are only partially borne by the members of the community.

With regard to the second factor determining the magnitude of the potential benefits from risk management strategies (i.e., the size of the individual's potential losses relative to his income), the amount of public infrastructure at risk per capita (or per household) may be quite large in some communities. The stock of fixed assets owned by state and local governments was on the order of $2 trillion in 1984; the national average for state and local infrastructure per capita was thus about $8000. For a family of four, that would imply a $32,000 share in state and local infrastructure. Most families would probably prefer to insure against a possible loss of their own property of that magnitude. Since losses to state and local infrastructure run about $1 billion annually (0.05 percent of the capital stock), the average annual loss to a family of four is about $16. Insurance against all risks from natural hazards to state and local infrastructure would thus probably cost less than $20 per year per household.

Insurance premiums of that magnitude would appear to be modest, less than 2 percent of what many households spend annually for private insurance (medical, homeowners, automobile, life, and disability). Yet, as noted in Chapter 1, FEMA's proposal that state governments could afford to devote $1 per capita for disaster response and recovery was strongly opposed by state and local officials and was rejected by Congress. Such political opposition to state and local cost-sharing should not be interpreted, however, to mean that local residents cannot afford or are unwilling to pay for actuarially sound insurance against risks to public infrastructure if no other risk-sharing options are available to them.

In our 1988 survey of local government officials, we asked respondents what size of loss would be beyond their jurisdiction's ability to respond using already budgeted contingency funds. As discussed in Chapter 2, their response, on average, was $14 per capita, or $56 for a household of four. That is an estimate of affordable losses for a low probability event, not an estimate of what could be afforded on a regular basis, and appears to be unrealistically low. In many parts of the United States, $56 is roughly the price of a moderately-priced dinner out for a family of four; a loss of $56 could hardly be termed a "disaster" for most American households. Still, even this low estimate by government officials suggests that the insurance premiums required for actuarially-sound insurance against risks to public infrastructure are probably affordable by most households.

The national averages for per-capita state and local infrastructure at risk obscure the fact that some communities have much more infrastructure per capita than others and that the infrastructure in some communities is much more at risk from natural hazards than that in other communities. The size of these potential losses thus suggests that if local communities were themselves responsible for coping with the damages from natural hazards, the potential benefits from risk reduction strategies could be significant in communities with large amounts of public infrastructure at high risk.

However, even in high-risk communities actuarially-sound insurance against the risks to public infrastructure from natural hazards is still likely to be affordable. This is particularly true if we consider the size distribution of losses to public infrastructure between 1980 and mid-1987. Figure 8.2 illustrates the relationship between (1) losses to public infrastructure in cities in the United States with populations above 2500 on a per capita basis, and (2) the cumulative percent of such losses. Only about 10 percent of the total losses occur in communities with per capita losses above $50. The premiums required for households to insure against catastrophic losses to public infrastructure would be only a small fraction of that required to insure against all losses.

Policy Options from an Economic Perspective

In the preceding discussion of the cost of risk to individuals, we assumed that the local community bore the entire burden of coping with losses to public infrastructure. In fact, as we have seen, the current federal programs of disaster assistance and subsidized flood insurance do much to reduce the cost of those risks, spreading them across all citizens. Thus, the first question to ask is whether there is anything wrong in economic terms with the current policies for coping with infrastructure losses.

Federal disaster relief policy provides a form of insurance for local governments, but from an economic perspective it is flawed for two main reasons. First, much of the federal attention is focused on small losses with few if any economic benefits (where "economic benefits" are defined in terms of the welfare changes specified in the previous section). Second, subsidized disaster relief programs do little to promote risk reduction efforts and may promote excessive, inefficient development in hazard-prone areas.

In addition to those economic problems, federal policy is inequitable because it results in reimbursements to governments that experience only small losses in large areawide disasters, but not to governments that experience small losses from other hazard events (e.g., "disasters" of less than "Presidential" magnitude). Also, costs to taxpayers in terms of federal tax liabilities do not reflect the degree of risk to which their local infrastructure is exposed. Taxpayers in relatively low-risk areas in effect subsidize taxpayers in high-risk areas. Since many high-risk areas— such as California—are also high-income areas, the current policy has the added inequity of poorer people subsidizing wealthier people. Both of the economic problems with current federal policy are discussed below.

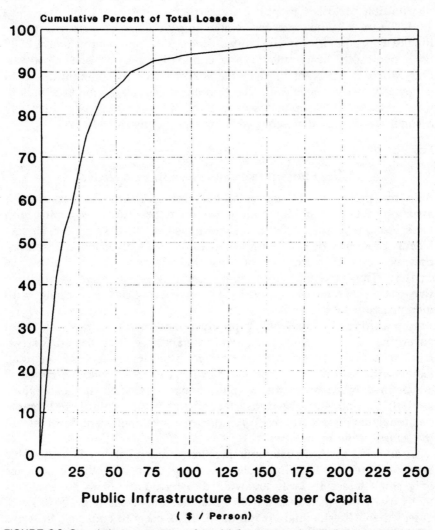

FIGURE 8.2 Cumulative percentage of total infrastructure losses by per capita infrastructure losses. Infrastructure losses include all public losses to natural disasters eligible for federal relief. Includes emergency services and debris removal as well as capital structures. Losses are for towns and cities over 2,500 in population.

A significant finding of this research is that most federally-designated "disasters" are not really disasters at all for many governmental units. The data presented in Chapter 2 show that two thirds of the state and local governmental units that experience losses large enough to merit a Presidential declaration suffered losses of less than $50,000. Losses of that size are not appropriately termed "disasters" even for citizens of a small city—much less a medium or large city—because the losses per capita are very small when they are spread across all taxpayers. There is no evidence nor any theoretical justification for believing that individuals would be risk-averse with respect to such small losses when they are shared with other members of their community. Because individuals are not risk-averse with regard to such small losses, there are no economic efficiency benefits associated with federal programs designed to spread such risks further across all taxpayers in the nation.

The administrative costs associated with federal assistance to communities which suffer small losses are obviously greater than any possible economic efficiency benefits associated with reducing the cost of risk from natural hazards. Federal assistance for such minor losses can only be regarded as a transfer payment, and there is little reason to believe that the equity consequences are on balance positive.

The policy conclusion is thus clear: federal policy should only address those cases with significantly higher losses. The size of loss above which federal involvement might be justified is a matter for further analysis, but, as discussed in the following section, it should clearly be related to the size of the per capita loss in a community. Damages of $10 million to roads and bridges in Los Angeles would have quite different implications than damages of $10 million to roads and bridges in Tyler, Texas or Chapel Hill, North Carolina, simply because the losses in Los Angeles can be spread across so many more people.

The second problem with current policies has been clear to most people for over twenty years: disaster relief and subsidized insurance, such as the National Flood Insurance Program, can increase losses because communities and individuals do not bear the full costs of their decisions to locate in areas susceptible to natural hazards. However, counterbalanced against the efficiency losses from such excessive development are the potential efficiency gains achieved by spreading the risks across many individuals.[5] The goal of federal policy should thus be to eliminate the efficiency losses from excessive development in hazard-prone areas while maintaining the efficiency benefits associated with spreading the risks of catastrasophic losses.

The obvious means of doing that is to ensure that all communities can purchase actuarially sound insurance against large losses from natural hazards. Actuarially sound insurance would require that rates be much higher in communities along the coast, along some rivers, and in earthquake zones. Such differential rates would be necessary to induce communities to keep facilities "out of harm's way," and thus avoid the efficiency losses associated with improper location incentives. Such insurance would also reduce the cost of risk by spreading it across individuals in many communities. If the price of hazards insurance reflected its true cost, insuring against small losses would be prohibitively expensive due to its high administrative costs.

One basic choice to be made by the federal government is whether or not to subsidize disaster relief, either in the form of insurance, grants, or low-interest loans. In fact there are few sound economic arguments in favor of subsidized federal disaster relief programs. Existing subsidies promote excessive development in hazardous areas and are an inefficient mechanism for compensating communities which typically only suffer small losses.

If the federal government does not subsidize disaster relief, it has two choices: (a) to offer communities actuarially-sound insurance against natural hazards, or (b) to leave the responsibility for managing the risks to states and local communities, pushing the problem back on lower levels of government. In practice, for a variety of reasons discussed in Chapters 6 and 9, neither local governments nor individuals are likely to purchase sufficient insurance to cover catastrophic losses to public infrastructure from natural hazards. If local governments will not participate in such an insurance program, the federal government finds itself in a situation in which in reality it may not have pushed the risk of infrastructure losses back on lower levels of government at all: whatever the stated policy, after a disaster strikes local communities may still have the political power to secure disaster assistance.

Although the recent trend in federal policy has been to push an increasing proportion of the risk to infrastructure from natural hazards onto state and local governments, it is not hard to understand the expectation of many local governments that the federal government will meet their needs for relief in times of a disaster. Sound policy requires that the federal government act to change such expectations. That cannot be accomplished simply by pushing the risk of natural hazards back on the communities and walking away from the problem. The federal government must also change its own behavior. For example, after the 1989 Loma Prieta earthquake in San Francisco, politicians of both parties rushed to offer federal disaster assistance to the region.

The difficulty the federal government faces is in a sense not so different from a mortgage company that requires that a prospective homeowner take out fire insurance on a new house in order to obtain the loan. If the homeowner does not carry fire insurance, it is the bank that is really at risk from a fire, not the homeowner, because in the event of a fire, many individuals would simply declare bankruptcy, thus pushing the loss back on the bank. As a result federally-insured home mortgages require that the buyer purchase such insurance. Similarly with risks from natural hazards, the federal government may ultimately be at risk, and thus has the right to ensure that local communities act responsibly in coping with catastrophic infrastructure losses from such hazards.

To a certain extent, federal policy has been moving in the right direction. The Disaster Relief Act of 1974 (Section 409 of the 1988 amendments to the act) requires as a condition for federal disaster loan or grant assistance that states must evaluate the risks from natural hazards where funds are to be applied and must take steps to mitigate the hazard through various means, including safe land use and constructions practices. Since 1981 FEMA has sent out interagency teams to provide post-disaster techncial assistance on methods of reducing future losses through the adoption of various mitigation measures. Our survey compared (1) communities that experienced a disaster and received federal aid, (2) communities that experienced a disaster and did not receive federal aid, and (3) communities that had not experienced a disaster. The results showed that communities that received federal aid were significantly more likely to adopt various mitigation measures (see Chapter 6). But, one of the main problems with the current federal policy is that the federal incentive only comes into play after a disaster occurs. One means of addressing that problem would be the enactment of eligibility requirements for disaster assistance that applied before disasters occurred. A difficulty, however, is that it is only after a disaster that local officials tend to pay attention to the threat. Therefore, even if predisaster eligibility requirements were adopted, they might well be ignored by many local governments.

Local Impacts: An Illustration from California

To illustrate how one might begin to identify communities that would benefit most from participation in a scheme designed to insure against losses to public infrastructure, we compiled data from 38 counties in California that received federal disaster assistance aid in either 1980, 1982, or 1983.[6] These 38 counties represent two thirds of the counties in California and over 90 percent of the state's population. The California State Controller's Annual Report for 1982–83, *Financial Transactions Concerning Counties of California*, provides county population estimates (as of June 30, 1983), as well as information on the value of assets owned by each county government, the assessed value of private property, and property tax delinquency as a percentage of the tax levy. From the

FEMA data files, we also obtained information on the total losses from disasters in California in 1980, 1982, and 1983 disaggregated by county.

Table 8.1 presents the information on the counties' estimated 1983 population, the dollar value of the losses suffered, the number of loss events, and the total amount of federal disaster assistance. In general, the counties with the largest populations suffered the largest losses from disasters and received the most federal aid. That is probably due to a combination of reasons: (1) counties with large populations generally cover a larger area and thus have more area at risk than smaller counties; (2) larger counties typically have more sophisticated local governments and are probably more adept at receiving federal assistance, and (3) counties with large populations are in higher risk areas along the coast and near serious earthquake faults.

Table 8.2 presents information on the total value of county-owned fixed assets, the value of private property, the ratio of private property to county-owned fixed assets, and the delinquency rate on local property taxes as a percent of the total tax levy. As one would expect, the value of county-owned assets and the assessed value of local property are generally proportional to county size. However, the ratio of locally-assessed property to governmentally-owned fixed assets shows substantial variation across counties. For example, in Alameda County the assessed value of privately-owned property is 448 times the value of county-owned assets, while in Trinity County it is only 29 times as large. The property tax delinquency rate also shows variation across counties.[7]

Table 8.3 presents the information in Tables 8.1 and 8.2 on a per capita basis. The first column shows the dollar value of county assets at risk per capita in each of the 38 counties. The estimates of the assessed value of private property per capita exhibit surprisingly little variation across counties. The most striking feature of these data is the overall low value of county-owned assets at risk per capita: the mean value is only $239. The assessed value of privately-owned property (mean = $24,428 per capita) is generally over 100 times greater than the value of county-owned assets. These low estimates of county-owned assets at risk per capita are in large part due to the fact that counties in California do not have many urban responsibilities; those tend to be handled by cities and special districts.

Ideally we would like to have data for the value of all governmentally-owned infrastructure assets in each county; those data are unfortunately not readily available. If we compare, however, our estimate of the average value of all governmentally-owned infrastructure (including federal) of $8000 per capita with the assessed value of property per capita in these California counties, the assessed value of private property is still more than three times the size of publicly-owned infrastructure. The risk of

TABLE 8.1
Federal Disaster Assistance Versus Eligible Losses
in Selected California Counties

County	Population	Eligible Losses	Federal Aid
Alameda	1,145,117	$3,553,913	$2,755,902
Colusa	14,179	$547,284	$410,464
Contra Costa	681,580	$4,381,384	$3,286,042
Del Norte	18,648	$182,534	$136,901
Fresno	545,957	$3,851,933	$2,888,953
Glenn	22,555	$212,388	$159,293
Humboldt	111,215	$2,305,752	$1,729,315
Imperial	100,005	$985,037	$738,779
Kern	442,773	$4,575,682	$3,431,763
Kings	79,486	$541,475	$406,108
Lake	42,220	$838,230	$628,672
Los Angeles	7,763,792	$11,948,322	$8,793,778
Marin	223,849	$6,918,661	$5,261,481
Mendocino	70,385	$1,314,267	$985,702
Merced	146,320	$206,962	$155,221
Monterey	309,031	$381,110	$285,834
Napa	101,337	$413,318	$309,988
Orange	2,036,390	$16,127,250	$8,261,874
Riverside	731,173	$10,150,556	$7,396,124
San Benito	27,637	$362,635	$271,979
San Bernardino	985,880	$3,350,509	$2,842,031
San Diego	1,986,035	$26,222,378	$14,900,401
San Joaquin	381,512	$593,945	$439,167
San Luis Obispo	170,190	$3,096,019	$2,322,017
San Mateo	593,531	$5,757,526	$4,318,158
Santa Barbara	313,497	$1,919,404	$1,406,546
Santa Clara	1,343,103	$4,832,766	$3,624,581
Santa Cruz	200,288	$8,370,079	$5,993,484
Shasta	122,992	$543,481	$407,611
Solano	257,929	$1,327,984	$995,990
Sonoma	318,047	$962,962	$722,223
Stanislaus	286,364	$141,540	$106,155
Sutter	56,454	$153,139	$114,855
Tehama	41,877	$208,572	$156,428
Trinity	12,706	$303,484	$227,614
Tulare	263,017	$559,205	$419,404
Ventura	565,607	$3,825,850	$3,263,700
Yolo	118,922	$90,774	$68,081
Mean	595,568	$3,475,219	$2,384,806

Source: Unpublished records of Federal Emergency
Management Agency.

TABLE 8.2
Assessed Value of Private Property, County Assets,
and Property Tax Delinquency Rate in Selected
California Counties

County	Total Fixed County Assets	Value of Private Property (000's)	Ratio of Private/ Govt. Property	Delin- quency Rate
Alameda	$52,578,316	$23,559,111	448	3.785
Colusa	$6,434,307	$750,082	117	1.958
Contra Costa	$76,753,922	$19,118,326	249	3.515
Del Norte	$7,881,674	$337,654	43	5.236
Fresno	$70,413,133	$12,973,650	184	6.531
Glenn	$7,405,897	$783,746	106	5.654
Humboldt	$34,940,360	$2,106,748	60	5.135
Imperial	$33,768,639	$1,754,902	52	4.523
Kern	$141,465,568	$20,215,904	143	2.387
Kings	$24,170,391	$1,497,575	62	2.825
Lake	$9,448,271	$1,237,523	131	14.240
Los Angeles	$941,506,618	$169,969,220	181	4.883
Marin	$64,769,006	$7,541,851	116	3.006
Mendocino	$13,716,559	$1,685,045	123	9.205
Merced	$37,378,472	$2,948,580	79	2.569
Monterey	$59,757,046	$6,992,454	117	3.585
Napa	$25,424,820	$2,538,125	110	4.294
Orange	$195,375,014	$56,953,967	292	4.502
Riverside	$125,903,216	$17,573,297	140	4.351
San Benito	$5,540,154	$623,061	112	4.780
San Ber- nardino	$161,949,916	$17,996,254	111	6.136
San Diego	$399,145,313	$43,218,217	108	5.314
San Joaquin	$57,299,592	$7,677,610	134	4.622
San Luis Obispo	$52,581,962	$3,805,530	72	6.791
San Mateo	$144,353,116	$7,677,610	53	2.880
Santa Barbara	$62,629,834	$8,547,542	136	4.441
Santa Clara	$284,340,357	$34,874,618	123	3.047
Santa Cruz	$34,709,728	$4,797,524	138	8.335
Shasta	$31,616,521	$2,587,018	82	7.625
Solano	$43,418,967	$5,147,943	119	4.045
Sonoma	$63,158,936	$8,260,680	131	4.312
Stanislaus	$40,520,837	$6,042,027	149	4.956
Sutter	$13,177,568	$1,552,835	118	2.713
Tehama	$12,816,233	$893,344	70	5.945
Trinity	$9,656,869	$282,929	29	8.112
Tulare	$50,505,451	$4,583,457	91	4.793
Ventura	$126,313,544	$14,417,582	114	4.097
Yolo	$22,200,649	$2,762,807	124	2.053
Mean	$93,290,205	$13,849,641	125	4.926

Source: State of California.

TABLE 8.3
Per Capita Estimates of County Assets, Private
Property, Losses from Natural Hazards, and Federal
Aid in Selected California Counties

County	County Assets Per Capital	Private Property Per Capita	Losses Per Capita	Federal Aid Per Capita
Alameda	$46	$20,574	$3	$2
Colusa	$454	$52,901	$39	$29
Contra Costa	$113	$28,050	$6	$5
Del Norte	$423	$18,107	$10	$7
Fresno	$129	$23,763	$7	$5
Glenn	$328	$34,748	$9	$7
Humboldt	$314	$18,943	$21	$16
Imperial	$338	$17,548	$10	$7
Kern	$319	$45,657	$10	$8
Kings	$304	$18,841	$7	$5
Lake	$224	$29,311	$20	$15
Los Angeles	$121	$21,893	$2	$1
Marin	$289	$33,692	$31	$24
Mendocino	$195	$23,940	$19	$14
Merced	$255	$20,152	$1	$1
Monterey	$193	$22,627	$1	$1
Napa	$251	$25,046	$4	$3
Orange	$96	$27,968	$8	$4
Riverside	$172	$24,034	$14	$10
San Benito	$200	$22,544	$13	$10
San Bernardino	$164	$18,254	$3	$3
San Diego	$201	$21,761	$13	$8
San Joaquin	$150	$20,124	$2	$1
San Luis Obispo	$309	$22,360	$18	$14
San Mateo	$243	$12,935	$10	$7
Santa Barbara	$200	$27,265	$6	$4
Santa Clara	$212	$25,966	$4	$3
Santa Cruz	$173	$23,953	$42	$30
Shasta	$257	$21,034	$4	$3
Solano	$168	$19,959	$5	$4
Sonoma	$199	$25,973	$3	$2
Stanislaus	$142	$21,099	$0	$0
Sutter	$233	$27,506	$3	$2
Tehama	$306	$21,333	$5	$4
Trinity	$760	$22,267	$24	$18
Tulare	$192	$17,426	$2	$2
Ventura	$223	$25,490	$7	$6
Yolo	$187	$23,232	$1	$1
Mean -	$239	$24,428	$10	$8

Source: State of California and unpublished records of
Federal Emergency Management Agency.

natural hazards to public infrastructure—particularly state and local infrastructure—is thus only a fraction of the risk to individuals' private property.

Moreover, the magnitude of the total private and public losses suffered in these counties from 1980–83 are very small on a per capita basis (Table 8.3, columns 3 and 4). For example, over the four-year period from 1980-1983, Los Angeles County suffered total losses of almost $12 million. However, that amounted to only $1.54 per capita, or $0.38 per capita per year. In the smaller counties a single loss can have a much greater per capita impact. For example, Colusa County suffered a single loss of $547,284; with only 14,179 residents, the per capita loss was $39. Still, over the four-year period this only amounted to about $10 per capita per year—hardly a catastrophic loss.

Data on losses experienced from the 1987 Whittier earthquake (see Chapter 3) support that conclusion. Los Angeles County experienced about $2.5 million in losses from the Whittier quake, but that was only $0.33 per capita. The City of Whittier itself experienced about $1.6 million in damages, but this was still only $22 per capita. Of course, Whittier residents were also residents of Los Angeles County, so they experienced both of those losses, plus any additional losses incurred by special districts in which they lived.

The losses incurred by California counties over this brief period from 1980 to 1983 are not representative of the expected annual losses likely to occur over a longer time horizon (e.g., we cannot ignore the potential losses from a large earthquake). However, the small magnitude of these per-capita losses serves to emphasize again that federal disaster assistance for such small losses cannot reasonably be expected to have any economic benefits in terms of risk spreading. Instead, local governments should be expected to deal with such losses using their own resources.

Similar calculations of the per-capita value of publicly-owned infrastructure at risk which included the assets of all state and local government jurisdictions—not just those of counties—could help identify areas that would benefit most from risk-spreading mechanisms, such as insurance. Local areas in greatest need of risk-spreading mechanisms would be characterized by (1) high probability of disasters, (2) high levels of public infrastructure at risk per capita, and (3) low overall per capita income (a high-income jurisdiction could self-insure against higher losses per capita than a low-income jurisdiction).

An examination of the composition of these figures on the value of county-owned assets in California serves to emphasize a final point: that the value of much of the assets of state and local governments are land, bridges, water and sewer systems, and roads and highways. Most natural hazards threaten only a very small portion of this capital stock, even in a limited geographic area. In other words, citizens are not actually at risk of losing all of their governmentally-owned assets, even in severe disaster events. In that sense, local governments of even relatively small communities can to an extent self-insure against small damages; they only need insurance against the most catastrophic losses.

Toward Efficient Public Policy

The fundamental dilemma for federal policy identified in this book is how to get communities to assume responsibility for risks *before* disasters happen when in fact they are, for whatever reasons, largely unwilling to do so. Indeed, the fact that individuals are typically unwilling to purchase insurance against losses to their private property from natural hazards—much less for losses to public infrastructure—raises the question of what normative basis exists for any federal government intervention. If individuals or local communities do not want to insure against natural hazards, why should the federal government insist they do so? Does such behavior in fact indicate that individuals are not risk-averse (in which case there are no economic efficiency benefits from risk spreading mechanisms)?

In our view, such a conclusion would be unwarranted. Given the existing uncertainty with respect to how individuals perceive and respond to the risks from natural hazards, federal policy makers have two basic options: (1) they can accept individuals' expressed preferences regarding risks to their community's infrastructure from natural hazards, or (2) they can judge these preferences to be confused, irrational, strategically motivated, or poorly informed. In our opinion, preferences regarding risks of losses to public infrastructure, if they have been formed at all, are likely to be poorly informed. How many people know even approximately the value of their share of the stock of public infrastructure in their community or the probability that it could be destroyed or damaged by natural hazards?

Not only are preferences regarding risks to public infrastructure from natural hazards likely to be poorly informed, but if the community were to be responsible for coping with such risks, the individual would face great uncertainty with regard to how such losses would be distributed among members of the community in the event of a disaster. For example, there would be a stronger incentive for renters than for property owners to move away from a community after a disaster struck. Since a high proportion of local government expenditures is financed with property tax revenues, which raise rents, renters would be less likely to support pre-disaster hazard reduction expenditures.

The individual is thus doubly at risk: from the natural hazard and from the political process. In some communities the individual would have little assurance that he would be treated fairly. Because the process by which losses to public infrastructure would be allocated among citizens is rarely clear to individuals or specified in advance of a disaster, individuals may hope that they will not have to bear their fair share of the losses or may feel they can act strategically to reduce their share of this community burden. In either case they may understate their preferences for reducing the cost of the risk. Information on existing preferences regarding risks to public infrastructure is thus unlikely to provide a convincing normative basis for policy.

In the absence of informed preferences regarding risks to public infrastructure, responsible policy can best be based on an ethically defensible proposition about how individuals would wish other citizens in their community to behave with respect to the risks to public infrastructure from natural hazards. We feel that most citizens would agree that risks to their shared public property should not be valued less than risks to individuals' private property, on a per unit of valuation basis. In other words, if a family's share of the public infrastructure stock in its community was $32,000, it should not treat this share of common property any differently with respect to risk than, for example, its own house. Both are assumed to be equally valuable for the economic and social well-being of the family.

If that proposition was accepted and used as a basis for hazard management policy, it would have important implications for federal, state, and local policy makers. Most individuals are risk-averse with respect losing a large portion of their net wealth (such as a house, car, or savings account) due to illness or disability and would insure against such losses. If that same degree of risk-aversion was used to value risks to public infrastructure, it would provide policy makers with a criterion with which to judge how much insurance a community should carry against losses to its public infrastructure from natural hazards. For example, a community with $75,000 of public infrastructure at risk per household would require a much more effective risk management strategy than a community with $2000 of infrastructure per household at risk.[8] Federal policy could perhaps legitimately allow the latter community to not participate or to opt out of a national insurance program against losses to public infrastructure from natural hazards. However, based on the proposition the households *should* be risk-averse with respect to catastrophic losses to public infrastructure, the first community would clearly need substantial amounts of insurance if it were in a high-risk area.

In our judgment, the most effective way the federal government can (1) reduce the efficiency losses associated with excessive development in hazardous areas and (2) achieve the efficiency benefits associated with spreading risks is to ensure that local governments with large amounts of public infrastructure at risk per capita participate in either a national or a state insurance scheme with actuarially-sound premiums assigned to specific communities. That would require that the federal government make participation in such an insurance scheme a condition to receive benefits from another federal assistance program. The inequitable allocation of the costs of the current federal program would also be addressed by an actuarially-sound insurance program.

It is still an open-question whether the efficiency and equity benefits of such an insurance program would be worth the costs of identifying hazards, rating all infrastructure's susceptibility to loss, and administering the scheme. If an actuarially-sound insurance scheme proved politically or administratively unworkable, the worst inefficiencies in the current federal disaster relief policy could be removed by simply raising the minimum loss standards (in per capita terms) for federal asssitance and broadening the eligibility requirements. Both of those changes could be designed to stimulate state and local governments to design and locate public infrastructure so that it would be "out of harm's way" and reasonably safe from loss. An increase in the minimum loss threshold (above which a community would be eligible for federal assistance) could be coupled with an increase in eligibility for such assistance so that assistance would be provided to all communities which suffered losses above a threshold amount, not just those in Presidentially-declared disaster areas. Such a broadening of eligibility might make the increased threshold more popular politically because although some local governments would get less assistance (i.e., those with small losses in jurisdictions which would have been Presidentially-declared disaster areas), some would receive more federal assistance (i.e., those areas with large losses in jurisdictions that would not have been declared disaster areas by the President).

Notes

1. This section is based on the standard microeconomic approach to the treatment of risk. The example presented parallels the presentation in Layard and Walters (1978: Chapter 13).

2. Risk pooling involves spreading the risks of many identical, independent risks over many people.

3. Risk spreading involves distributing the losses from one risky outcome over many people.

4. If individuals are not risk-averse, i.e., if they are risk-neutral or actually enjoy taking risks, then, of course, their welfare cannot be increased by risk-spreading or risk-pooling mechanisms designed to reduce the cost of risk. In that case there are no economic benefits associated with such risk management strategies.

5. As discussed in the previous section, the efficiency gains from risk spreading are only applicable to catastrophic losses, not the small losses currently covered by the Federal Emergency Management Agency.

6. The data cover the period 1980–1983; no disaster relief was provided to California counties in 1981.

7. We have included the delinquency rate here as a measure of county-level fiscal stress, but differences may be due more to the level of enforcement efforts than to general economic conditions.

8. Estimates of public property at risk would have to be coupled with information on the likelihood of damage to calculate actuarially sound premiums.

9

Local Decision Makers' Willingness to Share Risks

In the previous chapter, we concluded that to foster economic efficiency and equity, federal policy should encourage local governments to share further in the risks of large losses from catastrophic events. The federal government took a limited step in that direction with passage of the Stafford Act in 1988. By withdrawing federal aid for any dollar losses that could have been covered by insurance, Congress now hopes to induce local governments to insure their property against losses from natural hazards. As we argued in Chapter 6, however, local governments' lack of response to the incentive in the 1974 disaster assistance legislation indicates that this latest incentive may not have the desired effect. If that is true, what measures are likely to increase the feasibility of insurance as a local hazard management tool? In this chapter we address that question by examining a variety of factors that could stimulate local officials to recommend the purchase of insurance.

The Decision to Purchase Flood and Earthquake Insurance

This analysis focuses on 224 respondents in our 1988 survey of local officials who said they had participated in decisions to purchase or not purchase hazards insurance. Among those respondents, 71 percent (159) recommended that their jurisdiction purchase flood or earthquake insurance and 29 percent (65) recommended against buying insurance. Those recommendations are clearly influential: 76 percent of the jurisdictions where officials recommended insuring public property against losses from natural hazards actually carried such insurance versus only 28 percent of the jurisdictions where officials recommended against insurance. Nevertheless, the fact that some officials recommend against hazards insurance and some officials' recommendations to purchase insurance are not heeded results in less than optimal coverage. As we

TABLE 9.1
Insurance Purchase Recommendations Versus Status
as Jurisdiction: Aided, Refused Aid, or Having
No Disaster

Status of Federal Relief	Respondent's Insurance Purchase Recommendation		
	Against	For	Total
Aided	25%	75%	100%
Aid Refused	30%	70%	100%
No Disaster Declared	33%	67%	100%

Chi Square = 1.21, df = 2, p = .55, n = 224

Source: Survey of 481 local officials, summer 1988.

reported in Chapter 6, less than half of the local governments we studied
are insured against losses in natural disasters.

Federal policy for encouraging local governments to share risks to
public property from natural hazards is predicated on a rational incentive.
That incentive is the denial of federal relief for insurable losses to local
government property. Federal officials believe that penalty for not ac-
quiring insurance will evoke the desired local response; that is, local
officials will behave like rational decision makers and purchase hazards
insurance.

Prior to the Stafford Act's passage, Federal Emergency Management
Agency staff described cities and counties as "taking a gamble" by
failing to purchase insurance after a Presidentially declared disaster.
Furthermore, they argued: "Local governments are taking a risk (by
failing to insure any facilities) because there are many more small floods
that will not be aided than floods that will be aided." (October 15, 1987
interview) Consistent with the findings reported earlier in Chapter 6,
however, neither the award nor refusal of Presidential disaster relief is
a good predictor of local officials' recommendations concerning insurance.
(See Table 9.1.)

Despite our finding that prior aided disasters and federal policy have had no discernible influence on observed insurance use, there are different types of both rational and situational motivations that could influence local insurance recommendations. Individual decision makers may vary in the importance they attach to each dimension of the decision. Prior research on individuals' and local officials' responses to choices about hazards management supports the following propositions:

First, individuals vary in the degree to which they are directly responsible for the safety of public property. We expect those with more direct responsibility to be more concerned about potential losses, to be more knowledgeable about potential risks of loss, and, therefore, to be more likely to recommend the purchase of hazards insurance. (Drabek, Mushkatel and Kilijanek 1983)

Second, there are judgments of the probability of experiencing a disastrous loss beyond local fiscal capacity, as well as the odds of actually receiving federal aid. Judgments of the probability of a significant damaging event are the conventional way in which risk is conceived. (Rowe 1977) It is well known that the general public has difficulty in using probabilistic information about risk, often even ignoring it completely in favor of other information about hazards. Trained professionals are more likely to take probability of loss into account (Slovic, Fischoff and Lichtenstein 1985), but there is also evidence that local government officials ignore risk information (e.g., see Chapter 6). We expect that when officials judge the probability of loss to be high, however, they will recommend the purchase of hazards insurance. But, we also expect that local officials will vary in the extent to which they have adequate technical information about risks. We expect that those officials with more adequate information will be more likely to support risk sharing measures like insurance than those officials with less adequate information.

Third, there are beliefs about the cost-effectiveness of insurance, compared to alternative methods of coping with anticipated public losses. Given equivalent judgments of risk among a group of decision makers, some may nonetheless prefer insurance because of the high judged cost of alternatives such as floodproofing of facilities. In addition, the rapid rise of insurance costs to local government in the last decade has made it an infeasible option in some cases, particularly for earthquake hazards.

Fourth, external requirements are imposed on local governments that may influence insurance preferences of decision makers. Underwriters of bond financing for major facilities require hazards insurance in some cases. The Disaster Relief Act itself is another externally imposed requirement.

Fifth, much recent research on individual decision making suggests that there are considerations beyond rational criteria that may affect choices about low probability, high consequence events like natural disasters. Because people have an observed difficulty in making probabilistic judgments about such infrequent events, they have been found to be influenced by other factors. Examples include the prior frequency of hazard events or social interactions that make images of the hazard more salient and real, although those factors are not strictly part of a rational estimate of risks. Such influences are considered in the assessment that follows.

Position in Local Government

We expected that officials with more direct responsibility for the safety of public property and with greater access to hazards information would be more likely than officials with broader responsibilities to favor purchasing hazards insurance. That in fact tends to be the case. Risk managers, finance directors and public works directors/emergency management officials were more likely than officials with more general responsibilities, such as city and county managers, to recommend the purchase of insurance, but as illustrated in Table 9.2, differences among officials in different positions are neither large nor statistically significant.

Judgments of Risk

We asked decision makers to judge the odds of experiencing a financially "disastrous loss" to public property in "any given year." That judgment was evoked after each respondent had estimated the dollar value of such a loss, as discussed in Chapter 2. The five choices we gave the respondents range from a 1 in 200 or smaller chance of disastrous loss to a 1 in 10 or greater chance of such a loss. Decision makers who recommended purchasing insurance judged the odds of disastrous loss to be much higher than the odds given by all other respondents. (See Table 9.3.) Decision makers who recommended against adoption made the lowest estimates of risk on average (and they account for more than half of the decision makers we queried). Other evidence suggests that there is a basis in fact for decision makers' estimates of risk. Thus, those who recommended the purchase of insurance worked for larger cities with more property at risk (average population size of 54,336 versus 32,008 for those who recommended against purchasing insurance) and in cities that suffered larger losses in previous disasters (an average of $357,461 versus $224,254). Those differences are statistically significant ($p < .001$).

TABLE 9.2
Insurance Purchase Recommendation by Position in
Local Government

Position in Local Government	Respondent's Insurance Purchase Recommendation		
	Against	For	Total
Risk manager	21%	79%	100% (n = 28)
Other (public works, planning, emergency management)	25%	75%	100% (n = 32)
Finance director	27%	73%	100% (n = 48)
City/county manager	33%	67%	100% (n = 62)
Elected official	36%	64%	100% (n = 22)
City/county clerk	42%	58%	100% (n = 24)

Chi Square = 5.04, p = .539, n = 216

Source: Survey of 481 local officials, summer 1988.

Another probabilistic judgment that may influence recommendations is the expectation of actually receiving federal aid in the event a disaster occurs. Judgments of the odds of aid in the event of a disastrous loss were made on a five-point scale ranging from "little chance" to "almost certain." In a separate analysis not shown here, we found that the judged odds of receiving federal aid are strongly related to prior aid history ($p < .001$). Fifty-three percent of the respondents who worked for cities and counties that had received aid in the past judged its likelihood in a future disaster as probable (though only 11 percent judged aid as "almost certain"). But among jurisdictions that had been refused aid in the past, only 29 percent judged the odds as being in favor of receiving aid in the event of a future disaster. The jurisdictions with no disaster from 1980–87 were only slightly more optimistic—32 percent judged

TABLE 9.3
Insurance Purchase Recommendation by Judged Odds of
Experiencing a Disastrous Loss to Public Property in
Any Given Year

Perceived Odds of a Disastrous Loss in Any Given Year	Respondent's Insurance Purchase Recommendation		
	Against	For	Total
A 1 in 10 or Even Greater Chance of Disastrous Losses (or 10%)	0%	100%	100% (n - 10)
Around 1 in 20 Odds (or 5%)	18%	82%	100% (n - 17)
Around 1 in 50 Odds (or 2%)	5%	95%	100% (n - 20)
Around 1 in 100 Odds (or 1%)	25%	75%	100% (n - 52)
Around 1 in 200 Odds (or 0.5%)	40%	60%	100% (n - 121)

Chi Square - 17.61, $p < .001$, n - 220

Source: Survey of 481 local officials, summer 1988.

the odds to be in favor of aid. Those findings suggest that relief creates an expectation that, if needed, federal aid will be forthcoming in the future, and thus it could be a disincentive to the adoption of risk-sharing or risk-mitigation strategies.

As we show in Table 9.4, however, the judged odds of future aid have no relationship to recommendations on disaster insurance protection for public property. Those decision makers who recommended insurance adoption were actually more likely to judge the odds of aid as more favorable, although the difference is not statistically discernible from zero ($p = .59$).

TABLE 9.4
Insurance Purchase Recommendation by Judged Odds of
Receiving Federal Disaster Assistance for Public
Property Losses

Perceived Odds of Receiving Federal Disaster Assistance	Respondent's Insurance Purchase Recommendation		
	Against	For	Total
Federal Aid Is Almost Certain	35%	65%	100% (n = 17)
It Is Uncertain, But I Think Odds Are in *Favor* of Getting Aid	22%	78%	100% (n = 68)
Odds Are Even -- A Toss-Up	34%	66%	100% (n = 50)
It Is Uncertain, But I Think Odds Are *Against* Getting Aid	25%	75%	100% (n = 48)
Little Chance of Federal Aid	29%	71%	100% (n = 34)

Chi Square = 2.79, p = .594, n = 217

Source: Survey of 481 local officials, summer 1988.

An important consideration in evaluating these judgments of risk is the extent to which the decision makers may be well or poorly informed about the potential losses to public property from flood or earthquake hazards. Each was asked to rate the adequacy of information on potential losses from floods and earthquakes, respectively, on a five-point scale (the choices include "very adequate," "somewhat adequate," "somewhat inadequate," "very inadequate," and "no information available." We excluded from this analysis those cases in which respondents claimed there is no flood or earthquake hazard present and those who said they

TABLE 9.5
Insurance Purchase Recommendation by Rating of
the Adequacy of Flood and Earthquake Hazards
Information Available

Type of Information	Mean Rating of the Adequacy of Information by Respondent's Insurance Purchase Recommendation[a]			
	Against	For	T-value	Significance
Flood Hazard Information	3.4	3.5	0.726	.469
Earthquake Hazard Information	2.8	2.6	0.240	.811

Source: Survey of 481 local officials, summer 1988.

[a] Scale: 1 – no information available; 2 – very
inadequate; 3 – somewhat inadequate; 4 – somewhat
adequate; 5– very adequate.

didn't know what information might be available. Thus, for flood hazard
information, the effective sample is about 84 percent of all responses
(184 cases) and for earthquake hazard information the sample is 148
(about 66 percent of the sample).

Although those decision makers who recommended insurance adoption
rated the information on flood hazards available to them as slightly
more adequate than others, that difference is not significant (p = .47)
nor substantively important. (See Table 9.5.) All respondents rated flood
hazard information as being, on average, between "somewhat adequate"
and "somewhat inadequate." Our findings for earthquake hazard information are similar. There is no difference in ratings between officials
who did and did not recommend the purchase of earthquake insurance.
In the case of earthquake hazard information, however, average ratings
are somewhat lower than for flood hazards, as illustrated in Table 9.5.

In sum, then, the differences in hazard insurance recommendations cannot be ascribed to inadequate information among those decision makers who were aware of such information.

That finding is further corroborated by two additional questions posed to local officials. We asked officials to agree, disagree, or claim neutral opinions in response to the following statements: "Technical studies of the flood (earthquake) risk are important information in our decisions about buying flood (earthquake) insurance." For flood hazards, 67 percent of those who recommended against purchase and 69 percent of those who recommended for purchase agreed with the statement. The pattern of responses to the same question about the value of technical studies of earthquake hazards is similar, although a lower proportion of officials thought such studies were important: 62 percent of the officials who recommend insurance coverage agreed that technical studies provide important information and 53 percent of those recommending against insurance purchase agreed.

Cost Considerations

The preceding discussion indicates that among the risk factors we examined judgments of higher odds of disastrous damages are related to insurance recommendations. Another possible explanation for variation in the recommendations is the perceived cost of insurance and its comparative value compared to a feasible alternative, such as retrofitting structures to make them less susceptible to damage. To examine that, we asked decision makers to agree, disagree, or claim neutral opinions in response to the following statements about flood and earthquake insurance costs: "The cost of flood (earthquake) insurance is too high for public property." The modal response to both statements was one of neutrality. That indicates that many local officials have not formed strong opinions about the cost of hazards insurance. (See Table 9.6.)

Some officials nevertheless do have strong opinions about insurance costs: 18 percent agreed strongly to the statement that flood insurance costs are too high and the same percent agreed strongly to the statement that earthquake insurance costs are too high. In both cases those officials were much more likely than those who did not feel strongly that costs were too high to recommend against purchasing hazards insurance (that difference is statistically significant for flood insurance [p = .038] but not for earthquake insurance). When the whole distribution of attitudes toward costs is considered, however, the relationships between attitudes toward costs and recommendations regarding the purchase of insurance are not statistically significant, as shown in Table 9.6.

TABLE 9.6
Insurance Purchase Recommendation by Rating
of the Cost of Flood and Earthquake Insurance

Response to State-ment Regarding Cost of Insurance	Respondent's Insurance Purchase Recommendation		
	Against	For	Total
The Cost of Flood Insurance Is too High for Public Property			
Agree Strongly	44%	56%	100% (n - 56)
Agree Somewhat	23%	77%	100% (n - 39)
Neutral	29%	71%	100% (n - 84)
Disagree Somewhat	13%	87%	100% (n - 23)
Disagree Strongly	22%	78%	100% (n - 9)

Chi Square - 8.06,
p - .089, n - 211

The Cost of Earthquake Insurance Is too High for Public Property

	Against	For	Total
Agree Strongly	40%	60%	100% (n - 20)
Agree Somewhat	21%	79%	100% (n - 24)
Neutral	31%	69%	100% (n - 39)
Disagree Somewhat	29%	71%	100% (n - 17)
Disagree Strongly	33%	67%	100% (n - 12)

Chi Square - 1.97,
p - .741, n - 112

Source: Survey of 481 local officials, summer 1988.

A second question probed the relative cost of insurance compared to the alternative of retrofitting facilities (flood- and earthquake-proofing). Again the modal responses were ones of neutrality; apparently most decision makers have not formed opinions about the relative costs of insurance and retrofitting. (See Table 9.7.) Those who felt strongly that there are no particular cost advantages in insurance over retrofitting, however, were much more likely than other decision makers to recommend against purchasing insurance. That does not necessarily mean that those decision makers or their jurisdictions have adopted structural modifications to reduce hazard consequences, however; the correlation coefficients between attitudes regarding cost advantages of insurance vs. retrofitting and actual retrofitting are low (less than r = .15) and not significantly greater than zero.

External Requirements

Judgments of probable losses and cost considerations could be less important to decision makers for whom hazards insurance adoption is the result of externally imposed requirements. Underwriters for bond financing for major public facilities require disaster coverage, for example, but those requirements have not had a large effect on the purchase of hazards insurance. Only 13 percent of our respondents reported that their jurisdiction had purchased flood insurance because of bond requirements; only 16 percent said their jurisdiction had purchased earthquake insurance for that reason.

Disaster Assistance Act rules are another type of external requirement that mandates insurance as a condition for receiving federal aid for disaster losses. When we asked if flood insurance had been purchased only because of that requirement, however, just 14 percent of the respondents agreed that was the case. Thus, the federal insurance purchase requirement has some influence on local governments' behavior, but it seems to have an influence on only a small percentage of localities. A much large proportion of local decision makers do not appear to give it much consideration at all, as they can neither judge it to be the single influence on insurance decisions nor judge it to be but one consideration among several.

Although not a requirement in the legal sense, the recommendations of local governments' insurance carriers are another external influence. For flood insurance, 45 percent of our respondents reported that insurance carriers' recommendations influenced their decisions to purchase or not purchase coverage. Insurance recommendations, however, do not automatically translate into decision makers' recommendations for the purchase of hazards insurance. As shown in Table 9.8, for both flood and

TABLE 9.7
Insurance Purchase Recommendation by Rating of the
Cost of Retrofitting Structures to Reduce Losses

Response to State-ment Regarding Costs of Retrofitting	Respondent's Insurance Purchase Recommendation		
	Against	For	Total
The Costs of Flood-proofing Are so High That Insurance Is a Better Alternative			
Agree Strongly	21%	79%	100% (n - 19)
Agree Somewhat	22%	78%	100% (n - 55)
Neutral	29%	71%	100% (n - 77)
Disagree Somewhat	27%	73%	100% (n - 40)
Disagree Strongly	53%	47%	100% (n - 17)

Chi Square - 6.77, p - .148, n - 208

The Costs of Quake-proofing Are so High That Insurance Is A Better Alternative			
Agree Strongly	26%	74%	100% (n - 19)
Agree Somewhat	16%	84%	100% (n - 25)
Neutral	27%	73%	100% (n - 45)
Disagree Somewhat	50%	50%	100% (n - 12)
Disagree Strongly	63%	37%	100% (n - 8)

Chi Square - 9.09, p - .059, n - 109

Source: Survey of 481 local officials, summer 1988.

earthquake insurance, the respondents most likely to have recommended against coverage were those who either agreed strongly or disagreed strongly that insurance carriers' recommendations influenced their insurance decisions.

Situational and Organizational Factors

One of the most consistent findings regarding decisions about hazards coping behavior is that people and organizations often take action only after the risk has been made more salient to them. Of course, experiencing a disastrous loss is one means by which that occurs. Individuals have been found to increase their adoption of hazards insurance immediately after an event (Kunreuther et al. 1978), and local governments have been found to increase disaster preparedness and hazard mitigation efforts in the wake of an emergency (Burby et al. 1988; Kartez and Kelley 1988; Berke, Beatley and Wilhite 1988). Capitalizing on this "window of opportunity" when local officials are receptive to change is a major reason for new federal incentive funding for hazard mitigation under the 1988 Stafford Act (see Chapter 1).

Researchers have also found, however, that individuals and local public officials are influenced by their social environment when assessing the need to act on risks. In their study of homeowners' willingness to purchase flood and earthquake insurance, for example, Kunreuther and associates (1978) found that individuals who "know someone" who has experienced disaster losses are significantly more likely to purchase insurance. Kartez and Lindell (1987; Kartez and Kelley 1988) found that local government administrations that have experienced recent disasters are more likely to improve preparedness efforts when personnel have interacted and shared perceptions about the experience. Even inexperienced administrations are more likely to take hazards adjustment actions when the organizational social environment makes the hazards more salient and real.

One general explanation for that phenomenon is that individuals and organizations operate under conditions of bounded rationality. That limits the attention they give to events and expectations that fail to exceed some threshold for attention. (March and Simon 1958; Kiesler and Sproull 1982). Low probability natural disasters are particularly likely to be screened out and ignored: "In other words, there may be a threshold below which individuals effectively assume the probability of an event to be zero due to the mental costs of attending to such an event" (Hogarth and Kunreuther 1988: 30). However, knowing someone for whom low probability events have become real, or participating in frequent organizational activities that make expectations about the events

TABLE 9.8
Insurance Purchase Recommendation by Rating of
the Influence of Insurance Carriers on Insurance
Purchase Decisions

Response to Statement Regarding Carrier Influence	Respondent's Insurance Purchase Recommendation		
	Against	For	Total
Our Insurance Carrier's Recommendations Influence Our Decisions on Buying (or Choosing Not to Buy) Flood Insurance			
Agree Strongly	41%	59%	100% (n = 27)
Agree Somewhat	16%	84%	100% (n = 68)
Neutral	27%	73%	100% (n = 55)
Disagree Somewhat	27%	73%	100% (n = 30)
Disagree Strongly	48%	52%	100% (n = 31)

Chi Square = 13.18, p = .010, n = 211

Our Insurance Carrier's
Recommendations Influence
Our Decisions on Buying
(or Choosing Not to Buy)
Earthquake Insurance

	Against	For	Total
Agree Strongly	57%	43%	100% (n = 14)
Agree Somewhat	12%	88%	100% (n = 33)
Neutral	33%	67%	100% (n = 42)
Disagree Somewhat	0%	100%	100% (n = 6)
Disagree Strongly	44%	56%	100% (n = 16)

Chi Square = 14.24, p = .007, n = 111

Source: Survey of 481 local officials, summer 1988.

more prominent, may reduce the effort necessary to acknowledge the previously rather unimportant information about risk.

In the present study, we asked local decision makers to identify which of six organizational activities related to hazard management they have participated in. As shown in Table 9.9, we found no association between participation in such activities and officials' recommendations to purchase or not to purchase hazards insurance. We should note, however, that organizational participation strongly differentiates officials who were involved in insurance decisions from those who were not; local officials active in hazard management activities also tend to be those involved in insurance decisions. But, the pattern of results in Table 9.9 does not suggest that local officials recommend against insurance purchase because hazards fail to be attended to by the respondents because their governments were not involved in organizational activities that made the hazard more salient.

However, local management and finance officials were not heavily involved in organizational activities related to hazards in general. Particularly noteworthy is the very low proportion—less than one sixth—who participated in making hazard vulnerability analyses. Those analyses have received greater emphasis in federal and state government guidelines in recent years and provide the most relevant information for local managers making decisions about potential losses to public property. Although participation in emergency preparedness activities (e.g. exercises and plans) and informal communications can increase the attention fiscal managers give to local facility risks, the lack of involvement in preparing hazard analyses stands out as a deficiency across the board.

Another way in which the relevant local officials can become more aware of the risks of natural hazards to public property, and hence be more likely to recommend the purchase of hazards insurance, is through experience acquired in general risk management activities. In recent years local governments have become more involved in risk management because of the rising costs of liability insurance, greater legal requirements for workplace safety at public facilities, and a growing appreciation for the magnitude of routine losses from lax safety. When hazards insurance recommendations are compared to current local use of five general risk management strategies, much the same pattern emerges as in the case of organizational hazard management activities. As shown in Table 9.10, respondents who worked in communities that were engaged in a variety of risk management activities were only slightly more likely than those who worked in communities that did not undertake those activities to have recommended the purchase of hazards insurance (and the differences are not statistically significant.

TABLE 9.9
Insurance Purchase Recommendation by Respondents'
Participation in Organizational Activities Related
to Hazard Management

Participation in Activities	Respondent's Insurance Purchase Recommendation			Chi Square	Prob- ability
	Against	For	Total		
All Respondents	29%	71%	100%	---	---
Respondents Who Participated In:					
Informal discussions among departments	24%	76%	100%	2.72	.10
In developing a "hazard mitigation plan"	29%	71%	100%	0.01	.91
In developing an "emergency operations plan"	31%	69%	100%	0.24	.63
In an annual emergency preparedness exercise	32%	68%	100%	0.33	.57
Developing vulnerability analyses	32%	68%	100%	0.17	.68
On a hazard management committee	34%	66%	100%	0.83	.36

Source: Survey of 481 local officials, summer 1988.

TABLE 9.10
Insurance Purchase Recommendation by Community
Involvement in Other Risk Management Activities

Participation in Activities	Respondent's Insurance Purchase Recommendation			Chi Square	Prob- ability
	Against	For	Total		
All Respondents	29%	71%	100%	---	---
Respondents Working in Communities that Use the Following Risk Management Measures:					
Retention of funds for self insurance	25%	75%	100%	1.71	.191
Participation in multi-city or multi-county insurance pool	25%	75%	100%	1.47	.226
Comprehensive liability insurance	28%	72%	100%	1.00	.317
Preventive maintenance to reduce liability for employee or citizen injury	29%	71%	100%	0.10	.741
Employee safety training	30%	70%	100%	0.44	.801

Source: Survey of 481 local officials, summer 1988.

Preferences for Alternative Ways of Sharing Risks

The final sections of this chapter examine local decision makers' preferences for alternative means of sharing the financial losses to public property from natural disasters. As discussed earlier in this book, those losses can be distributed in a number of ways. First, local governments can absorb the loss into the local budget, in which case all taxpayers are equally liable, at least to the extent that their existing local tax incidence is equal. Second, losses can be exported to the private insurance market or a municipal or county insurance pool to the extent vulnerable facilities are covered. Again, taxpayers share "equally" in general fund expenditures for insurance premiums. The third alternative is most unlike current practices in that it involves more selectively apportioning the costs of losses to those who benefit from the vulnerable public service facilities. That benefits-received approach can be based on geographic areas or it can be based on charges for service. One geographic approach would be to draw a special taxing district around properties that are served in areas of high risk to public facilities. A charge-for-services approach would add a surcharge to the rates for water, sewer or other vulnerable services. In either case, the revenue raised by those means could be used to either fund local government loss reserves or to pay for hazards insurance covering public property.

As shown in Table 9.11, none of the alternative methods we explored is viewed as feasible by local officials working in governments that are not already using it. On the seven-point feasibility scale we employed, local officials gave the highest feasibility ratings to participation in a city or county insurance pool for risks from natural hazards, but the averages of those ratings are below the mid-points (4.0) of the scales. The other measures, including using loss reserve funds and purchasing commercial hazards insurance, received average feasibility ratings well below the mid-point of the scale. The two measures designed to improve the equity of risk management by sharing costs with beneficiaries through special taxing districts or surcharges on to the rates for water, sewer and other public services are viewed as highly infeasible by the officials we queried.

Sources of Funds to Meet the Local Costs of Recovery

If local officials view transferring risks through insurance and sharing losses with beneficiaries as infeasible, how do they propose to deal with risks that are retained? That is not an unimportant question. When we looked in depth at losses in the Whittier Narrows earthquake in Chapter 3, for example, we found that state and local governments absorbed

TABLE 9.11
Local Officials' Estimates of the Feasibility of
Alternative Risk Sharing Methods

| | ------Feasibility Estimate[a]------ | | |
Risk Sharing Method	Disaster 1980-1986 No Federal Aid	Disaster 1980-1986 Aid Received	No Disaster 1980-1986
Participate in a Local Government Insurance Pool for Risks from Natural Disasters	3.5	4.2	3.9
Self Insurance with a Loss Reserve Fund	3.3	2.7	3.4
Purchase Commercial Flood or Earthquake Insurance	2.4*	3.0*	3.6*
Create a Hazard Area Special Taxing District to Raise a Loss Reserve Fund or Pay Insurance Premiums	2.0	1.8	2.0
Add a Surcharge to Rates for Water, Sewer or Other Services to Specifically Fund Disaster Loss Reserves or Insurance Premiums	2.4	2.4	2.5

Source: Survey of 481 local officials, summer 1988.

*Difference among three groups is statistically significant at .05 level on the basis of analysis of variance test.

[a]Mean feasibility estimate of officials in jurisdictions that are not using each measure. Estimate is measured on 7-point scale ranging from 1, not at all feasible, to 7, very feasible.

TABLE 9.12
Sources of Local Funding Officials Would Use in the
Event of a Natural Disaster

Source of Local Funds	Percent Who Would Recommend Use of Source of Funds		
	Disaster 1980-1986 No Federal Aid	Disaster 1980-1986 Aid Received	No Disaster 1980-1986
Transfers from Other Fund Categories in Budget	64%	68%	61%
Contingency Funds Budgeted Every Year	60	69	61
Revenue or Tax Anticipation Notes	37	35	32
Reserves Held for New Construction	32	43	38
One-time Tax Increase	35	29	29
Temporary Increase in Rates for Services	10	23	24

Source: Survey of 481 local officials, summer 1988.

*Difference among three groups is statistically
significant at .05 level on the basis of difference
of means test.

about two thirds of the public-sector costs of that disaster. Thus, federal disaster assistance still leaves state and local governments exposed to catastrophic financial losses and, if many of those governments won't or can't transfer that risk through insurance or other arrangements, then they need to be prepared to fund losses themselves.

We asked local officials about that directly; their responses are summarized in Table 9.12. Reflecting local officials' actual behavior in time of disaster (e.g., see Table 2.6), the only two sources of local funds a majority of the officials we queried would recommend for use in recovering from a natural disaster are transfers of funds already budgeted for other purposes and budgeted contingency funds. About a third said they would recommend the use of other sources of funds, if necessary; those include revenue or tax anticipation notes, one-time tax increases, and reserves held for new construction. Even fewer officials would recommend the use of temporary increases in rates for public services such as water and sewer.

Local officials' willingness to recommend that their governments purchase hazards insurance is related to their preferences for local funding sources. Namely, officials who would not recommend using temporary increases in service charges were significantly (p = .008) more likely than those who would use service charges to have recommended the purchase of hazards insurance. That is also true of officials who would oppose the use of one-time tax increases; they too were more likely to have recommended purchasing insurance, but that relationship is not statistically significant (p = .09). Those findings are reinforced by the association we found between officials' estimates of the feasibility of funding insurance premiums or reserves through special tax districts and their willingness to recommend the purchase of insurance; the more likely officials were to view that source of funds as infeasible, the more likely they were to have recommended the purchase of insurance (p = .019).

Those findings suggest that as long as local officials feel that through a combination of intergovernmental aid and the use of already available local funds they can recover from a natural disaster, they are prone to forego purchasing hazards insurance. But, the more officials feel that a disaster might result in increases in taxes or service charges, the more likely they are to recommend that their government insure itself against losses.

Conclusions

Federal policy encourages local governments to insure public property in identified hazard areas. But, our data indicate that simply legislating a weak federal mandate for local government hazards insurance to encourage risk sharing is having little effect. It is more difficult, however, to come to conclusions about what additional actions would further that aim. Among the myriad of factors we examined in this chapter, the only strong associations with local officials' willingness to recommend the purchase of hazards insurance are their perception of the risk of loss and cost-effectiveness of insurance. In other words, officials will recommend insurance when they feel it provides a good value. Since most officials perceive the risk of a disastrous loss from a natural hazard as low (e.g., 55 percent estimated the odds of such a loss as 1 in 200 or less in any given year), it is no surprise that less than half of the local governments we studied had purchased insurance.

The effect of perception of the hazard may be magnified by the number of veto points in local government decision processes. For example, studies about seismic hazard mitigation have found that although professional personnel judge the risks as important, elected officials are less supportive of costly or politically unpopular management actions. (Mushkatel and Nigg 1987) Thus, even though a risk manager or finance director perceives natural hazards risks and recommends the purchase of insurance, that recommendation may be thwarted by a chief administrator or elected officials to whom the risk of loss is much less evident.

Among the decision makers we studied, for example, 71 percent had recommended that insurance be purchased, but insurance was in effect in less than half of those cities and counties. Also, we found some evidence that city clerks, managers and elected officials may be much less favorable toward hazards insurance than risk managers, finance directors, and public works personnel. That may be evidence of another influence on mitigation policy found to be important in a few other recent studies: the presence of a well-placed advocate is important to adoption of hazard-related local policy. (Alesch and Petak 1986; Berke and Beatley 1989) To the extent that officials with broad responsibilities are least likely to be advocates of risk sharing policies, little action can be expected. The present study did not allow us to test that proposition further, however.

The availability of federal and state disaster assistance may account for some decisions not to purchase hazards insurance, but the evidence in that regard is far from clear. Several officials serving governments that suffered losses in the Whittier Narrows earthquake told us unequivocally that their governments did not carry insurance because federal and state aid would meet their needs. Also, we found that local officials would be more interested in insurance if they thought that losses would require increases in local taxes or service charges; but a majority felt that contingency funds and fund transfers would be adequate to meet most losses. Federal aid does not seem to contribute to that perception, however. A large proportion of losses governments experience in natural disasters actually can be covered by contingency funds, as we demonstrated in Chapter 2. Also, we found that local officials serving disaster-stricken communities that were denied aid were no more likely to recommend the purchase of insurance than those serving communities that did receive aid. Thus, it seems unlikely that if federal disaster assistance was withdrawn many communities would rush to purchase insurance.

One avenue that merits further examination is to increase the attention given to hazards insurance in the context of other local government risk management activities. For example, the growth of local government interest in insurance pools indicates that it is a logical context in which to also promote insurance coverage of natural hazards. When we broached that possibility in informal discussions with the managers of several insurance pools, they indicated that risks from natural hazards might well be worth their attention. But, that will not occur automatically, as the following example illustrates. A major project by Oklahoma State University Cooperative Extension in conjunction with the Public Risk Management Association (PRIMA) has recently been directed at improving the general risk management capabilities of smaller local governments, with support from the W. K. Kellogg Foundation. Information on natural hazards vulnerability analysis and risk management choices, however, is given very scant attention (even less than special events such as fairs and parades). Thus, there seems to be a role for federal, state, university, and professional association technical assistance directed toward the risk management community and local officials in general. That potentially would be most effective for smaller jurisdictions, where we found that lack of a professional advocate for managing risk is most typical but per capita losses in natural disasters are largest.

To conclude, then, it appears to us that hazards insurance coverage and risk sharing is unlikely to increase markedly at the local level without a strong federal mandate. Since most local officials do not believe that their governments will experience a loss, the present mandate, which uses eligibility for disaster assistance as an incentive, is ineffective. Most local officials do not believe they will ever suffer a loss or need such aid. A more effective incentive would be to condition all federal grants-in-aid for infrastructure on local certification that hazards insurance was in place for all insurable public property. Local officials, our findings show, are particularly sensitive to increasing the burden on taxpayers by using fees for service or special tax assessments to fund losses from disasters. Those who view such increases as undesirable were significantly more likely to view insurance as feasible. Decreasing federal assistance that reduces local tax and capital investment costs would be more likely to motivate local officials to consider sharing hazard losses through insurance than would the current policy of denying relief for uninsured losses. That and other ideas for increasing local governments' attention to risk sharing are discussed further in the concluding chapter to this book.

10

Intergovernmental Considerations

This chapter focuses on the prospects for adopting hazard management policies. We highlight a neglected area of the debate over appropriate policies to manage losses from natural disasters—the political and organizational conditions associated with risk management decision making. Given the notion of risk as the possibility of loss under conditions of uncertainty (Denenberg et al. 1964), decision making in the natural hazards policy arena is different from making decisions under clearer conditions in more stable, less complex situations. Political and institutional obstacles to intergovernmental cooperation are numerous. In this chapter we examine a variety of factors that ease and inhibit policy development for risk management and the range of policy options that are realistically available at the national, state, and local levels.

Characteristics of the Policy Arena

There is little agreement about the nature of the risks that stem from natural hazards, their costs, and what to do about them. Under normal circumstances, few citizens place a high priority on any phase of emergency management. Although those same individuals expect their government leaders to effectively manage disasters that occur, they rarely link long-term planning, such as that involved with any risk management program, with crisis events. Much of that disparity is explained by the nature of risk assumption by individuals and governments and the effects of social values on the interplay of groups, including governments, in society.

Individual Assumption of Risk

Knowledge or belief about the seriousness of threats, as well as the subjective probability of experiencing a damaging loss, influences adoption and implementation of mitigation strategies (such as a risk management program) by individuals, organizations, and communities. Empirical evidence regarding the extent and even the direction of those beliefs is mixed. The ways that people's intuitive inferences, predictions, probability assessments, and diagnoses do not conform to the laws of probability theory and statistics (Kahneman, et al 1982) make public policy choices difficult. In addition, most individuals simply do not have precise enough data on either damages or mitigation costs to be able to make rational decisions. (Milliman 1983) However, if people simply discount the probability of loss from infrequently occurring events, there will be little concern with hazards. (Wright, Rossi, Wright, et al. 1979)

The ability to estimate risk, perceived causes of hazard extremes, experience (including the frequency and severity of losses), and other factors contribute to the formation of risk perception. Intellectual limitations, the need to reduce anxiety, and information availability often lead to risk denial and to unrealistic oversimplification of complex problems. One bias associated with information availability, for example, is the difficulty of imagining low-probability, high-consequence events happening to oneself. Many floodplain residents are reluctant to buy low-cost flood insurance, for example. (Kunreuther et al. 1978)

The high tolerance levels for risks held by most individuals historically has made restrictive mitigation policies politically infeasible. As a result, one frequently practiced hazard mitigation strategy is simply to inform people of the risk and leave it to their own calculations of costs and benefits as to how to adjust. Reliance on an information-based mitigation strategy, however, is becoming politically unrealistic. The costs of exposure to hazards are not borne solely by individuals who often knowingly subject themselves to the risk. The costs of rescue, cleanup, and reconstruction, for example, are shifted wholly or in part to society as a whole.

As we noted in Chapter 1, those external diseconomies have led to shifts in federal policy over the past twenty years. The government is turning to a wider variety of natural hazard mitigation techniques, often regulatory in nature. Less emphasis is being placed on costly and questionably effective construction projects, which benefit hazard-zone occupants but are paid for by society, and more emphasis is being placed on building and other regulations that internalize external costs. The federal government has become more aggressive in demanding compliance with the National Flood Insurance Program (NFIP), the major incentive for community adoption of regulatory measures to deal with flood hazards. It also has increased state and local cost-sharing requirements for flood control projects. And, federal disaster relief policy is changing as well, with important cost-sharing provisions imposed on state and local governments as a major theme.

Although cost containment has driven federal policy in recent years, the irreversibility of certain decisions regarding low-probability, high-consequence events and the inability to reverse catastrophic events with any large degree of success raise significant questions about using efficiency as the sole criterion for evaluating policy choices. (Ricci, et al. 1984; Shrader-Frechette 1985; Waller and Covello 1984) Mitigation policies and disaster relief questions pose the classic problem of social regulation. How should the costs of the problem be distributed? How much avoidance of risk is necessary, given the enormous costs of unperfected solutions? Who should bear the costs of remedying undesirable consequences of past practices? The ethical character of the dilemma raises questions regarding the present generation's right to impose the uncertainties associated with their decisions on future generations, as well as consideration of the distributional impacts of decisions. (Cigler 1988a)

Governmental Assumption of Risk

The high tolerance for risk by individuals is linked to increased governmental concern for the costs of individual risk assumption borne by society. From the national government's perspective, natural hazards are a serious problem, presenting staggering economic losses each year. As one moves to lower levels of government, the damages experienced become fewer from that level of government's vantage point (i.e., the national government is affected by all disasters in the U.S., each state is concerned with the aggregate of disasters in that state, and so forth), meaning that local governments may be the least likely to perceive of hazards as important problems. In the preceding chapter, for example, we presented data showing that most local decision makers do not perceive risks from natural hazards, even when their government has experienced large losses in a disaster. In effect, then, perceived risk shifts from one level of government to another, generally becoming steadily less as one moves from the national to the local level.

The paradox for mitigation effectiveness is that the governments least likely to perceive risk management as a key priority—local governments—are at center stage in terms of responsibility for policy implementation. Local governments shoulder the bulk of responsibilities for disaster preparedness and response. Nonstructural mitigation measures, such as altering land use and building codes, are also traditionally local responsibilities.

A wealth of empirical studies have concluded that dealing with natural hazards has low priority on most local governments' formal agendas (e.g., Burby and French 1981; Burby and French et al. 1985; Drabek, Mushkatel, and Kilijanek 1983; Wright, et al. 1979; Wyner 1984). Our 1987 survey of planners and public works directors from communities recently experiencing disasters revealed that only for flood events were more than half of the respondents (53 percent) "moderately to very concerned" that a disaster would actually occur during the next year. The "moderately to very concerned response" rate was 34 percent for hurricanes, 21 percent for coastal storms, and 19 percent for earthquakes. Even in these high risk communities, only 14 percent of the officials thought spending to deal with threats posed by natural disasters was "very important." And, in fact, as we reported in Chapter 6, most communities have done relatively little and are generally unprepared for natural disasters.

The real or perceived low probability of disasters (e.g., see Chapter 9), and low visibility of most mitigation measures contribute to low salience local hazards politics. Lacking widespread public support, policy entrepreneurs rarely emerge to promote local programs or policies. It follows that local public decision makers, who demonstrate low interest in mitigation in general, would not likely be motivated to plan for future infrastructure losses through the development of risk management programs.

Prevailing American attitudes toward personal property and government regulation also work against local adoption of many mitigation strategies. In addition to the technical problems of successfully identifying and predicting risk (see Chapter 7), decision making is constrained by political, organizational and legal factors associated with the natural hazards policy arena. On the one hand, highly developed political coalitions promoting local mitigation are rare, due to the low probability of disaster events and the human tendency to discount their probability. On the other hand, interest groups opposing mitigation strategies (some developers, builders, real estate interests, etc.) are well organized and perceived as obstacles to development of mitigation measures. (Cigler, Stiftel, and Burby 1987; Wyner 1984)

Only a third of the local officials we surveyed in 1988 thought it would be politically feasible for their governments to maintain a loss reserve fund, compared to 44 percent who judged that option infeasible. Seventy-nine percent judged the option of creating a hazard area special taxing district to raise revenue for a loss reserve fund or hazards insurance to be infeasible. More promising for the development of alternative policy options, however, was the response by 41 percent that participation in an insurance pool that covered natural hazards would be politically feasible. However, a fourth of the respondents (27 percent) judged that option as politically infeasible as well.

The uneven distribution of natural hazards across political units hampers the development of mitigation strategies. Variation in risks means that uniform desires by state or local governments to implement or enforce mitigation measures cannot be assumed. That characteristic of hazard events, in addition, constrains both horizontal and vertical intergovernmental cooperation in developing insurance pools or other mechanisms requiring the sharing of risk. The only area of widespread agreement among respondents was that asking the private sector to assume more costs was a politically volatile issue.

The uncertainties of data and events contribute to high information costs for elected officials, reducing interest and action in hazards policy development. Since future infrastructure losses from natural disasters are so difficult to estimate, there is little incentive for local governments to include this topic in their planning for other types of liability. We would expect to find local decision makers surprised to learn of the relatively low average annual losses for public infrastructure. (As noted in chapter 2, we estimated the average annual loss per county between 1980 and mid-1987 at $48,300 and per city and special district, under $7,000 per year for each government type.) With more accurate information made available to government decision makers, a broader array of policy options might be seriously considered.

Intergovernmental Issues

Five aspects of how governments have organized to deal with hazards work against cooperation among and between governments. (1) Existing governmental programs are based on legislation addressing specific hazards (e.g., floods, earthquakes) that vary among states and local governments. (2) Hazards officials are a diverse group, with physical planners and financial planners and risk managers, for example, rarely working with other emergency management officials. (3) Most hazards officials devote only part-time effort to hazards policies, complicating opportunities for coordination. (4) The engineering, scientific, and economic expertise needed to deal successfully with hazards is limited at the local level and fragmented by academic disciplines. (5) Interaction among and between technical staff and public decision makers is not well established. (Cigler 1988a) Those factors place serious constraints on opportunities for intergovernmental hazards management programs. In addition, however, the formulation of intergovernmental programs must deal with difficult tradeoffs between the equity and efficiency of public policy.

Equity Considerations

The problem of public infrastructure is especially troublesome since many types of public structures (bridges, roads, buildings) were built early in U.S. urban development when location in hazardous areas (riverine and coastal waterfronts, for example) was dictated by the technology of the times (i.e., waterways as the primary mode of transportation). The constraints imposed by past decisions and the location and design of existing facilities, however, do not apply to decisions regarding new facilities. For much of their new public infrastructure, local governments can exercise discretion in its location and design. Facilities can be located away from hazardous areas, and funds can be expended to design structures so that they are less susceptible to loss. State and federal agencies can impose conditions on loans, grants, and permits to restrict service in hazardous areas (for example, federal flood insurance cannot be sold in areas designated under the Coastal Barrier Resources Act). The location of public facilities—schools, post offices, libraries, etc.—away from hazardous areas also discourages private development in hazard-prone areas. (Burby and French et al. 1985; Federal Emergency Management Agency 1986)

The fact remains, however, that many public buildings and other structures were built when water was the major mode of transportation, and the necessity of face-to-face interaction to conduct the public's business placed public structures close to transportation routes and therefore in hazardous areas. As explained in Chapter 2, almost half of all losses incurred by state and local governments in Presidentially declared natural disasters between 1980 and mid-1987 were associated with damages to highways, roads and streets. Those facilities necessarily serve private buildings constructed in an earlier era. We expect local and state officials to argue that damages to their infrastructure are not solely their responsibility, since technological necessity led to the location of many structures that helped build the nation's economy. In addition, serious questions of equity arise, especially those relating to intergenerational policy burdens, when economic efficiency calculations alone guide policy. Again, who should bear the consequences of policies and actions made in an earlier era?

Much is still unknown about the distribution of impacts—both of disasters and of disaster assistance—across income classes and geographic areas. Federal or state disaster assistance to relatively poor communities without an adequate tax base for financing even the costs of a minor disaster may be, in effect, a form of "urban renewal" and thus may be truly redistributive in effect. If, as some suggest, lower-income individuals are more likely to incur damages from a natural disaster than other income groups because of location in more hazardous areas, poorer quality housing, and so forth, then the governments representing those individuals may be less able to bear the costs of damages to their own infrastructure due to a weaker tax base, relative to other communities. However, as we reported in Chapter 2, our data do not provide evidence that losses to the public sector fall particularly heavily on poorer communities. While, the correlation between state per capita income and federal disaster assistance received between 1980 and mid-1987 for losses to the public sector is positive, it is not large ($r = +.104$). Thus, it is difficult to conclude that federal disaster assistance is regressive.

Efficiency Considerations

The relatively small financial losses experienced by most governments (less than $50,000 for two-thirds of state and local governmental entities experiencing natural disasters between 1980 and mid-1987), and the catastrophic losses (averaging over $10 million per occurrence per government) experienced by a few others (.03 percent or 27 units absorbing 26 percent of total losses among over 6,816 state and local governments experiencing natural disasters between 1980 and mid-1987) suggest competing arguments. We argued in Chapter 8 that from an efficiency perspective the more typical small losses should be absorbed solely by the government at risk. The rarer catastrophic losses are more troublesome. Our data suggest that it would be politically difficult for governments within a metropolitan area or state, for example, to be willing to cooperate via insurance pooling or other shared risk mechanisms due to the unequal distribution of losses. For catastrophic losses, at least, it appears that victim governments would both be unable to shoulder the costs alone or to convince others units at their governmental level to join with them in sharing the risk of future losses. The dominant call for federal (and state) bailout when a catastrophic event occurs, then, is obvious.

Multiple hazard management is another approach that has some potential for increasing the efficiency of governmental efforts to cope with losses to infrastructure. A key policy question in designing risk management options, for example, is whether to protect against single hazards (flood protection, earthquake protection, for example) or to develop options based on estimations of loss frequency and severity of all possible hazards. The Federal Emergency Management Agency has promoted multiple hazard management as an integrated or coordinated approach that addresses the full range of hazards to which communities are prone. Multiple hazard mitigation is the component of multiple hazard management concerned with reducing the long-term adverse impacts of the full range of hazards within a community, state, region, or the nation as a whole. A multiple hazards approach is appealing, since it focuses attention on the full range of hazards, allows for consideration of the interaction among hazards, and offers increased opportunities for greater efficiency in the use of finances, personnel, and other resources. (Cigler 1988b)

The many commonalities among hazards (Perrow 1984) make multiple hazards approaches feasible for some disaster response functions, such as communications. But, an integrated multiple hazard approach to mitigation is more problematic due to the complexity within and between hazard types—natural and technological. As reported in more depth in other chapters, our survey of communities with recent hazard experiences shows great differences among them in terms of the types of hazards experienced, their frequency, and resulting damages. In turn, local willingness to undertake various types of mitigation measures is affected by officials' perceptions of risk, as is willingness to participate in insurance arrangements that require cooperation with other communities that might not have the same experiences. Also, we found that federal efforts to foster mitigation following a disaster have some effect in stimulating local governments' attention to the specific hazard that caused the disaster, but not on other hazards facing those same governmental units. Thus, federal aid for a hurricane stricken community such as Charleston, South Carolina, helps that community mitigate future losses from hurricanes, but it does nothing to foster preparedness for an earthquake, which also poses a severe threat to public property in Charleston.

Our 1987 survey of planners and public works directors shows that floods are perceived to be more likely to occur than earthquakes. Forty-five percent of the respondents said the probability of significant flood damages was .01 or greater in the next year; sixty-five percent said the probability of earthquake damage was less than a .001. The challenge to multiple hazard mitigation, including the ability to analyze risk and to ensure commitment from diverse communities, is great. The vast differences among communities in their hazard vulnerability and experiences suggest obstacles in developing risk management programs that combine hazards. It may be that more piecemeal, hazard specific approaches are both technically and politically more realistic.

Local Officials' Perspectives

At present, the low salience of hazards management policy, the variation in hazard risks among communities and states, and the unpredictability of certain classes of hazards helps lead to a local ideology that federal (or state) disaster assistance is both necessary and expected. Our survey of risk managers and finance directors from communities recently experiencing disasters demonstrates their expectations that the federal government should take the lead in disaster assistance. As we reported in Chapter 2, when we asked officials what sources of funding they used in financing reconstruction of public facilities, 51 percent mentioned federal grants as "very important" and 43 percent gave the same rating to state grants. Grants were much more important than loans, with only 8 percent mentioning federal loans and the same number citing state loans as "very important."

In that same survey we asked local risk managers and finance directors "Would you favor or oppose revision of disaster assistance legislation which would make participation in a natural hazards insurance pool a condition for receiving assistance for the repair of public facilities damaged by natural hazards?" Their responses do not indicate either a strong interest in increased local assumption of the costs of relief, nor strong opposition to such policy. Among 146 respondents, 42 percent favored the insurance pool as a condition for federal assistance, 39 percent opposed it, and 19 percent offered no opinion. Thirty-five percent also favored a similar condition for state disaster assistance, 43 percent opposed it, with 22 percent offering no opinion. Overall, strong support for either the federal or state pool was voiced by only 14 percent of the respondents. Of course, the respondents may be familiar with the realities of gaps in revenue needed to finance losses, but they are not the elected officials who make public policy.

Still another indicator of the perceptions of officials depending on the level of government which they represent is the gap between requests for major or emergency disaster declarations made by governors and those granted presidential declarations. Of 725 such gubernatorial requests made from 1971 through 1981, for example, 20 percent were granted neither Presidential declarations nor agency approvals leading to Small Business Administration loans. (May 1985) Between 1980 and 1985, federal officials reported to us that approximately 50 percent of the gubernatorial requests for Presidential disaster declarations were denied.

Political and Organizational Factors

In addition to factors associated directly with the probabilistic nature and resultant psychology of natural hazards, various characteristics of and trends in governmental organization affect prospects for risk management policy adoption. Some trends increase the likelihood of policy reform, while others will likely hamper policy making.

Changing Intergovernmental Roles

The reductions in federal disaster relief discussed here are part of a larger reduction in federal aid to state and local governments and a changing national role in general. While the debate continues regarding the impact of recent federal policies, the overall shift in the federal system toward decentralization of policy to subnational units has been modest. The serious nature of the national budget deficit, however, suggests that there is less room than in past eras to undertake new initiatives that involve expenditure of national dollars, regardless of any political will to do so. Substance abuse, AIDS, and pollution control, as examples, are higher on the political agenda than issues such as the development of a catastrophic insurance or other program to deal with public infrastructure losses due to natural hazards. Any funding available to deal with the infrastructure loss problem, moreover, would likely come out of existing programs that have survived the political challenges of the 1980s.

The "zero-sum" quality of the national government's role in the federal system has the effect of maintaining existing commitments, whether they are effective or not, and excluding new initiatives, whether they are meritorious or not. A key concern is whether there will be a similar pattern in state and local governments, which are being asked to assume a larger role in service delivery (such as for all phases of emergency management, including disaster relief) and social regulation. It is uncertain whether the changing national role in the federal system will have a long-term effect that unleashes subnational innovation or constrains it.

Federal funding cuts may well prove to be the obstacle making it impossible for new programs in the hazards management area to be successful. A case in point is the Dam Safety Act of 1986 (Title XII of PL 99-662). In 1987, the Office of Management and Budget offered support for only partial funding of the law, with monies allotted solely for updating the national inventory of dams and for training programs. Appropriations for state dam safety programs, the most important aspect of the law for the states (and the largest dollar amount), were not included in federal budget requests. The Administration's position was that dam safety is a state issue; however, the states maintain that at this point in their fledgling programs federal funds are necessary to boost the programs to a point where they can be self-supportive. With the federal budget deficit as large as it is, programs such as hazard mitigation are often the first to be eliminated.

Some bright signs in this potentially static federal system relate to the relative strengths and weaknesses of the national, state, and local governments, based on recent performance. For the question of hazard management, especially the mitigation and reconstruction phases, assessments must be made of which particular functions individual levels of government are or are not well equipped to handle.

The National Government

The government's domestic expenditures are concentrated on redistributive activities and have promoted equity across regions, states, and localities (i.e., the more nationalized a redistributive governmental activity is, the less variation in benefits based on place of residence). (Albritton and Brown 1986) To attract political support, redistributive programs are often broadened to benefit larger constituencies, thus diminishing the degree of redistribution as well as becoming very costly. While the national government is the key vehicle for equity and redistribution, the enormous costs are obvious.

For the natural hazards policy arena, much more information is needed about the equity effects of federal disaster assistance and of new proposals, such as our suggestion, made in Chapter 8, for shifting from relief to mitigation and insurance as a way of dealing with losses to public property in natural disasters. Clearly, for public infrastructure losses, as with individual losses, questions relating to intergenerational impacts of policies and practices and their equity effects are a key concern. Without achieving a niche in the redistributive policy arena, new federal disaster policy initiatives will not likely occur. If any redistributive effects favor wealthier states or communities, such policy options become even more unlikely to be accepted.

Another area of consideration for a national role is as "insurer of last resort." The growing liability insurance crisis in the U.S. has spawned calls for more government insurance programs. One option relevant to the problem of losses to public infrastructure would be substitution of a catastrophic insurance program for federal disaster relief. The key advantage of such a program would be its ability to make insurance both available and affordable to state and local governments experiencing the rare catastrophic event. While addressing the affordability problems of subnational units, such a program could end up subsidizing the program's insured. Recent changes in the National Flood Insurance Fund, which requires federal subsidies of approximately $150 million annually, suggest that a new catastrophic insurance program would be difficult to enact. The cumulative loss for the National Flood Insurance Fund was projected to be $1.4 billion at the end of 1988. The deficit has been partially financed through appropriations of $1.2 billion. The national government's goal in recent years has been to reduce that subsidy by increasing revenues from premiums and taking other steps to reduce losses.

The rationale behind the planned phase-out of the subsidy is the authorizing legislation's requirement of distributing burdens equitably among those protected by flood insurance and the general public. The recent changes will presumably reduce the general taxpayer's burden and offer a more equitable sharing of the costs of losses between general taxpayers and insureds. If that same rationale were applied to the public assistance disaster relief program, there might be strong federal support for expanding the flood insurance program to include a broader spectrum of losses to public property or losses to public and private property from other disaster agents, particularly if an expanded program was self-supporting.

The national government's reluctance to subsidize the NFIP, and presumably any new proposals, is not based solely on potential costs. Ideally, insurance should promote public health and safety by policing insureds to ensure minimization of risk. Insureds who fail to minimize risks, for example, would find insurance coverage more difficult to obtain and more expensive. Calculations of the costs of a new catastrophic insurance program, therefore, would need to consider the additional funds, personnel and resources necessary in the regulatory area. (U.S. Department of Justice, 1986)

Another issue for any catastrophic insurance program relates to the difficulties cited earlier that arise from differences among various types of hazards. The imperfections of data gathering and uncertainties of disaster events once again suggest that single-hazard approaches (flood insurance, earthquake insurance, etc.) may be more feasible than any combined approach.

A criticism of any governmental hazards insurance program, regardless of any conditions for mitigation activities it might require, is that it might operate as a disincentive to mitigation since insureds would receive the benefit of a risk transfer (to government, in the case of individuals and to another level of government in the case of states and localities) without any strong checks upon their conduct. During the 1980s, the national government began to sue local governments to recover insurance losses attributable to local governments' failure to comply with requirements of the NFIP. A massive investment of litigation resources might be required to ensure governments' compliance with a large catastrophic insurance program's mitigation requirements.

State Governments

State governments have moved from the backwaters of American federalism through a professionalization revolution that has made their policy and management capabilities impressive. (Advisory Commission on Intergovernmental Relations 1985; Bowman and Kearney 1986) One area of especially aggressive policy development has been the promotion of economic development. (Dubnick and Holt 1985; Anton 1987; Osborne 1988) Increased activity in service delivery and social regulation have led to state innovations in the area of environmental protection (Rabe 1986), and recent Environmental Protection Agency mandates require innovative financing for water and sewer facilities, such as revolving loan funds. While the states have always had a limited capacity to promote redistribution (due to wide disparities across states in their fiscal capabilities as well as their political will), increased citizen pressures for more state involvement in non-redistributive policy areas are occurring. The deterioration of America's infrastructure is a case in point, with recent experience suggesting that the national government will offer little financial help.

Natural hazards policies at the state government level, as with their local governments, have always been hampered by their low priority on political agendas and the difficulty of linking them to other policies perceived to be more salient. If policy can be effectively linked to the broader infrastructure policy arena, or to the more general area of state promotion of economic development, however, the likelihood of policy action in the natural hazards arena might be increased. For example, the state of Washington's innovative infrastructure trust fund provides moneys for local flood control projects.

The key point is that policy implementation research has shown linkages among policies are a key ingredient to success. To date, no policy entrepreneurs have emerged to translate the issue of public infrastructure losses from natural disasters into proposals linked to a broader policy arena already high on state governments' agendas. (Cigler 1987)

Many states have an uncoordinated maze of regulations and fragmented building construction programs as part of their capital facilities development process. These states have not surveyed the condition, operations, and maintenance of state-owned buildings, for example, and are ill-equipped to devise alternative strategies for dealing with potential losses to their infrastructure. While more attention has been focused on roads, bridges, and water and sewer facilities, the maintenance and repair needs of state-owned buildings are often neglected. In addition, unlike the federal government, most states do not have uniform procedures for selecting designers based on qualifications and experience with capital improvement projects. Nor are there systematic procedures for evaluating the work performed on capital improvement projects. Until such basic problems as those are addressed, we believe it is unlikely that many states will move toward innovative options for dealing with future losses to much of their own infrastructure from natural disasters. Further complicating the level of state government concern is the fact that many states are moving toward leasing buildings for government activities from the private sector.

The states, of course, also have a continuing role in easing risk management for their local governments, especially in offering technical assistance for hazard mitigation. In a number of cases, however, rather than easing local hazards management, states create obstacles. Some states, for example, lack enabling legislation authorizing local pooling for risks. Some states prevent local governments from creating capital reserves to finance future capital expenditures. That has a negative impact on small communities that are otherwise unable to enter the bond market or use a "pay-as-you-go" approach to financing infrastructure. As a result, many communities "hide" capital reserves for financing future infrastructure needs within the operating budget in the form of contingency reserves, which entails some risk that the reserves will be depleted and funds used for non-capital purposes. In those states, legal restraints would have to be removed before any risk management options requiring reserve funds for infrastructure losses could be created. (See Rosenberg and Rood 1985.)

Local Governments

There are more than 80,000 governmental units that can suffer losses to their infrastructure from natural hazards. A serious mismatch frequently exists between a governmental unit's responsibilities and its fiscal or management capacity. For most local governments, fiscal stress and cut back management have become routine. In addition, there is considerable variation across types of infrastructure and, within types, across facilities owned and maintained by different government agencies. (See chapters 2 and 3.) Those facts, along with the unpredictability of disaster events and uneven occurrence of losses across entities, suggests that piecemeal, rather than comprehensive, policy options often are more feasible at the local level.

That is, in undertaking financing that requires shared risk, school districts or water districts may be more likely to cooperate with each other than municipalities and school districts or counties and municipalities. The common sense reasoning is that homogeneity of participants is a condition of successful shared risk approaches. As such, similar hazard vulnerability or experience, as well as similar type of government (general purpose or special purpose) are important considerations.

Population size and fiscal resources are important because large governments can consider self insurance, either individually or in groups, but small governments have more difficulty in generating the necessary contribution volume (premiums) for developing a shared risk approach such as government pooling. An established program of intergovernmental cooperation would ease the formation of programs for shared risk, but local governments in the United States do not have strong records in cooperative service delivery and other shared modes of governance.

Good data are necessary for development of risk sharing mechanisms. Few local governments, however, have developed even an inventory of their infrastructure, since cost accounting is not used to measure public assets for depreciation purposes as in the private sector. (The same conclusion holds for state governments.) Without records on what is owned, its value, and its maintenance history, any financial planning is difficult. In addition, most local governments budget on a line-item, object of expenditure basis. That approach does not provide a basis for accurate analysis of infrastructure investment decisions. Furthermore, capital improvement plans, the basis for analyzing public facilities in terms of needs, priorities, and fiscal capacity, are not commonly used by small local governments. (Cigler 1987)

Insufficient planning capacity, weak policy and program coordination, fragmented organizational responsibilities, poor financial management, and other basic management and organizational concerns are too often evident at the local level, and they make governmental entities ill-equipped to develop and evaluate policy options for managing risk. Unfortunately, in addition, the smaller, especially non-metropolitan, governments are most likely to possess a wide array of administrative inadequacies. (Sokolow and Honadle 1984; Cigler 1987)

Because there are more small governments than any other type, administrative inadequacies loom as a significant set of obstacles to local risk management decision making. The smallness of most governments, as mentioned earlier, makes it financially unlikely that they can develop self insurance programs or participate in programs requiring high reserves. Similarly, their capacity to perform vulnerability analyses is weak, as is their experience with innovative modes of working with the private sector.

Governmental professionalization is associated with larger units of local government. The average population of jurisdictions where professional risk managers served as respondents to our 1988 local government survey, for example, was over 135,000. But, more than 90 percent of the municipal and town/township governments in the United States serve communities of less than 10,000 people. More than 80 percent of municipal governments serve fewer than 5,000 people each, and about 30,000 local governments are ZEG's—zero employee governments. (Schenker 1986) More than three-fourths of county governments serve populations of less than 50,000 people. Approximately one-third of the U.S. population lives in rural areas, and approximately two-thirds of all governmental units exist there. Most local governments, inside and outside of metropolitan areas, serve small populations and have limited management capacity. (Cigler 1989)

Those facts lead to serious reservations about either the technical or the fiscal capability of most local governments to practice risk sharing through transfer of risk to governmental pools. However, they might not inhibit local government participation in an insurance program sponsored by the federal government, if adequate incentives for participation (or penalties for nonparticipation) accompanied the program, or in an insurance pool composed of small local governments with similar exposures to loss.

In the absence of new federal insurance initiatives, the insurance liability crisis in the U.S. may, in fact, provide an opportunity to link the problem of disaster-caused losses to public property to a problem of greater salience to local officials. Municipalities are among the groups hardest hit by problems of liability insurance affordability, availability, and adequacy in general. Several hundred municipal insurance pools exist, for example, to resolve that problem. Participation in an existing pool would likely increase a local government's interest in pooling for natural hazards losses. If personnel responsible for existing arrangements were made aware of relevant data on average annual losses to public infrastructure from natural hazards, they might be willing to incorporate those risks of infrastructure losses into some existing pools. Although the differential effects of disasters work against interlocal cooperative efforts, the potential cost savings from pooling, opportunities for assured availability of hazards insurance, creation of loss prevention incentives through increased communication among pool members and as an incentive for lower claims experience, and other benefits are worth exploring.

The hazards insurance area would not likely generate opposition from the private sector. The greatest anticipated problem would be in generating enough members and creating a reserve capacity to deal with catastrophic losses.

In Chapter 2 we pointed out that infrastructure losses from natural hazards are far below levels of normal repair and replacement costs associated with infrastructure. That fact will not necessarily motivate local officials to action, however. While it suggests a manageable problem, the reality remains that political rewards for dealing with infrastructure are traditionally lacking and the time horizons of local officials command attention to immediate problems, not events that might occur in the future.

Implications for Alternative
Risk Management Approaches

This chapter has examined the characteristics of physical hazards that shape policy making for mitigation and recovery, as well as characteristics of the general political and institutional environment in which governments operate. We have demonstrated that the opportunities for risk management are many, but the obstacles great. There are great disparities among governmental units in terms of exposure to risk, losses experienced, financial and technical capability, and the subjective assessments of policy options. A reasonable approach for any government, policy advocate, or governmental decision maker is to first recognize the gamut of options theoretically available for dealing with the infrastructure loss problem so that a systematic assessment of criteria for choosing options can evolve.

Transferring Risk

As we noted in Chapter 4, pooling options are becoming increasingly attractive alternatives for municipal liability insurance as the cost of coverage is often significantly less than is coverage on the traditional insurance market (no longer available to many governments), and the coverage itself is much broader and better adapted to the risks that a local government is attempting to insure. Most of local government insurance pools buy reinsurance, however, through the same market as the private insurance industry that is retrenched. Furthermore, pools often engage in the same investment and marketing practices that led to the problems in the private insurance industry, and as a result the pools are restricting their coverage much as in the private insurance industry.

For those reasons, along with the unique problems of the natural hazards policy arena and great differences among and between governmental units, it is unclear to us whether such pools can be used to insure against public infrastructure losses from natural disasters, a very high risk area. Any of the public pools would have to be capable of identifying hazard vulnerability, establishing sound methods for hazard risk reduction, and ensuring that required mitigation measures are actually used by participants. Accomplishing those tasks would be very difficult. But, there are serious questions of equity and morality if mitigation standards are not required and a "no-fault" system is used instead.

As explained here and in previous chapters, the most popular way of transferring risk from natural hazards is via disaster assistance programs sponsored by the federal and state governments. Our surveys of local officials, moreover, suggest the continued popularity of such approaches.

Government insurance programs (sometimes a condition of disaster assistance) are also a way of transferring risk. The most widely used risk transfer device is the National Flood Insurance Program, which contains provisions requiring some local risk assumption and adoption of hazard mitigation regulations. Other federal and state insurance or disaster assistance programs can have conditions of aid, such as deductibles, required mitigation programs, and so forth. Here, the question of "fault" looms large, with the argument of many, including the Reagan and Bush Administrations, that subsidized government insurance often punishes those who have done nothing wrong (general taxpayers), simply because they have the collective resources to compensate those who have done wrong (located in hazardous areas, for example). That criticism, of course, also applies to federal disaster assistance.

As explained in this chapter, the "fault" question with regard to public infrastructure losses from natural hazards is especially complicated due to locational and policy decisions made in earlier eras. It may be unreasonable to make the citizens of an unfortunate government that is the victim of a catastrophic event bear all costs due to past decisions of local officials to locate facilities in hazardous areas or to fail to build those facilities to adequate standards. However, how much of those costs should others shoulder? The question of fault also applies to insurance measures. How, for example, are participants in an insurance program to be monitored for enforcement of mitigation standards? Clearly, future policy in this area of risk transfer will likely relate to questions of deductibles, caps, and mitigation, which, as we suggested in Chapter 8, make eminent sense from an economic efficiency perspective.

Another risk transfer device, noted in Chapters 5 and 9, would be to levy fees or other exactions on people who benefit from location in hazardous areas to be used in hazard mitigation, purchasing hazards insurance or reconstructing public facilities damaged by natural hazards (that would be a risk transfer since part of the cost of the risk is transferred to the private sector). Those risk funding mechanisms can easily be linked to existing comprehensive planning procedures, capital facilities planning, and other local activities. Again, the smallness of most governments and the political sensitivity of cost shifting to the private sector (e.g., see Chapter 9) suggests that as a potentially controversial risk funding mechanism. Local governments can, however, simply recognize the need to adjust existing exactions to reflect the potential for hazard-related reconstruction costs and earmark those funds for risk management purposes, rather than attempt to develop unique programs for funding hazards management and reconstruction.

Risk Reduction

The most diverse category of risk management options relates to risk elimination or reduction to prevent loss. This includes the activities and programs generally referred to as hazard mitigation—flood control and other measures to manage the forces of nature; land use policies, building code and construction codes to protect against floods, hurricanes and earthquakes; public and employee education programs; and greater use of disaster planning services, for example. As stated earlier, we still know relatively little about the costs or benefits of many mitigation techniques. However, a loss reduction plan is the key to any other type of risk management program. A mitigation plan is necessary for successful risk funding schemes, so as to reduce premiums, for example, or to ensure equity across those sharing in the payments for losses. The question of monitoring mitigation plans looms as an important policy issue for intergovernmental cooperation through risk sharing at both the horizontal (within a metropolitan area, for example) and vertical (national-state-local) levels.

Risk Elimination

This option refers to locating new structures outside of flood-prone or other known hazardous areas and relocating existing structures to reduce risks. That is frequently a wise choice for new construction, but it can be very costly, and as a result is little used, in handling risks of loss to existing structures. It would be a very unlikely candidate to serve as a "condition" of assistance or participation in a risk transfer program.

Risk Assumption

This category includes no-insurance or "going bare" (i.e., hoping that a disaster does not occur) and self insurance (by setting up a reserve fund to cover uninsured costs or paying them out of operating expenses). As explained earlier, the uncertainties of hazards occurring and the lack of existing data to estimate possible losses make this an unreliable approach if not used in combination with other options. But, our survey data show that no-insurance for natural hazards losses is a very frequently used option among local governments and that the use of reserve funds to deal with such losses is similarly not widespread (see Chapter 6). Local governments are also unlikely to adopt new mitigation measures even after a disaster strikes. Trends in the federal system, however, show growing interest in increasing deductibles, reducing coverage, and other loss control mechanisms the involve risk assumption as an incentive to promote more mitigation activity.

Because governmental entities vary so widely in their needs for risk management, it is unlikely that comprehensive solutions to the infrastructure loss problem will emerge. However, as governmental units perform vulnerability studies, the frequency and severity of their risk and its relationship to each risk management method can be assessed. For example, public entities experiencing high-frequency/low-severity risks or those with low-frequency/low-severity occurrences may want to make closer examination of the variety of risk reduction, elimination, or assumption options. Alternatively, governmental units with high-frequency/high-severity occurrences or low-frequency/high-severity occurrences would examine transferring by commercial insurance, insurance pooling, or other methods of sharing risk.

Some likely scenarios serve as examples. A community in the low-frequency/low-severity risk category might logically choose to retain the risks while another with high-frequency/low-severity experiences might also wish to retain. Entities classified as low-frequency/high-severity might find it more useful to do the necessary analyses regarding options to eliminate, transfer, or reduce risk. Finally, high-frequency/high-severity entities would likely give further consideration to elimination and reduction of risk. These steps seem to be pre-conditions for selecting or advocating alternative policy approaches.

Conclusions

We think it is likely that risk management options for dealing with infrastructure losses will evolve on a piecemeal rather than comprehensive basis. One promising strategy for policy development would be linkage of this policy area to related policies that are higher on governments' agendas--the need to reduce the costs of government through improved efficiency, the general infrastructure deterioration problem, economic development, or even the development of state revolving funds for water and sewer facilities and other infrastructure (including infrastructure bond banks).

Policy debate will focus on questions of economic efficiency in the allocation of governmental funds, but equity issues will also be brought to bear. Normative questions about the respective roles of the national, state, and local governments in the federal system will dominate the debate. Policy options embraced by particular governmental entities will most likely be multi-tiered in terms of governmental roles. The complexity of the data and perception problems suggest a continued focus on single hazards, not multiple hazard approaches for risk funding. The physical characteristics of hazards themselves, along with the political environment in which decision making must occur, will lead to continued debate on the "fault" question, further highlighting interest in mitigation and risk funding policy options.

PART 4

Policy Futures

11

Future Directions
for Public Policy

This chapter examines a range of policy options for managing risk to public property from natural hazards. We summarize the major constraints to reform discussed in the preceding chapters and consider their implications for public policy. Given those constraints, we examine various policy alternatives for federal, state, and local policy makers within the framework of risk management strategies. Finally, we offer a proposal for reform of federal financing of disaster relief.

The Need for Change

The nation's policies for dealing with public losses in natural disasters are expensive, inequitable, and inefficient. Because of competing concerns and limited financial resources, however, policy makers at all levels of government have devoted few resources to reducing the risks of losses in natural disasters or righting the various flaws in current policies that we have discussed in this book. There are a number of reasons. At the state and local level, public officials underestimate the probability of loss, and without a strong constituency arguing for greater attention to natural hazards, they underinvest in insurance, loss prevention and other risk management strategies. At the federal level, public losses just are not large enough to attract the attention needed for reform.

Public losses in natural disasters are enormous—we estimate them conservatively at about $1 billion per year—but from some perspectives that is not a large amount. As we noted in Chapter 2, for example, losses from natural hazards represent only one half of one percent of the $2 trillion plus (in 1980) capital stock of public property. It is far less than normal costs associated with depreciation of that capital. The portion of the federal budget spent on disaster relief is small—less than one-half of one percent. And, the losses to local governments averaged over all governmental units are also small—only $50,000 for counties and less than $10,000 for other types of entities. When measured against the financial demands posed by problems such as the fight against drugs or reducing the national debt, losses to governments from natural hazards may seem minor and not worth a lot of attention.

Nevertheless, few would argue for continuing policies and practices that are inequitable and inefficient. In the previous chapters we described how current disaster relief financing can create inequities in a variety of ways. For losses to public property, the prime concern is how communities or individuals not at risk effectively subsidize those at risk. A community, for example, that locates infrastructure near an earthquake fault zone or in a floodplain is much more likely to receive disaster assistance for destroyed government property than a community that is more prudent with its capital stock. Similarly, within a community individuals who locate in hazardous zones effectively put public works such as the streets and water and sewer lines serving their property at risk of loss. Those individuals benefit from the amenities of the high risk area, but they pass the costs of the risk on to society as a whole. Once, people viewed natural disasters as "acts of God" with no possibility of government or individual responsibility or fault. That perception has changed. Careful consideration shows that hazards are the product of the interaction of the environment and society, and that individuals and government can increase or decrease the degree of risk.

Equity issues are complicated by uncertainty and long time horizons. Construction in hazardous zones implies a risk not a certainty. Avoiding all building in an area could be undesirable if the risk is quite small. The person determining the risk and the one who bears the cost, however, are usually not the same. Also, whether people now living in hazard areas should be penalized for housing patterns shaped by decisions in the past is a difficult question. But, if adjustments are not made now, when the risks are known, then governments knowingly create problems for future generations. Despite those complications, we believe the level of inequity that exists with present policy toward hazards and public losses merits reform.

The policies of the federal government and many states also create inefficiency. Relying heavily on financial relief, for example, reduces the incentives for local governments to adopt risk elimination and reduction strategies that could reduce losses. Although data on the effectiveness of various mitigation strategies are very limited, estimates indicate reductions in losses of between 15 and 40 percent are possible. (Petak and Atkisson 1982) Unrestricted disaster relief payments also make it easier for local officials to ignore alternative risk transfer strategies such as insurance pools. Finally, failure to assign the costs of locating in hazardous areas to the residents adds to inefficiency in locational decisions. As we noted in Chapter 10, the nature of risk and uncertainty complicate natural hazards policy making. Efficiency should not be the sole criterion for choices, but it should be an important concern for decision makers.

Constraints on Policy Choices

The range of policy options is extensive. Various factors constrain whether those options can reach the public agenda, however, and what form the policies take. The agenda setting process is complex, and issues must meet certain conditions before they can be considered. (Mittler 1988) Previous chapters have identified many constraints that will shape the policy futures for hazards management. Four of these constraints are critical: (1) lack of information, (2) lack of resources, (3) fragmented policy setting, and (4) low salience. Clearly they are interdependent and reinforce each other at times.

Lack of Information

Risk management first requires that decision makers identify exposure to risk. As we discussed in Chapter 7, analyzing exposure requires information about the hazard, the capital at risk, and the relationship between hazard and damage. Policy makers, especially at the local level, have little of the required information. But, as we demonstrated in Chapter 9, they often do not realize the limitations in their ability to make rational choices in devising how to respond to threats posed by natural hazards. Also, not enough is known about the effectiveness, cost, and requirements of alternative risk management strategies. Lacking both an adequate understanding of risks and an adequate basis for choosing among risk management strategies, decision makers are apt to underestimate the risk to public property and to give inadequate consideration to policy alternatives and their consequences.

Collection and dissemination of information may be a valuable way to further risk management. The federal government has played a significant role with regard to assembling information about hazards, particularly floods as part of the National Flood Insurance Program. Thus, it is not surprising to us that respondents to our surveys generally showed more awareness of and responsiveness to flood risks than other hazards. There are several reasons why that is the case but information availability is almost certainly an important one. Equally important as the provision of better information, however, will be efforts to increase its salience to local officials.

Lack of Resources

Governments at all levels do not have unlimited resources to devote to social problems. The federal budget deficit severely limits policy options requiring substantial additional outlays. Cuts in existing relief and mitigation programs are not improbable. Many states and localities are similarly constrained. Limited management and technical personnel is a difficulty at the local level as well. Many communities cannot afford to hire the staff to match the responsibilities assigned to local governments. Communities also may not have the resources to collect information, evaluate alternatives, and implement policy options.

Financial limitations make it unlikely that new approaches such as a national insurance program that covered all hazards will be adopted because of the probable need for significant outlays to cover start-up costs. Risk management strategies such as restrictive zoning and stricter building codes that have only minimal public costs may be more popular in comparison, even though they engender opposition from the private sector. At the same time, however, that opposition limits the potential effectiveness of those measures in practice. Furthermore, small localities have a very limited capacity to adopt nonstructural mitigation strategies, but those are the jurisdictions that suffer the highest losses per capita, as we reported in Chapter 2. Technical assistance and managerial direction for hazards policy is apt to come from federal and state levels because of limited local staff available to work on hazard management programs.

Fragmented Policy Setting

Natural hazards policy making is fragmented among federal, state, and local levels of government, between different agencies at each level, and between the public and private sectors. The Building Seismic Safety Council, which was created in 1979 under the auspices of the National Institute of Building Sciences, for example, is made up of over 58 separate organizations that must agree on new standards to improve seismic safety of buildings. To actually apply any new standards they agree upon, the standards must be modified in over 16,000 code issuing jurisdictions in the nation, some at the state level, some at the local level, and some at both. (Dillon 1985) In addition, many federal agencies have their own construction requirements.

Differing priorities, perceived responsibilities, and resources cause separate units to pursue uncoordinated and even conflicting policies. The Federal Emergency Management Agency, for example, encourages the adoption of land use restrictions to reduce flooding while the Army Corps of Engineers encourages local governments to share the costs of flood control structures that will encourage floodplain development.

Federal efforts such as the National Earthquake Hazard Reduction Program encourage the adoption of stricter building codes to promote seismic safety while local governments hesitate to apply those measures because they may hinder economic growth. Regulatory approaches to hazards management are usually delegated to local officials, but as we demonstrated in Chapters 6 and 9, local officials often do not view natural hazards as a serious threat. Even agencies with similar mandates may have different priorities leading one to pursue financing strategies while the other focuses on mitigation with little or no effort made to harmonize the policies.

The possibility of coordinated comprehensive policy for natural hazards is low given the piecemeal nature of the policy process. The federal government has the greatest resources, but its ability to play a more active regulatory role is limited. Consideration of the impact of policy options on other governmental units as well as the interaction of different policies should become increasingly important.

Low Salience

Our survey of local officials and numerous other studies clearly show risk management related to natural hazards is of low priority for most policy makers. The current system fosters this inattention in part because localities lack incentives for addressing hazards. Federal and state disaster relief transfers risk away from communities struck by catastrophic events. Believing they are protected against large disasters, local officials have little reason to take corrective measures that could be costly, distracting, or unpopular. The uncertainty of natural hazards also lessens their importance to policy makers. As discussed in Chapters 9 and 10, people have a poor understanding of their exposure to loss. Furthermore, addressing low probability events is politically difficult; costs are incurred now, but the benefits are to be realized in some uncertain future.

We believe more of the risks posed by natural hazards should be returned to localities by reducing federal and state disaster relief funds for small losses (see Chapter 8). However, given the limited and contradictory information about how people respond to risks, the net result may not be more efficient behavior unless such a move is accompanied by substantial technical assistance or other measures to convince local governments that they should attend to potential losses from natural hazards. Direction and impetus for reform will probably have to come from hazard professionals primarily located at the federal or state level. And, actual adoption of policies may require a disaster or similar "window" to stimulate the public and politicians. Issue definition and preparation, however, is the responsibility of professional staff, and they need to have done their homework so that they can offer appropriate recommendations when the opportunity presents itself. (Mittler 1988) Linkage of hazards policy to other issues such as infrastructure rebuilding and expansion, community planning, and environmental protection also may be crucial for raising the salience of natural hazards.

Policy Futures

Given the constraints to policy innovation, changes to correct the flaws in public policy we have uncovered in this book are likely to be piecemeal. Comprehensive reform is unlikely given limited resources and the low priority of this issue. New policy will depend on the continued commitment to efficiency and equity by personnel within public agencies rather than on outside interests. Federal and state governments are in the best position to instigate and guide most changes although the process will clearly be intergovernmental with the success of implementation dependent on local actions. We think it is also likely that the basic approach to hazards policy will continue shifting from distributive measures such as disaster relief and structural protection to regulatory measures such as mandatory insurance, more stringent building and design codes and standards, and zoning. Finally, the need to connect hazards risk management to other issues that are more salient to policy makers will be important. With those considerations in mind, we next examine five interrelated policy options.

Identifying Exposure to Risk

It is important to identify the exposure of governments to risks from natural hazards. There are four reasons. First, information about risk exposure can foster political support. Increasing the awareness of the threats and potential losses can generate commitment from the public and policy makers for reform. Second, determining the nature of the risk will narrow policy choices. Appropriate options for a low frequency/low severity hazards are dissimilar from those for high frequency/high severity threats. Earthquake risks need to be addressed by policies different from flood risks. Third, many options require risk exposure information for implementation. Establishing a hazards insurance pool for communities, for example, would necessitate being able to determine differing levels of risk. Fourth, risk exposure information is necessary to avoid wasting public funds on risk avoidance and risk reduction when the risk, in fact, is slight.

Assessing exposure to risk requires knowledge about the nature and severity of the potential hazard, the types and amounts of capital at risk, and the relationship between hazard intensity and damage to property. The availability of that information varies significantly with data on the severity of the hazard most likely to be deficient. Information about the hazard and damage functions can probably best be collected and distributed by federal agencies and state governments. Economies of scale and limited technical expertise make more centralized efforts preferable. Assembling data on the location and value of public property should be a local task given that localities have great variability in capital stock and that they already have (or should develop) some type of property inventory. The types of information and assistance that are needed must be shaped by which risk control policies are contemplated.

To further identify risk exposure, federal and state policy could focus on collecting data on hazards, sponsoring research to determine damage functions, developing practical risk analysis methods for local officials, and providing technical assistance. (For ideas about how to disseminate technical information to local infrastructure managers, see Nigg 1986.) To varying degrees those tasks already are being done with some hazards and in some parts of the country. The National Flood Insurance Program has provided most communities seriously at risk from floods with some flood hazard information (Burby and French 1985), and where state mandates require it, such as in California, earthquake hazard information is increasingly available. As we noted earlier, that may explain part of the reason local officials are more likely to have addressed flood hazards than other environmental risks and why officials in California have begun to address earthquake hazards that, in other states, are usually ignored. Extension of federal and state efforts to similar approaches with other hazards would probably yield worthwhile results. Support for informational activities represents a subsidy for at-risk communities, but to the extent that dissemination of this information promotes more effective local risk control, the cost may be lower than disaster assistance.

Localities need to increase their knowledge of the amount and types of public property at risk. Given the low priority of hazards management on local agendas, that will not be easy. As we discussed in Chapter 7, the specific component approach to risk analysis (the most accurate) would be quite costly due to the level of detail on the capital inventory that would be required. Other approaches would be less costly but would also be less accurate. The level of detail needed depends on the risk control policies of interest. In order to ensure that information about capital facilities and their vulnerability to loss is available to decision makers, disaster or technical assistance from federal and state sources may need to be conditioned on local efforts to assemble that information.

Also, vulnerability assessment might be attached to the broader issue of public infrastructure policy. Public agencies are apt to increase efforts to keep track of the condition and value of property in order to increase the efficiency of capital stock management. Information collection for hazards management could be part of that work with only marginal added costs. The greater salience of infrastructure issues on the public agenda could pull hazards management along. Similarly, a large national effort has been underway for two decades to upgrade and rehabilitate the nation's infrastructure. Bridges, sewage treatment, water treatment, and other facilities have attracted federal aid for that work. Federal assistance should be conditioned on the concurrent assessment of the vulnerability of aided infrastructure to loss and retrofits to reduce vulnerability where that is cost effective. That, in fact, has been suggested with regard to federal transportation investments (see Gordon 1987 and Martin, Lame and Crouse 1987), and the advice seems equally applicable to other infrastructure.

Elimination of Risk

Elimination of risk refers to locating or reconstructing buildings and other public works so as to minimize exposure to hazards. For existing infrastructure that would require relocation or retrofits, and frequently neither is a viable option, since the cost of relocating or strengthening buildings, roads, and other public property to totally eliminate the threat of loss is usually prohibitive. Furthermore, relocation is difficult because areas that are already developed can not easily be stripped of the public infrastructure without also removing private homes and businesses. The political, economic, and social implications make that alternative nearly impossible.

For new construction, eliminating risk is politically feasible in many communities. The primary method for control is restrictive land use and building regulations. One projection of reductions in losses from tsunami, storm surge, and riverine flooding by banning new development in hazard areas after 1980 is 30 percent or $2.4 billion per year by the year 2000 for public and private property. (Petak and Atkisson 1982; also see Sheaffer and Roland 1981)

Prohibiting development in certain areas has limitations as a risk control strategy, however, since not all natural hazards can be localized to a suitable degree. Areas at risk from riverine flooding, storm surge, and landslides can usually be determined with acceptable accuracy for small areas, but the area threatened by earthquakes and tornadoes is typically so extensive as to make banning development infeasible except in very limited areas, such as those subject to soil liquefaction and directly adjacent to fault lines. Proscribing development in heavily urban areas with hazards may be unacceptable for economic reasons as well.

Leaving land within a flood zone empty (even if a flood has wiped out the previous structures) might be undesirable. The potential economic benefits associated with new construction may outweigh the risks from flooding. In that case, cities might choose to ignore the risk or rely on other forms of risk control. However, the land may have value in an undeveloped state that goes beyond risk control. Recreation or environmental protection may be other alternative and simultaneous reasons for prohibiting new construction. Also many creative communities have discovered that banning construction on undeveloped land may attract development on adjacent, less hazardous land or in other forms such as increased tourism. (See Kusler 1982a and Kusler 1982b.)

Risk elimination policy options are again marked by the need for intergovernmental action. Implementing restrictive building and land use regulations traditionally is left to local governments. Due to the low priority of hazards management, however, the competing concerns for economic development and private property rights frequently make localities reluctant to ban new construction. Remember that our 1988 survey of local officials revealed that fewer than half of the local governments we queried had adopted measures to eliminate or reduce risks from natural hazards (see Chapter 6). But, the benefits and costs of this strategy typically extend across political boundaries. The value of undeveloped land, as we mentioned above, often extends beyond risk control to environmental concerns, and environmental benefits often transcend city lines. Because of that, a number of states have enacted legislation to protect particularly sensitive environments. Finally, if local decision makers choose to ignore the risk altogether, they have effectively transferred it and its cost to federal and state disaster assistance programs.

Risk elimination strategies should be used more frequently. Because of the need for intergovernmental action, federal and state incentives and mandates to ensure that localities consider this strategy are necessary and need to be increased. Federal disaster relief and the National Flood Insurance Program already contain provisions that are designed to encourage localities to avoid new construction in flood-prone areas. However, those incentives are not particularly effective; there is ample evidence, for example, that the National Flood Insurance Program has not halted development in flood zones. (Burby and French et al. 1985; Burby et al. 1988) That failure may not be due to inappropriate incentives but stronger competing economic forces. Consequently, strengthening the incentives for local risk elimination may not be effective, but it should be evaluated by federal policy makers.

States can effectively encourage restrictive zoning through comprehensive planning requirements or environmental restrictions. Requirements to ban all new development in clearly defined hazardous areas would not be practical because of the extreme variety in local physical and social needs. However, by forcing localities to consider the best use of undeveloped land through both planning and environmental impact assessment requirements (an approach used by the state of California), states increase the likelihood that risk elimination will be considered. Linkage of hazards management to planning and environmental protection concerns also is an important aspect of this policy strategy.

The National Flood Insurance Act authorizes FEMA to require similar measures as a condition for community participation in the NFIP, but the agency has yet to require community planning for flood hazard areas. The experiences of California and states with similar mandates indicate to us that planning could be an effective tool for fostering greater attention to risk elimination. Because of that, we think FEMA should explore using its authority to mandate such planning.

Reduction of Risk

Reduction of risk through hazard mitigation is an essential part of any hazards management policy. Not all losses can be avoided, but preventing or reducing damage lowers the cost of disaster response and recovery (paying now to avoid paying more later). Mitigation also is important for ensuring equity when the financing of risk is shared by multiple parties. Unfortunately, only limited data are available on the costs and benefits of alternative mitigation strategies. Lack of knowledge about which policies are effective, what they cost, and how they compare is a serious deficiency.

Federal policy focuses on reducing future risks primarily by influencing the location and design of new development. In the case of flood and hurricane risks it does that through Executive Order 11988, which requires federal agencies to avoid uneconomic, unnecessary and hazardous use of floodplains, and the National Flood Insurance Program, which includes location and design standards for public buildings and for public infrastructure associated with land development projects. The federal flood insurance program, however, does not insure a variety of infrastructure—roads, utility lines, water and sewage treatment plants, storm drainage, for example—and as a result does not affect the design standards applied to those facilities. In the case of earthquake hazards, the federal government does not mandate location and design standards at all. Instead, through the National Earthquake Hazard Reduction Program (initiated with the Earthquake Hazards Reduction Act of 1977) the government has fostered the development of new design standards and their adoption by the national building code organizations and state and local governments. (Fratto 1987)

Federal efforts to foster risk reduction in new development do not appear to be very effective. The process of code revision is painfully slow, given the fragmented character of the regulatory system and a lack of consensus about the cost effectiveness of more stringent standards to reduce losses from earthquakes, floods, and other natural hazards. (Dillon 1985; Mushkatel and Weschler 1985) In general, progress occurs not as a result of federal persuasion but as a policy response to each new catastrophic event that demonstrates the inadequacies of existing standards and raises, for a short time, the political salience of the hazard. Furthermore, as we reported in Chapter 6, many local governments have ignored the risks of catastrophic losses from natural hazards. Thus, much stronger mandates for risk reduction, possibly attached to federal grants-in-aid for infrastructure, seem necessary to us.

If reform is limited to standards attached to new construction, however, it will be decades before risks to infrastructure are reduced significantly. That stems from the fact that risk exposure represented by new infra-structure is dwarfed by the exposure represented by existing public works at risk from natural hazards. Thus, Sheaffer and Roland (1981) demonstrated that even with the application of Draconian land use regulations, average annual flood losses would not be reduced substan-tially. In short, then, risk reduction measures limited to new construction will not have much effect on annual losses to the public sector.

Reducing losses to existing property at risk is infinitely more difficult than dealing with new construction. The dimensions of the problem are suggested by these statistics on the U.S. highway system (recall from Chapter 2 that highways absorbed over half of total infrastructure losses between 1980 and mid-1987): 3.87 million miles of roadways, of which only 683,000 are in urban areas; and 563,000 bridges, of which 105,000 are structurally deficient. (Fratto 1987) Thus, just identifying vulnerable public works—a step we recommended earlier in this chapter—is an enormous job. Once that is accomplished, finding the funds and political will to undertake cost effective retrofits will be a substantial challenge for policy makers at all levels of government.

Nevertheless, institutional mechanisms are in place to foster greater attention to risk reduction. The Federal Highway Administration, for example, has considerable influence on engineering and construction practices of states and local governments. FHWA has developed methods for evaluating risks from natural hazards based on economic optimization analysis of costs and benefits. In the case of flood hazards, for example, the agency mandates least cost analyses that take into account total costs, including flood damages, over the projected life of a structure. (Federal Highway Administration 1980) In general, federal aid highways allow conveyance of 100-year floods without damage. Most states, however, require bridges for nonfederal highways to pass somewhere between the 25- and 100-year storm and culverts that can be replaced more frequently may be designed for 10- to 50-year storms. (Sheaffer et al. 1976) The problem is this: over half of national flood losses result from events that exceed all of those standards (i.e., from floods with a lower than 1 percent chance of occurring in any given year). Thus, reduction of flood losses to highways may require the application of stricter standards than are now typical.

The case of earthquake risks to highways suggests that public agencies can be persuaded of the cost effectiveness of more stringent standards to reduce the risk of loss. After the San Fernando earthquake in 1971, for example, the California Department of Transportation re-evaluated its standards for bridges that prior to the large losses in that earthquake had seemed adequate (losses over the preceding forty years had been only $100,000). (Gates 1987) Based on new standards, CALTRANS retrofitted bridges throughout California. Also, those revised standards were subsequently modified and adopted by the Association of State Highway and Transportation Officials for national use. ASHTO revised the standards again in response to new standards promulgated by the Applied Technology Council in 1981 and, we suspect, they may be strengthened further after technical analyses of losses to the highway system from the 1989 Loma Prieta earthquake in the San Francisco region.

Federal and state influences on the design and retrofitting of highways illustrate the potential for policy leadership that could occur across a number of infrastructure systems. The U.S. Environmental Protection Agency, for example, sets standards for the design of sewage and water treatment plants and will have an increasing impact on the design of stormwater management facilities. The agency has paid attention to flood hazards in the past, but its primary concern has been the effect of flooding on wastewater treatment effectiveness and not property damage; thus, its standards could be reviewed and, if appropriate, strengthened. (Sheaffer et al. 1976) The U.S. Department of Housing and Urban Development's minimum property standards have influenced the standards for buildings employed by the four principal national building codes (Southern Standard Building Code, Uniform Building Code, BOCA Basic Building Code, and National Building Code). Those codes have traditionally not paid much attention to flood or earthquake hazards, but through the leadership of the National Earthquake Hazard Reduction Program, Building Seismic Safety Council, and other organizations that situation is likely to change dramatically. (See Building Seismic Safety Council 1986.)

We believe that risk reduction will become an increasingly important policy strategy as the portion of the nation's population at risk from natural hazards continues to escalate. Through the National Flood Insurance Program and the National Earthquake Hazard Reduction Program, both of which are housed in the Federal Emergency Management Agency, mechanisms are in place to move forward with a unified national program to reduce losses from natural hazards. The lack of attention to hazards at the state and local level, which we have documented amply in this book, emphasizes the critical importance of federal leadership in dealing with losses to the public sector. We believe it is very important that Congress provide adequate funding for those programs as a way of avoiding much larger expenditures on disaster relief.

Assumption of Risk

Even with the most effective loss reduction techniques, disasters will still occur. Local governments can either pass the risk on to someone else or assume the risk. Assumption of risk is not always a planned strategy. Inadequate risk identification or hazards mitigation may unexpectedly expose a locality to financial loss. Local officials in our 1987 survey indicated very strongly that assuming financial risks was much less desirable than transferring risk by relying on federal and state disaster relief (see Chapter 2). As long as there are few restrictions on disaster relief, localities have little incentive to assume more risk or to pass risk backward to hazard area property owners, who after all, are frequently the main beneficiaries of infrastructure located in and serving hazardous areas. The ability of local governments to assume more risk will depend on the severity and frequency of the hazard and the financial resources of the government.

Most communities can cover the costs of low-severity events. Forcing or enticing them to assume the risks associated with high-severity events should lead to more efficient decisions about the location and design of public facilities. Given the contradictory results of the available research on how people respond to risk, however, the economic presumption of greater efficiency is not guaranteed. But, making localities assume more of their own risk can be justified on equity grounds as well. Communities should be expected to pay for their losses that do not exceed the financial resources of their government.

Federal and state disaster relief could be restructured to not provide assistance for small losses—for example, losses up to $10 or $15 per capita—thus making localities assume that risk. Relatively small risks of that magnitude are arguably not a financial disaster when spread across all of the residents of a community. Most localities already recognize the need to be prepared for some unexpected expenses and should be able to handle those costs. Local government costs now reimbursed through federal disaster relief, however, are highly skewed toward small losses. As we noted in Chapter 2, approximately two thirds of the governments receiving federal aid for losses in natural disasters between 1980 and mid-1987 had losses under $50,000, and over 20 percent had losses under $5,000. Most communities can cover losses of that magnitude.

Measures such as per capita losses or losses as percentage of budget would give consideration to differing abilities to pay. Using measures such as per capita losses recognizes the importance of considering the severity of disasters for a local community (see Wright et al. 1979 for a discussion of impact ratios). Our case study of the Whittier Narrows earthquake (reported in Chapter 3), for example, found that while the City of Los Angeles had eligible losses twice as high as the City of Whittier, Whittier's per capita losses were 21 times greater. Arguably, Los Angeles' loss was not catastrophic and perhaps should have been a local responsibility in spite of its size.

An alternative approach would be for federal and state disaster relief to require more cost sharing from states and localities. Federal relief covers 75 percent of eligible losses. Changing that to a lower share would make localities assume more risk. A sliding percentage based on local ability to finance the loss would be a further variation. FEMA has made similar proposals in the last ten years but encountered resistance from states and local governments, particularly on increasing state and local cost sharing. (Settle 1990) Given the political support for disaster relief and lack of financial alternatives, there are political limits to how much risk could be shifted back to communities. However, changes in that direction should certainly give localities more incentive to adopt measures to reduce future losses.

Local governments have two policy options in assuming losses. The first is to treat the loss as an operating expense. The size and tightness of the budget are the factors that limit that choice. The larger the budget and the less competition for funds, the easier the operating budget option is. One rule of thumb suggests that no single loss should be greater than 1 percent of the annual operating budget; thus, the method is limited to small losses.

The second option is to cover losses from reserve or contingency funds. Those funds could be general purpose or targeted for hazards losses only. Given the uncertainty and low salience of natural hazards, a general purpose fund is the only feasible approach. The level of the reserve should be based on the risk exposure and the resources of the community. As noted in Chapter 4, a fund balance of 5 percent is the traditional recommendation for reserves to cover all contingencies, not just natural hazards. However if federal and state authorities elect or return more risk to localities, a higher balance may be needed. Small jurisdictions (which tend to suffer higher losses per capita in natural disasters) and poor communities may be less able to raise sufficient funds. To ensure equity state and federal policy must take account of local financial capacity.

The potential savings from self insurance through the use of reserves and contingency funds can be substantial when compared to regular insurance. If a locality assesses its risk as being high, however, self insurance may no longer be desirable. Obtaining catastrophic coverage, though, would generally be easier if the community has continued to assume some level of risk. Ensuring that localities have adequate reserves may be difficult, however. Again linkage with other concerns such as liability and aid for financing new infrastructure may be necessary in order for hazards management to be considered. The assumption of risk by a local government should be taken as part of a multiple strategy which also emphasizes mitigation measures.

Transfer of Risk

Whether due to risk aversion or the threat of catastrophic loss, governments may choose to transfer the risk of hazard losses to individuals, commercial insurance, or other governmental units. Federal and state disaster relief programs are the primary method by which risk is transferred for natural disasters. Transference of risk is not by itself inefficient. As discussed in Chapter 8, assuming individuals and communities are risk averse, risk-pooling or risk-spreading have economic benefits.

Local governments also can seek to transfer risks to public property to individuals. Rather than prohibiting development in hazardous areas, governments can use regulatory and taxing power to make the occupants bear the risk for public facilities located there. Our 1987 survey of local officials revealed that 80 percent of their governments required the private sector to provide or pay for public facilities serving new development. Furthermore, 65 percent required developers to meet special standards for infrastructure built in hazardous areas. Few governments, however, have tried to pass on such costs to current residents. When we asked officials responding to our 1988 survey about the use of special tax districts or user fees for natural hazards, both of which have theoretical appeal since the risks to public infrastructure would be borne by beneficiaries, they indicated neither would be feasible politically. In addition to political difficulties, the level of risk information necessary to implement such taxes may be beyond the technical capacity of most localities, and they are also expensive to administer. Furthermore, such taxes could be regressive in some communities while progressive in others. All of those factors make this option unlikely for wide adoption at this time.

Transferring risk to commercial insurers does not offer a complete alternative for managing natural hazards risks but should be used more. Commercial insurance generally does not cover damage to roads, debris removal, or emergency services, and those costs represent more than three-fourths of the public losses incurred. Commercial insurers also have been reluctant to cover all natural hazards because losses from some hazards, such as earthquakes, are not independent and may result in extensive claims with potentially catastrophic losses to the insurance industry. Despite those limitations, governments can make greater use of commercial insurance. But, our survey results reported in Chapter 9 indicate that as long as the purchase of insurance is voluntary and federal and state disaster relief are available, low perception of the risk of loss in combination with multiple veto points in local government will limit sharply the use of insurance in the management of risks from natural hazards. Reducing disaster relief in and of itself is not likely to stimulate the voluntary purchase of insurance because government officials, like private individuals, simply ignore the probability of loss.

Transferring all risks of loss from natural hazards to public insurance, as advocated by Petak and Atkisson (1983), has promise, but except for the small proportion of risk covered by the National Flood Insurance Program, it is as yet untried. Another possibility is to transfer risk to an insurance pool. Because of unavailability and dissatisfaction with private insurance, communities too small to self insure have formed insurance pools in the last fifteen years. Pools have been established primarily for workers' compensation and liability risks. In spite of the potential advantages of lower cost, professional management, and greater control than commercial insurance, it is unclear to us whether a natural hazards pool could work. The nature of hazards creates two major obstacles not found with other types of pools. First, natural disasters are often catastrophic and affect large areas. A pool would probably have to cover several states or even be national in scope in order to ensure that large losses could be spread sufficiently. Second, the level of risk is extremely variable among communities. The ability to determine relative levels of risk would be necessary to equitably assess rates and mitigation needs (as we showed in Chapter 7, that should be feasible technically though expensive). Failure to account for differences might lead to low participation or adverse selection. However, the costs of identifying relative levels of risk for insurance purposes may discourage consideration of this approach.

A variation on risk pooling would be for the federal government to participate in order to overcome the obstacle to pooling created by high severity events. The federal government with its greater resources would act as a reinsurer or simply assume large losses. Local governments would be required to participate in an insurance pool covering moderate losses and to assume small losses. If such a program required additional federal outlays due to expanded coverage of local losses or demands for additional administration, its acceptance by Congress is doubtful. The federal deficit makes significant extension of federal responsibilities nearly impossible. To the extent self-insurance and a pool reduced claims for disaster funds, however, substitution of federal outlays would minimize that difficulty. Regardless, as with a regular insurance pool, concerns about equity may create problems that cannot be addressed easily. For the near future any type of insurance pool for hazards risk is unlikely. The obstacles and uncertainly make this choice infeasible. Nevertheless, the potential is substantial and many parties remain interested. Further research is needed to determine the needs and feasibility of a risk pool for natural disasters.

One final method for transferring risk would be to extend the National Flood Insurance Program to other hazards. As mentioned earlier, the NFIP may reduce demands for disaster relief by transferring costs to those at risk. But the program has not halted development in flood zones and may have encouraged more building. Furthermore, even with subsidized flood insurance, losses from flooding still absorbs the largest share of disaster relief. Expansion to other hazards is likely to further increase federal financial obligations.

Changes in federal and state disaster relief have already been discussed under assumption of risk. Because of the intergovernmental and interdependent nature of hazards policy, reform of disaster relief may be the critical issue. Local governments have developed the expectation that after a disaster federal aid will follow. Because of the forces limiting change, disaster relief will continue to be a major focus of risk management. However, more efficient and equitable outcomes will necessitate altering communities' reliance on federal funds. Facing only limited risk, localities have little incentive to adopt mitigation options, self insurance, or risk sharing pools unless required to do so as a condition for federal aid. Clear and definite changes in federal and state disaster relief policy can create that incentive by increasing the degree of risk assumed by

localities and by conditioning eligibility for federal aid on the adoption
of additional risk reduction measures.

A Proposal for Reform of Federal Disaster Relief

After considering the different constraints to policy options for managing natural hazard risks and examining the distribution of losses reimbursed by federal funding, we believe there is a need for reform of current federal disaster relief. A tentative proposal which improves equity and efficiency is offered here to stimulate discussion.

A two- or three-tiered system for financing public infrastructure losses should replace the current federal program. These tiers would be determined by a measure of the severity of public losses. As mentioned earlier, the concept of an impact ratio (resources lost/resources available) (Wright et al. 1979) is compelling as it recognizes that the severity of losses for communities varies significantly. Federal policy should be altered to recognize such variations and take different approaches for different levels or tiers of losses.

A variety of alternative formulations of such an impact ratio are possible. We believe that losses per capita weighted by per capita income makes the most sense. Losses per capita is simple to calculate and easy to understand. A simple measure minimizes complicated regulations and formulas which eases the burden on federal, state and local officials for determining eligibility and coverage. As noted in several places, local officials are often frustrated by not knowing whether they qualify for disaster relief. Shifting to an impact ratio also improves equity by providing aid for small localized disasters that have high impacts but which are not large enough to warrant a Presidential disaster declaration. Such communities are presently not eligible for federal relief. Because of differing abilities to pay, a per capita loss measure should account for income variations across communities. Other more involved impact ratios are likely to correlate highly with a per capita measure but be more complex or reflect differences in public spending philosophy which should not be the basis for variations in assistance.

In its simplest form, we would suggest a two-tier system with a hazard losses deductible. Communities would be responsible for the first $X per capita in infrastructure losses. Communities below that threshold would be responsible for all losses. Communities above the threshold would only be responsible for the first $X after which the federal government would cover 100 percent of eligible losses. The threshold amount would vary depending upon the community income level. For example, a community with an income level twice the national average would have a deductible of $2X, while a community with half the national income average would have a deductible of $.5X. All communities would thus face the same level of financial risk regardless of the size of the loss. No community would at risk for more than the deductible amount.

Determining the appropriate deductible amount will require further research. As discussed in Chapter 8, per capita deductibles on the order of $50 ($200 for household of four persons) might be comparable to the levels of risk commonly assumed with various types of individual insurance. However, since losses under this plan would be faced by all persons simultaneously (similar to everyone in a city having a car accident the same day) that might be too high. Additionally, a proportion of individuals in the community would also be facing private losses and that may argue further for a lower deductible.

For the period 1980 to mid-1987, 2,272 reimbursements were made to cities and towns with population of 2,500 or more that suffered losses totalling $347 million. If those communities received 75 percent of their eligible losses in aid, federal payments would have totaled $260 million. For illustrative purposes, Table 11.1 provides results of a simulation of the changes that would occur with our proposed reform of federal disaster relief policy with various deductible levels in comparison with current federal reimbursement of 75 percent of eligible losses. If a $5 deductible (weighted for community income differences) had been in effect during the period 1980 through mid-1987, only 37 percent of the communities that received federal disaster assistance would have been eligible for aid, and total federal payments to those communities would have been 66 percent of the payments that were made under current federal policy. With a deductible of $25, less than 7 percent of the communities would have had losses above the deductible, and federal payments would have been reduced to 19 percent of those made with the current policy.

Even modest deductibles could significantly reduce federal outlays while at the same time reimbursing local governments for 100 percent (rather than 75 percent) of eligible costs for losses above the deductible. This two-tiered proposal would reduce the number of local governments receiving aid but would thereby focus relief assistance more clearly on only those communities that truly suffered a disastrous loss. By making all localities bear the risk for non-disastrous losses, the relief policy we propose would give local governments an increased incentive for taking appropriate risk management actions, such as more restrictive zoning, special building codes, or insurance coverage where available. The proposal maintains aid for hard-hit communities but is structured to equitably and efficiently distribute the bulk of risk back to local governments. Because of the large reductions in federal relief costs possible,

TABLE 11.1

Simulated Disaster Relief Payments for Losses to Cities of
2,500 or More Population in Natural Disasters, 1980 - 1987[a]

Deductible[b]	Number of Cities Aided	Percent Receiving Federal Assistance	Federal Assistance Payments (millions)	Percent of Current Aid
$ 0 (Current Policy)	2,272	100%	$ 260.0	100%
$ 5	829	37%	$ 171.9	66%
$10	454	20%	$ 116.3	45%
$15	301	13%	$ 85.1	33%
$20	226	10%	$ 64.0	25%
$25	167	7%	$ 48.6	19%
$50	72	3%	$ 21.8	8%

[a]This simulation examines losses in Presidentially
declared disasters only. Since losses to cities in
smaller disasters that did not merit a Presidential
disaster declaration would be covered by the relief policy
we propose, the number of cities aided and amount of
federal assistance payments would increase somewhat had
information for those cities been available. That
increase would not be large, however, because the per
capita deductibles would eliminate all but the most hard-
hit communities from federal assistance.

[b]The listed deductible is a nominal amount. The actual
deductible for each city is the nominal deductible
multiplied by an adjustment factor (national per capita
income/city per capita income).

federal policy could be further altered to expand assistance for the hardest hit communities. For example, with a deductible of $25 the federal government could cover not only the depreciated cost of lost infrastructure as an eligible loss (the current policy) but also some portion of the replacement cost as well.

A variation on this two-tiered proposal would be a three-tiered approach. Federal disaster relief would be set up following the two-tiered approach with a high deductible such as $50 per capita. Eligible losses above that level would be covered at 100 percent by federal relief payments. All communities would also be eligible to participate in a federal hazards insurance program for public infrastructure losses. Under this insurance program communities would still have to meet a modest per capita deductible, $10 for example. After that level of loss, the insurance program would cover losses up to the $50 per capita level at which point traditional relief would take over. To receive insurance payments, however, communities would have to pay a premium. Because of the relief for large disasters and the deductibles for small disasters, the insurance program would only be covering about 25 percent of current federal disaster relief payments. Thus, the annual premium rates would be very modest and affordable, probably between 5 and 15 cents per capita. In order to encourage enrollment in the insurance program, participation might be a condition for disaster relief. However, it might also be acceptable to just let communities decide for themselves if avoiding these intermediate risks was worth the small insurance premium.

This three-tiered system is thus set up with a low risk level where communities bear the risk (below $10 per capita in the example), an intermediate risk (between $10 and $50 per capita) where the risk is covered by insurance or self-insured if a community so chooses, and high risk (above $50 per capita) where traditional relief kicks in. Because of the specific and unpredictable nature of large disasters, relief rather than insurance will probably always be a better way to finance losses for extreme events. Because this proposal, like the two-tiered proposal, will reduce federal disaster relief outlays, federal subsidies for startup costs and possibly initial administration may be desirable. As with the two-tiered proposal, this policy would offer improvements in equity and efficiency as well as reduce federal expenditures. However, the difficulty and responsibility of administering an insurance program may not be worth the gains over the simpler two-tiered proposal.

Appendix A
Questionnaire for 1987 Survey
of Risk Managers/Finance Directors

PUBLIC FACILITY RISK MANAGEMENT

> Questionnaire for
> **Risk Managers/Directors of Finance**

Conducted By

Center for Urban and Regional Studies
University of North Carolina at Chapel Hill

In Cooperation With

California Polytechnic University, San Luis Obispo
North Carolina State University
Washington State University

Supported By

National Science Foundation
Washington, DC 20550

May 1987

Public Facility Risk Management

Public Facility Risk Management　　　　1

WHAT THIS SURVEY IS ABOUT

- This survey is designed to provide information about local governments' approaches to coping with potential losses to public facilities from natural disasters such as earthquakes, floods, hurricanes, and landslides.

- We are particularly interested in your government's procedures in financing and managing capital assets and your experiences with past natural disasters. We would also like your opinions about the feasibility of insurance and other methods of dealing with catastrophic losses to various types of public facilities not currently insurable, such as streets and storm drainage works.

WHAT WILL BE DONE WITH THE INFORMATION

- Statistical summaries of your opinions and approaches to dealing with potential losses will be put together in a report that will be presented to CONGRESS, FEDERAL, STATE, AND LOCAL AGENCIES that are responsible for disaster assistance programs and to various professional associations that are helping with this study.

- NO INFORMATION YOU GIVE US WILL BE REVEALED TO ANYONE IN A WAY THAT CAN IDENTIFY YOU.

HOW YOUR GOVERNMENT WAS CHOSEN TO FILL OUT THIS QUESTIONNAIRE

- Your government was selected at random from a list of local governments that have received federal assistance in recovering from a natural disaster during the period 1981 through 1985.

- Because governments were selected by chance, the results will provide an unbiased picture of local experiences in coping with potential losses to public facilities from natural disasters.

HOW TO FILL OUT THE QUESTIONNAIRE

- Most of the questions can be answered by circling a number or word that corresponds to your answer; for example:

  What is the population of your jurisdiction?

  1 Less than 10,000

  (2) 10,000 – 24,999

  3 25,000 – 49,999

  4 50,000 – 99,999

  5 100,000 or more

PLEASE ANSWER EVERY QUESTION THAT APPLIES TO YOUR GOVERNMENT

IF YOU HAVE ANY QUESTIONS ABOUT THE SURVEY CALL DR. RAYMOND J. BURBY COLLECT AT (919) 962-3074.

The first series of questions deals with natural hazards that threaten your government and the public facilities it owns and operates. We are interested in your government's attitudes towards hazards and its experiences with actual disasters since 1980.

1. How would you characterize the degree of risk each of the following hazards presents to your government's public buildings and other infrastructure? If you do not have precise information about each hazard, please make your best guess.

	Circle One for Each Hazard			
Coastal Storm	Very Threatening	Somewhat Threatening	Slightly Threatening	Not at All Threatening
Earthquake	Very Threatening	Somewhat Threatening	Slightly Threatening	Not at All Threatening
Flood	Very Threatening	Somewhat Threatening	Slightly Threatening	Not at All Threatening
Hurricane	Very Threatening	Somewhat Threatening	Slightly Threatening	Not at All Threatening

2. Over the next year, what is your best guess of the odds of each of the following natural hazards causing significant damage—damage beyond your government's ability to finance repairs and reconstruction—to buildings and other infrastructure it owns?

	Circle One for Each Hazard					
Coastal Storm	Zero, No Chance	1 in 10,000	1 in 1000	1 in 500	1 in 100	1 in 10 or greater
Earthquake	Zero, No Chance	1 in 10,000	1 in 1000	1 in 500	1 in 100	1 in 10 or greater
Flood	Zero, No Chance	1 in 10,000	1 in 1000	1 in 500	1 in 100	1 in 10 or greater
Hurricane	Zero, No Chance	1 in 10,000	1 in 1000	1 in 500	1 in 100	1 in 10 or greater

3. How concerned would you say your government is that a disaster resulting from each of the hazards listed below will actually occur during the next year? (Circle one answer for each hazard; if a hazard poses no threat at all to your government, circle N/A to the far right.)

	Circle One for Each Hazard				
Coastal Storm	Not at All Concerned	Slightly Concerned	Moderately Concerned	Very Concerned	N/A
Earthquake	Not At All Concerned	Slightly Concerned	Moderately Concerned	Very Concerned	N/A

	Circle One for Each Hazard				
Flood	Not at All Concerned	Slightly Concerned	Moderately Concerned	Very Concerned	N/A
Hurricane	Not at All Concerned	Slightly Concerned	Moderately Concerned	Very Concerned	N/A

4. In comparison with your government's spending to alleviate other problems, in your opinion how important does it consider spending to deal with threats posed by natural hazards? (Circle)

1 Very unimportant
2 Somewhat unimportant
3 Neither important nor unimportant
4 Somewhat important
5 Very important

Federal records indicate that your government experienced a

_____ coastal storm
_____ earthquake
_____ flood
_____ hurricane

disaster in 19_____ .

THE REMAINING QUESTIONS IN THIS SECTION DEAL WITH THAT SPECIFIC DISASTER.

---

5. First, please circle all of the following public facilities owned or operated by your government that you know were damaged in that event. If you don't know of any that were damaged, circle 13.

1 Public buildings
2 Streets, roads, or sidewalks
3 Bridges
4 Water treatment plant
5 Water distribution lines
6 Sewage treatment plant
7 Sewer lines
8 Electric power lines or substations
9 Storm drainage/flood control facilities
10 Parks and recreation facilities, including buildings
11 Stadiums, convention centers, etc.
12 Other (e.g., ports, airports) (Specify: _____)
13 Don't know of any facilities that were damaged

6. In round numbers, what would you estimate was the total direct cost (exclude cleanup and indirect costs) of reconstructing public facilities owned by your government that were damaged in that disaster? (If you are unable to make this estimate, circle 1 below)

TOTAL COSTS OF RECONSTRUCTION: $ _____

1 Unable to estimate costs

7. Were any facilities owned by your government abandoned (not repaired or reconstructed) after being damaged in that disaster? (Circle)

1 No
2 Don't know
3 Yes

a. What would you estimate was the total repair/replacement cost of those facilities? (If you are unable to make this estimate, circle 1 below)

REPAIR/REPLACEMENT COST FOR ABANDONED FACILITIES: $ _____

1 Unable to estimate costs

b. Why were facilities abandoned? (Circle all that apply; if you do not know, circle 6)

1 Not cost effective to repair
2 No longer needed by government
3 Funds for repair/reconstruction not available
4 Too susceptible to recurring damage in future
5 Other reasons (Specify: _____)
6 Don't know

8. In financing reconstruction of public facilities, how important was each of the following sources of funds? If it was very important, circle 1; if it was very unimportant, circle 5. If it was somewhere in between, circle 2, 3 or 4. If the funding source was not used, circle N/A. If you do not know whether it was used or how important it was, circle D/K.

	Circle One for Each Source of Funding						
	Very Important				Very Unimportant		
Insurance	1	2	3	4	5	N/A	D/K
Insurance pools	1	2	3	4	5	N/A	D/K
Federal disaster assistance grants	1	2	3	4	5	N/A	D/K
Federal disaster assistance loans	1	2	3	4	5	N/A	D/K

| | Circle One for Each Source of Funding | | | | | | |
	Very Important				Very Unimportant		
State disaster assistance grants	1	2	3	4	5	N/A	D/K
State disaster assistance loans	1	2	3	4	5	N/A	D/K
Local contingency funds	1	2	3	4	5	N/A	D/K
Reserves accumulated for capital construction	1	2	3	4	5	N/A	D/K
General obligation bonds	1	2	3	4	5	N/A	D/K
Revenue bonds	1	2	3	4	5	N/A	D/K
One-time charges levied on benefited parties (special assessments, etc.)	1	2	3	4	5	N/A	D/K
Emergency taxes or user fees	1	2	3	4	5	N/A	D/K
Other sources of funds (Specify: _____)	1	2	3	4	5	N/A	D/K

9. How long did it take to receive funds from each of the following sources of disaster assistance? (Circle one for each source; if the source of assistance was not used, circle N/A; if you do not know how long it took to receive funds, circle D/K)

	Circle One for Each Source of Assistance					
Commercial insurance	Under 1 Month	1-3 Months	4-6 Months	Over 6 Months	N/A	D/K
Insurance pool	Under 1 Month	1-3 Months	4-6 Months	Over 6 Months	N/A	D/K
State government	Under 1 Month	1-3 Months	4-6 Months	Over 6 Months	N/A	D/K
Federal government	Under 1 Month	1-3 Months	4-6 Months	Over 6 Months	N/A	D/K

10. What methods were used for interim financing of public facility repair and reconstruction costs prior to the receipt of federal or state aid? (Circle each that you know was used; if you don't know if any of them were used, circle 6)

1 Funds on hand
2 Emergency taxes or user fee surcharges
3 Borrowing from banks or public credit markets
4 Delayed payment of bills
5 Other (Specify: _____)
6 Don't know of any that were used

11. Did any of the following problems hinder repair and reconstruction of public facilities that were damaged in that disaster? (Circle each that you know was a hindrance; if you don't know of any of them that were a hindrance, circle 8)

1 Delays in receiving outside financial assistance
2 Timing of disaster late in fiscal year
3 Low level of contingency funds available
4 Lack of reserve funds for repair/reconstruction of facilities
5 Lack of adequate insurance
6 Loss of tax revenues from damaged private property
7 Other factors (Specify: _____)
8 Don't know of anything that hindered repair and reconstruction

12. In hindsight, what is the single most important step your government could have taken to be more prepared to meet the costs of that disaster?

_____

_____

_____

Now we would like to turn to risk management policies being pursued by your government. Questions in this section deal with your approach to risk management and your opinions about ways of dealing with risk of catastrophic losses to public facilities that are not currently insurable.

1. In your opinion what is the relative importance to your government of providing protection against each of the following types of risk? If it is very important, circle 1. If it is very unimportant, circle 5. If its importance falls somewhere in between, circle 2, 3, or 4.

| | Circle One for Each Type of Risk | | | | |
	Very Important				Very Unimportant
Comprehensive liability	1	2	3	4	5
Environmental pollution	1	2	3	4	5
Damage to real property	1	2	3	4	5
Damage to personal property	1	2	3	4	5
Loss of income	1	2	3	4	5

2. In round numbers, how much did your government spend on the following categories of risk management costs during the past fiscal year?

Risk management personnel: $ _____

Property insurance: $ _____

Liability insurance: $ _____

Retrofitting or relocating facilities to reduce risks: $ _____

3. Of the total pool of resources devoted to risk management by your government, what share would you estimate is devoted to each type of risk?

	Percent of Risk Management Resources
Comprehensive liability	_____ %
Environmental pollution	_____ %
Damage to real property	_____ %
Damage to personal property	_____ %
Loss of income	_____ %
Other risks (Specify:	
_____	
_____)	_____ %
Total (should add to 100%)	_____ 100%

4. Which of the following liability/property loss control methods are being used by your government? (Circle **each** that is used; if you don't know of any that are used, circle 9)

1 Employee safety program
2 Preventive maintenance program
3 Retrofit of buildings and other facilities to reduce risk of loss
4 Relocation of buildings and other facilities to less hazardous areas
5 Elimination of activities to reduce risk of loss
6 Sale or transfer of assets to reduce risk of loss
7 Flood control or flood warning system
8 Other (Specify: _____)
9 Don't know of any that are used

5. Have vulnerability analyses (analyses of the probability of loss and likely amount of damage from natural hazards) been conducted for any of the following types of public facilities owned by your government? (Circle number by **each** facility that you know has had a vulnerability analysis performed; if you don't know of any, circle 13)

1 Public buildings
2 Streets, roads, or sidewalks
3 Bridges
4 Water treatment plant
5 Water distribution lines
6 Sewage treatment plant

7 Sewer lines
8 Electric power lines or substations
9 Storm drainage/flood control facilities
10 Parks and recreation facilities, including buildings
11 Stadiums or convention centers
12 Other facilities (Specify: _____)
13 Don't know of any vulnerability analyses

6. For each type of capital asset owned by your government, please indicate **all** of the risk management approaches that are being used for that type of facility. If you don't know of any being used for a particular type of facility, circle D/K. If your government does not own that type of facility, circle N/A.

Public	Circle Approach(es) Being Used for Each Facility					
	Property Insurance	Contingency Fund	Reserve Fund	Loss Control	D/K	N/A
Public Buildings	Property Insurance	Contingency Fund	Reserve Fund	Loss Control	D/K	N/A
Streets, roads, and sidewalks	Property Insurance	Contingency Fund	Reserve Fund	Loss Control	D/K	N/A
Bridges	Property Insurance	Contingency Fund	Reserve Fund	Loss Control	D/K	N/A
Water treatment plants	Property Insurance	Contingency Fund	Reserve Fund	Loss Control	D/K	N/A
Water distribution lines	Property Insurance	Contingency Fund	Reserve Fund	Loss Control	D/K	N/A
Sewage treatment plants	Property Insurance	Contingency Fund	Reserve Fund	Loss Control	D/K	N/A
Sewer lines	Property Insurance	Contingency Fund	Reserve Fund	Loss Control	D/K	N/A
Electric power lines/substations	Property Insurance	Contingency Fund	Reserve Fund	Loss Control	D/K	N/A
Storm drainage/flood control	Property Insurance	Contingency Fund	Reserve Fund	Loss Control	D/K	N/A
Parks/recreation facilities	Property Insurance	Contingency Fund	Reserve Fund	Loss Control	D/K	N/A
Stadiums, convention centers, etc.	Property Insurance	Contingency Fund	Reserve Fund	Loss Control	D/K	N/A

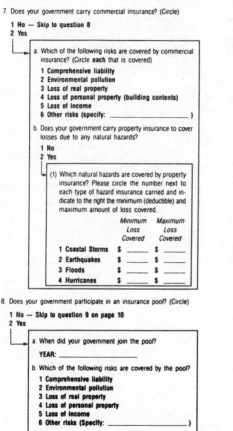

7. Does your government carry commercial insurance? (Circle)

1 No — Skip to question 8
2 Yes

    a. Which of the following risks are covered by commercial insurance? (Circle **each** that is covered)

      1 Comprehensive liability
      2 Environmental pollution
      3 Loss of real property
      4 Loss of personal property (building contents)
      5 Loss of income
      6 Other risks (specify: _____)

    b. Does your government carry property insurance to cover losses due to any natural hazards?

      1 No
      2 Yes

        (1) Which natural hazards are covered by property insurance? Please circle the number next to each type of hazard insurance carried and indicate to the right the minimum (deductible) and maximum amount of loss covered.

	Minimum Loss Covered	Maximum Loss Covered
1 Coastal Storms	$ _____	$ _____
2 Earthquakes	$ _____	$ _____
3 Floods	$ _____	$ _____
4 Hurricanes	$ _____	$ _____

8. Does your government participate in an insurance pool? (Circle)

1 No — Skip to question 9 on page 10
2 Yes

    a. When did your government join the pool?

      YEAR: _____

    b. Which of the following risks are covered by the pool?

      1 Comprehensive liability
      2 Environmental pollution
      3 Loss of real property
      4 Loss of personal property
      5 Loss of income
      6 Other risks (Specify: _____)

    c. What was the amount of your government's payment to the pool in the last fiscal year?

      PAYMENT TO POOL IN LAST FISCAL YEAR:
      $ _____

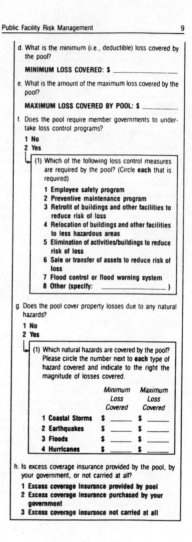

    d. What is the minimum (i.e., deductible) loss covered by the pool?

    MINIMUM LOSS COVERED: $ _____

    e. What is the amount of the maximum loss covered by the pool?

    MAXIMUM LOSS COVERED BY POOL: $ _____

    f. Does the pool require member governments to undertake loss control programs?

      1 No
      2 Yes

        (1) Which of the following loss control measures are required by the pool? (Circle **each** that is required)

          1 Employee safety program
          2 Preventive maintenance program
          3 Retrofit of buildings and other facilities to reduce risk of loss
          4 Relocation of buildings and other facilities to less hazardous areas
          5 Elimination of activities/buildings to reduce risk of loss
          6 Sale or transfer of assets to reduce risk of loss
          7 Flood control or flood warning system
          8 Other (specify: _____)

    g. Does the pool cover property losses due to any natural hazards?

      1 No
      2 Yes

        (1) Which natural hazards are covered by the pool? Please circle the number next to each type of hazard covered and indicate to the right the magnitude of losses covered.

	Minimum Loss Covered	Maximum Loss Covered
1 Coastal Storms	$ _____	$ _____
2 Earthquakes	$ _____	$ _____
3 Floods	$ _____	$ _____
4 Hurricanes	$ _____	$ _____

    h. Is excess coverage insurance provided by the pool, by your government, or not carried at all?

    1 Excess coverage insurance provided by pool
    2 Excess coverage insurance purchased by your government
    3 Excess coverage insurance not carried at all

9. Does your government maintain a loss reserve fund for risks you assume rather than covering them through insurance or pooling? (Circle)

1 No — Skip to question 10
2 Yes

a. What is the current magnitude of that(ose) fund(s)?

CURRENT LOSS RESERVE FUND: $ _____

b. What is the desired magnitude of that(ose) fund(s)?

DESIRED LOSS RESERVE FUND: $ _____

c. How many years did/will it take to reach that desired fund level?

YEARS: _____

d. Are any restrictions placed on the use of loss reserve funds? (Circle)

1 No
2 Yes
(1) Please explain briefly.

10. Does your government maintain one or more capital facilities maintenance/replacement/reconstruction reserve fund that could be used to finance the reconstruction of public facilities damaged in natural disasters? (Circle)

1 No
2 Yes

11. Finally, we are interested in your views on buying insurance coverage for different layers of risk to public facilities from earthquakes, floods, hurricanes and other natural hazards.

Imagine that the following layers of special coverage for natural hazards were available for losses to capital assets owned by your government. You may elect to purchase any combination of layers or none at all for natural hazards losses.

Please indicate which layers you would purchase for your government if this coverage were available, considering your level of exposure to loss and your budget for risk management. Circle "Yes" or "No" for each layer of coverage.

Would You Purchase?		Payable Loss Layer	Annual Cost to Government
Yes	No	$10,000 to $500,000	$1,750
Yes	No	$500,000 to $2 million	$4,000
Yes	No	$2 million to $5 million	$8,000
Yes	No	$5 million to $10 million	$13,000
Yes	No	$10 million to $20 million	$25,000
Yes	No	$20 million to $50 million	$80,000
Yes	No	$50 million to $100 million	$135,000

12. To wrap up this subject, we would like you to think about the following methods for anticipating and paying for costs of reconstructing public infrastructure damaged by natural hazards. We are interested in whether any of these methods are more politically feasible for your government than others. Please circle 1 if you believe a method is not politically feasible and 5 if you think it is highly feasible. Circle 2, 3, or 4 if you think its feasibility falls in between those extremes.

	Not Feasible				Highly Feasible
a. Maintain loss reserve fund financed from general revenue	1	2	3	4	5
b. Purchase commercial insurance (flood, earthquake, etc.)	1	2	3	4	5
c. Participate in state-sponsored natural hazards insurance pool	1	2	3	4	5
d. Participate in federally sponsored natural hazards insurance pool	1	2	3	4	5
e. Impose impact fee on new private development in hazardous areas to raise revenues to finance a loss reserve fund or pay for hazards insurance for public facilities	1	2	3	4	5
f. Create a hazard area special taxing district to raise revenue for a loss reserve fund or hazards insurance	1	2	3	4	5

13. Finally, would you favor or oppose revision of disaster assistance legislation which would make participation in a natural hazards insurance pool a condition for receiving assistance for the repair of public facilities damaged by natural hazards? (Circle for both federal and state legislation)

Participation in Insurance Pool a Condition of Federal Assistance
1 Strongly favor
2 Favor somewhat
3 No opinion
4 Oppose somewhat
5 Strongly oppose

Participation in Insurance Pool a condition of State Assistance
1 Strongly favor
2 Favor somewhat
3 No opinion
4 Oppose somewhat
5 Strongly oppose

The last section of this questionnaire deals with certain fiscal characteristics of your government.

1. During the previous fiscal year (FY 85–86), what was the total amount of general fund expenditures by your government?

   GENERAL FUND EXPENDITURES: $ _____

2. At the end of the previous fiscal year (FY 85–86), what was the fund balance in the general fund?

   GENERAL FUND BALANCE: $ _____

3. What were total capital expenditures from your government's own-source current revenues (exclude bond proceeds) during the previous fiscal year (FY 85–86) for:

   a. Facilities, such as streets, financed from sources other than user charges?

   CAPITAL EXPENDITURES IN FY 85–86: $ _____

   b. Facilities, such as water and sewer mains, financed from user charges?

   CAPITAL EXPENDITURES IN FY 85–86: $ _____

4. Does your government use a fixed asset accounting system (i.e., an accounting system that includes a listing of all property and facilities, their estimated value, and depreciation schedules)? (Circle)

   1 No
   2 Yes

5. Does your government operate its own pension system? (Circle)

   1 No
   2 Yes

   └── a. What percentage of accrued pension liabilities are actuarially funded at this time?

   PERCENT ACTUARIALLY FUNDED: _____ %

6. Is your government subject to a debt limit? (Circle)

   1 No
   2 Yes

   └── a. What is the limit of bonded indebtedness?

   DEBT LIMIT: _____

   b. What percent of your debt limit has been used up by past borrowing?

   PERCENT USED _____ %

7. What is the current credit rating of your government? (Circle for Standard & Poor's and/or Moody's ratings)

Standard & Poor's	*Moody's*
1 AAA	1 Aaa
2 AA	2 Aa
3 A	3 A
4 BBB	4 Baa
5 BB	5 Ba
6 B	6 B
7 Other	7 Other

8. What is the proportion of long-term debt outstanding to the full market value of property in your jurisdiction?

   PROPORTION OF LONG-TERM DEBT TO FULL MARKET PROPERTY VALUE:

   _____ %

9. What is the proportion of annual general obligation, tax-supported debt service payments to property tax revenues?

   PROPORTION OF DEBT SERVICE PAYMENTS TO PROPERTY TAX REVENUES:

   _____ %

10. Please circle each of the following positions that your government employs:

    1 Manager/chief administrative officer
    2 Finance director
    3 Budget officer
    4 Risk manager
    5 Public works director
    6 City/county engineer
    7 Planning director

11. What is your position with your government?

    POSITION: _____

Thank You For Your Assistance

Please seal and drop this questionnaire in the mail. Postage has been prepaid.

Appendix B
Questionnaire for 1987 Survey
of Public Works/Planning Directors

PUBLIC FACILITY RISK MANAGEMENT

Questionnaire for Public Works/Planning Directors

Conducted By

Center for Urban and Regional Studies
University of North Carolina at Chapel Hill

In Cooperation With

California Polytechnic University, San Luis Obispo
North Carolina State University
Washington State University

Supported By

National Science Foundation
Washington, DC 20550

May 1987

Public Facility Risk Management

WHAT THIS SURVEY IS ABOUT

- This survey is designed to provide information about local governments' approaches to coping with potential losses to public facilities from natural disasters such as earthquakes, floods, hurricanes, and landslides.

- In this questionnaire, we are particularly interested in learning about your government's procedures in managing capital assets, regulating new development, and your experiences with past natural disasters.

WHAT WILL BE DONE WITH THE INFORMATION

- Statistical summaries of your opinions and approaches to dealing with potential losses will be put together in a report that will be presented to CONGRESS, FEDERAL, STATE, AND LOCAL AGENCIES that are responsible for disaster assistance programs and to various professional associations that are helping with this study.

- NO INFORMATION YOU GIVE US WILL BE REVEALED TO ANYONE IN A WAY THAT CAN IDENTIFY YOU.

HOW YOUR GOVERNMENT WAS CHOSEN TO FILL OUT THIS QUESTIONNAIRE

- Your government was selected at random from a list of local governments that have received federal assistance in recovering from a natural disaster during the period 1981 through 1985.

- Because governments were selected by chance, the results will provide an unbiased picture of local experiences in coping with potential losses to public facilities from natural disasters.

PLEASE ANSWER EVERY QUESTION THAT APPLIES TO YOUR GOVERNMENT

IF YOU HAVE ANY QUESTIONS ABOUT THE SURVEY CALL DR. RAYMOND J. BURBY COLLECT AT (919) 962-3074.

HOW TO FILL OUT THE QUESTIONNAIRE

- Most of the questions can be answered by circling a number or word that corresponds to your answer; for example:

  What is the population of your jurisdiction?

  1 Less than 10,000
  ②10,000 – 24,999
  3 25,000 – 49,999
  4 50,000 – 99,999
  5 100,000 or more

The first set of questions asks about your government's policies with regard to land use controls and new private development.

---

1. Does your government use any of the following devices to provide or pay for public facilities serving new development? (Circle **all** that you know are used; if you do not know of any being used, circle 10)

   1 **Special assessment districts**
   2 **Requirements in *subdivision regulations* that developers build specified public facilities, such as streets, and transfer ownership to your government (or pay fees in lieu of building public facilities)**
   3 **Requirements in *special use permits or other regulations* that developers build specified public facilities and transfer ownership to your government (or pay fees in lieu of building public facilities)**
   4 ***Negotiated agreements* that require developers to build specified public facilities and transfer ownership to your government (or pay fees in lieu of building public facilities)**
   5 **Public facility *impact fees or availability charges***
   6 **Ordinance requiring *adequate off-site facilities*, such as thoroughfares and water and sewer system capacity, before development permits are granted**
   7 ***Tax increment financing***
   8 ***Performance bonds* or equivalent in subdivision regulations or special use permits that require developers to complete public facilities or forfeit the bond**
   9 **Other techniques (Please specify: _____)**
   10 **Don't know of any being used**

8. What do you *think the odds are* that your government could experience natural hazard damages to its public property *at or above the "disastrous" level* in any given year?

> Please circle one answer that best applies
>
> 1 A 1 IN 200 OR EVEN LOWER CHANCE of DISASTROUS LOSSES (or 0.5%)
>
> 2 AROUND 1 in 100 ODDS (or 1%)
>
> 3 AROUND 1 in 50 ODDS (or 2%)
>
> 4 AROUND 1 in 20 ODDS (or 5%)
>
> 5 A 1 IN 10 OR EVEN GREATER CHANCE OF DISASTROUS LOSSES (or 10%)

9. If your government has losses *at or above your "disastrous" level* next year, what do you think the *odds* are that Presidential (federal) disaster aid funds would be granted for your public property losses?

> Please circle one answer that best applies
>
> 1 LITTLE CHANCE OF FEDERAL AID
>
> 2 IT IS UNCERTAIN, BUT I THINK ODDS ARE *AGAINST* GETTING AID
>
> 3 ODDS ARE EVEN — A TOSS-UP
>
> 4 IT IS UNCERTAIN, BUT I THINK ODDS ARE *IN FAVOR* OF GETTING AID
>
> 5 FEDERAL AID IS ALMOST CERTAIN

10. Does your city's budget include any contingency funds budgeted *specifically* for natural hazard damages to any of the following types of public facilities?

	CONTINGENCY FUND BUDGETED?	IF *YES*, HOW LARGE WAS FUND IN LAST BUDGET YEAR?
Damages to Public Buildings..	NO YES──────→	$ _____
Damages to Streets, Roads and Bridges..............	NO YES──────→	$ _____
Damages to Sewage and Water Treatment Plant or Mains & Lines.................	NO YES──────→	$ _____

> Officials responsible for financial matters are not always involved in natural hazards management, though your government may be different. Whatever the case, we would like your views on hazards management.

1. Listed below are some reasons for purchasing insurance against damage to public property from FLOODS, including floods from hurricanes and storms. Tell us if you agree or disagree with each statement.

Please circle an answer for each item

Our experience with past losses indicates we should have FLOOD insurance....	Strongly Disagree	Somewhat Disagree	Neutral	Somewhat Agree	Strongly Agree
The cost of FLOOD insurance is too high for public property...............	Strongly Disagree	Somewhat Disagree	Neutral	Somewhat Agree	Strongly Agree
Technical studies of the FLOOD risk are important information in our decisions about buying FLOOD insurance...............	Strongly Disagree	Somewhat Disagree	Neutral	Somewhat Agree	Strongly Agree
The costs of FLOODproofing are so high that insurance is a better alternative......	Strongly Disagree	Somewhat Disagree	Neutral	Somewhat Agree	Strongly Agree
Our insurance carrier's recommendations influence our decisions on buying (or choosing not to buy) FLOOD insurance.........	Strongly Disagree	Somewhat Disagree	Neutral	Somewhat Agree	Strongly Agree
We have FLOOD insurance for public property only because of federal Disaster Relief Act requirements.....	Strongly Disagree	Somewhat Disagree	Neutral	Somewhat Agree	Strongly Agree
We have FLOOD insurance for public property because underwriters of a local bond issue required it......	Strongly Disagree	Somewhat Disagree	Neutral	Somewhat Agree	Strongly Agree

> If your government has NO risks of EARTHQUAKE damage, please SKIP this question and go to the next question.

2. Listed below are some reasons for purchasing insurance against damage to public property from EARTHQUAKES. Again, please indicate agreement or disagreement.

Please circle an answer for each item

Our experience with past losses indicates we should have EARTHQUAKE insurance.............	**Strongly Disagree**	**Somewhat Disagree**	**Neutral**	**Somewhat Agree** **Strongly Agree**
The cost of EARTHQUAKE insurance is too high for public property..........	**Strongly Disagree**	**Somewhat Disagree**	**Neutral**	**Somewhat Agree** **Strongly Agree**
Technical studies of the EARTHQUAKE risk are important information in our decisions about buying EARTHQUAKE insurance...	**Strongly Disagree**	**Somewhat Disagree**	**Neutral**	**Somewhat Agree** **Strongly Agree**
The costs of QUAKEproofing are so high that insurance is a better alternative......	**Strongly Disagree**	**Somewhat Disagree**	**Neutral**	**Somewhat Agree** **Strongly Agree**
Our insurance carrier's recommendations influence our decisions on buying (or choosing not to buy) EARTHQUAKE insurance...	**Strongly Disagree**	**Somewhat Disagree**	**Neutral**	**Somewhat Agree** **Strongly Agree**
We have EARTHQUAKE insurance for public property because underwriters of a local bond issue required it	**Strongly Disagree**	**Somewhat Disagree**	**Neutral**	**Somewhat Agree** **Strongly Agree**

3. To your knowledge, have there been any studies (vulnerability analyses) of the natural hazard risks (the probability and amount of expected damages) to any of your public facilities? *(Circle)*

   1 NO
   2 YES
   3 DON'T KNOW

4. In your own opinion, how adequate is the available information on potential losses to your government's public facilities from floods and earthquakes?

Please circle one answer for each hazard

> For Floods:

1 **NO INFORMATION AVAILABLE**

2 **VERY INADEQUATE**

3 **SOMEWHAT INADEQUATE**

4 **SOMEWHAT ADEQUATE**

5 **VERY ADEQUATE**

6 **DON'T KNOW**

7 **NO FLOOD HAZARDS**

> For Earthquakes:

1 **NO INFORMATION AVAILABLE**

2 **VERY INADEQUATE**

3 **SOMEWHAT INADEQUATE**

4 **SOMEWHAT ADEQUATE**

5 **VERY ADEQUATE**

6 **DON'T KNOW**

7 **NO EARTHQUAKE HAZARDS**

5. In which of the following hazard management activities do you personally participate? *(Please circle ALL that apply or 8 if none apply).*

1 **ON A HAZARD MANAGEMENT COMMITTEE**

2 **IN AN ANNUAL EMERGENCY PREPAREDNESS EXERCISE**

3 **IN DEVELOPING A "HAZARD MITIGATION PLAN"**

4 **THROUGH INFORMAL DISCUSSIONS BETWEEN DEPARTMENTS**

5 **IN DEVELOPING AN "EMERGENCY OPERATIONS PLAN"**

6 **IN DEVELOPING DAMAGE OR VULNERABILITY ANALYSES FOR YOUR GOVERNMENT'S PUBLIC PROPERTY**

7 **IN PREPARING POST-DISASTER REQUESTS FOR STATE AND FEDERAL DISASTER ASSISTANCE**

8 **NONE OF THE ABOVE**

> We have a few final questions about different approaches to reducing losses to ALL PUBLIC FACILITIES that your government owns.

1. Which of the following hazard mitigation techniques have been used by your local government to reduce the future FLOOD damages to public facilities of any kind?

(Please circle each technique used by your government. If none is used, circle 10).

1 DAMAGE-RESISTANT DESIGN STANDARDS FOR NEW PUBLIC FACILITIES

2 MODIFICATIONS TO PRESENT FACILITIES (FLOODPROOFING, WINDPROOFING)

3 FACILITIES WERE MOVED TO LESS HAZARDOUS LOCATIONS

4 FLOOD CONTROL WORKS (DAMS, CHANNELS, LEVEES)

5 SHORELINE PROTECTION WORKS (SEAWALLS, RIPRAP, BREAKWATERS)

6 ZONING TO LIMIT DEVELOPMENT IN HAZARDOUS LOCATIONS

7 SUBDIVISION REGULATIONS THAT REQUIRE DEVELOPER-BUILT FACILITIES TO BE MORE RESISTANT TO FLOOD DAMAGE

8 ADOPTION OF A "FLOOD HAZARD MITIGATION PLAN"

9 LAND PURCHASES OR EASEMENTS THAT PREVENT BUILDING IN HAZARDOUS LOCATIONS

10 NONE OF THE ABOVE

2. Which of the following hazard mitigation techniques have been used by your local government to reduce the future EARTHQUAKE damages to public facilities?

If your area has no earthquake risks please circle #9 and skip to question three.

1 DAMAGE-RESISTANT DESIGN STANDARDS FOR NEW PUBLIC FACILITIES

2 STRENGTHENING OR REDESIGN OF PRESENT FACILITIES (QUAKEPROOFING)

3 FACILITIES MOVED TO LESS HAZARDOUS LOCATIONS

4 ZONING TO LIMIT DEVELOPMENT IN THE MOST HAZARDOUS LOCATIONS

5 SUBDIVISION REGULATIONS THAT REQUIRE DEVELOPER-BUILT FACILITIES TO BE MORE RESISTANT TO POSSIBLE EARTHQUAKE DAMAGES

6 AN EARTHQUAKE RISK OR "SEISMIC SAFETY" SECTION IN YOUR LOCAL LAND USE PLAN

7 LAND USE PURCHASES OR EASEMENTS THAT PREVENT DEVELOPMENT IN THE MOST EARTHQUAKE-DAMAGE PRONE LOCATIONS

8 NONE OF THE ABOVE

9 NO EARTHQUAKE HAZARDS IN OUR AREA

3. Listed below are risk management activities, for accident liability and employee safety, that some local governments are engaged in.

Please circle all that are used by your government.

1 **COMPREHENSIVE LIABILITY INSURANCE**

2 **RETENTION OF FUNDS FOR SELF-INSURANCE**

3 **EMPLOYEE SAFETY TRAINING**

4 **PREVENTIVE MAINTENANCE TO REDUCE LIABILITY FOR EMPLOYEE OR CITIZEN INJURY**

5 **PARTICIPATION IN A MULTI-CITY OR MULTI-COUNTY INSURANCE POOL**

6 **NONE OF THE ABOVE**

4. Finally, we would like you to imagine that your government is considering ways to financially cope with future losses to public facilities—*other than buildings*—due to natural hazards. Listed below are methods for funding those losses in advance. In your opinion, how feasible would it be for your government to use each of the methods listed? For example, if one method could not ever be used by your locality, circle a "1". If you are not sure whether a method is feasible or not, circle a "4", the middle number on the scale.

	Circle a number for each method						
	NOT AT ALL FEASIBLE					**VERY FEASIBLE**	
A Maintain a loss reserve fund financed from general revenues......................	1	2	3	4	5	6	7
B Purchase commercial flood or earthquake insurance........................	1	2	3	4	5	6	7
C Create a hazard area special taxing district to raise a loss reserve fund or pay insurance premiums.................	1	2	3	4	5	6	7
D Add a sucharge to the rates for water, sewer or other services to specifically fund disaster loss reserves or insurance premiums.............................	1	2	3	4	5	6	7
E Participate in a local government insurance pool for risks from natural disasters...............................	1	2	3	4	5	6	7

5. Of the five methods you just read about (above), **PLEASE CIRCLE THOSE THAT ARE BEING USED NOW** by your government *(Circle A, B, C, D and E as appropriate)*.

6. Please tell us the title of your own position (finance director, clerk, county commissioner, mayor, risk manager, etc.)

_____ **YOUR POSITION**

THANK YOU FOR YOUR PARTICIPATION IN THIS SURVEY

> **PLEASE FOLD THIS BOOKLET AND PLACE IN THE RETURN ENVELOPE WE SENT YOU—NO POSTAGE IS NECESSARY.**

If you are interested in more information about the issue of paying for natural hazard losses to public property. . . . .

We are looking for jurisdictions that may wish to participate in a more detailed analysis of the risks to their public facilities and the costs and benefits of different financial approaches to preparing for potential damages. The information resulting will be given to any participating communities to consider in their decisions about insurance, public works contingency funds and rate structures.

If you are interested, just note your name, title and a phone number.

NAME _____   TITLE _____

PHONE _____

COMMENTS WELCOMED

References

Advisory Commission on Intergovernmental Relations. 1985. *The Question of State Government Capability*. Washington, DC: ACIR.

Advisory Committee on the International Decade for Natural Hazard Reduction 1989. *Reducing Disasters' Toll: The United States Decade for Natural Disaster Reduction*. Washington: National Academy Press.

Alesch, Daniel J., and William J. Petak. 1986. *The Politics and Economics of Earthquake Hazard Mitigation*. Boulder: Institute of Behavioral Science, University of Colorado.

Algermissen, S. T., K. V. Steinbrugge, and H. L. Lagorio. 1978. "Estimation of Earthquake Losses to Buildings (Except Single Family Dwellings)." U.S.G.S. Open File Report 78–441. Washington, DC: U. S. Geological Survey.

All-Industry Research Advisory Council. 1986. *Catastrophic Losses*. Oak Brook, IL: All-Industry Research Advisory Council.

Alterman, Rachell, ed. 1987. *Private Supply of Public Services: Real Estate Development Exactions and Some Alternative Land Policies*. New York, NY: New York University Press.

American Planning Association. 1980. *Local Capital Improvements and Development Management*. Washington: U.S. Government Printing Office.

Anton, Thomas. 1987. "Economic Development, Employment and Training Policy and Federalism," *Policy Studies Review* 6, 4: 728–732.

Applied Technology Council. 1985. *Earthquake Damage Evaluation Data for California*. Report ATC-13. Redwood City, CA: Applied Technology Council.

Applied Technology Council. 1987. *Evaluating the Seismic Resistance of Existing Buildings*. Report ATC-14. Redwood City, CA: Applied Technology Council.

Association of Bay Area Governments. 1979. *Will Local Governments Be Liable for Earthquake Losses: What Cities and Counties Should Know About Earthquake Hazards and Local Government Liability*. Berkeley, CA: The Association.

Baker, Earl J., and Joe Gordon McPhee. 1975. *Land Use Management and Regulation in Hazardous Areas: A Research Assessment*. Boulder: Institute of Behavioral Science, University of Colorado.

Beatley, Timothy, and Philip R. Berke. 1989. "Seismic Safety Through Public Incentives: The Palo Alto Seismic Hazards Identification Program," College Station, TX: Hazard Reduction and Recovery Center, College of Architecture, Texas A & M University.

Beatley, Timothy, and David R. Godschalk. 1985. "Hazard Reduction Through Development Management in Hurricane Prone Communities: State-of-the-Art," *Carolina Planning* 11, 1.

Beavers, James E. 1985. "Current Practices in Earthquake Preparedness and Mitigation for Critical Facilities," in *Societal Implications: Selected Readings*. Earthquake Hazard Reduction Series 14. Washington, DC: Federal Emergency Management Agency.

Berg, Gregory. 1986. "Capital Markets Risk Financing," *Public Risk* (November/ December): 10–12.

Berke, Philip, and Jesus Hinojosa. 1987. "Local Planning Response to Earthquake Hazards," Completed research summary presented at the Natural Hazards Workshop, University of Colorado, Boulder, Colorado, July 19–22, 1987.

Berke, Philip, and Suzanne Wilhite. 1988. *Local Mitigation Planning Response to Earthquake Hazards: Results of a National Survey*. College Station, TX: Center for Hazard Reduction and Community Rehabilitation, Texax A & M University.

Berke, Philip, Timothy Beatley, and Suzanne Wilhite. 1988. "Influences on Local Adoption of Planning Measures for Earthquake Hazard Reduction," *International Journal of Mass Emergencies and Disasters* 7, 1: 33–56.

Bernstein, George. 1978. "Introduction," in *Disaster Insurance Protection: Public Policy Lessons*. New York: John Wiley & Sons.

Bickelhaupt, David L., and John H. Magee. 1970. *General Insurance*. Homewood, IL: Richard D. Irwin, Inc.

Bieber, Robert M. 1983. "Risk Management Cost Allocation," *Governmental Finance* (March): 27–29.

———. 1984. "Risk Management Services for Government," *Governmental Finance* (March): 31–34.

Black, Alan. 1968. "The Comprehensive Plan," in *Principles and Practices of Urban Planning*. Washington, DC: International City Manager Association.

Blair, M. L., and W. E. Spangle. 1979. *Seismic Safety and Land-Use Planning: Selected Examples from the San Francisco Bay Region, California*. Washington, DC: U.S. Geological Survey, Professional Paper 941-8.

Bolton, Patricia A., Susan G. Heikkala, Marjorie M. Greene, and Peter J. May. 1986. *Land Use Planning for Earthquake Hazard Mitigation: A Handbook for Planners*. Boulder: Natural Hazards Research and Applications Information Center, University of Colorado.

Bowman, Ann O'M., and Richard C. Kearney. 1986. *The Resurgence of the States*. Englewood Cliffs, New Jersey: Prentice-Hall, Inc.

Britton, Neil, G. E. Kearney, and K. A. Britton. 1983. "Disaster Response: The Perception of the Threat and Its Influence on Community Decision on Insurance," in John Oliver, ed., *Insurance and Natural Disaster Management*, Papers Presented at a Seminar, Townsville, July 1983. Townsville, Queensland, Australia: Centre for Disaster Studies, James Cook University of North Queensland, pp. 260–332.

Brown, Alex. 1985. "Self-Insurance Pooling Arrives in Colorado," In *Risk Management Today*. Natalie Wasserman and Dean G. Phelus, eds. Washington, DC: International City Management Association, pp. 65–76.

Building Seismic Safety Council. 1985. *NEHRP Recommended Provisions for Development of Seismic Regulations for New Buildings*. Washington, DC: Federal Emergency Management Agency.

———. 1986. *Improving the Seismic Safety of New Buildings: A Non-Technical Explanation of the NEHRP Recommended Provisions*. Washington, DC: Federal Emergency Management Agency.

———. 1987. *Abatement of Seismic Hazards to Lifelines: An Action Plan*. Washington, DC: Federal Emergency Management Agency.

Burby, Raymond J., and Steven P. French. 1981. "Coping with Floods: The Land Use Management Paradox," *Journal of the American Planning Association* 47 (3): 289–300.

Burby, Raymond J., and Steven P. French with Beverly A. Cigler, Edward J. Kaiser, David H. Moreau, and Bruce Stiftel. 1985. *Flood Plain Land Use Management: A National Assessment*. Boulder: Westview Press.

Burby, Raymond J., Scott A. Bollens, James M. Holway, Edward J. Kaiser, David Mullan, and John R. Sheaffer. 1988. *Cities Under Water: A Comparative Evaluation of Ten Cities' Efforts to Manage Floodplain Land Use*. Boulder: Institute of Behavioral Science, University of Colorado.

California Government Code. Chapter 7.5: Natural Disaster Assistance Act. Sections 8680-8692.

California State Senate. 1987. *An Act to Amend Section 8690.4 of the Government Code, Relating to Natural Disaster Relief, Making an Appropriation Therefore, and Declaring the Urgency Thereof, to Take Effect Immediately*. S.B. 6, 1987–1988 First Extraordinary Session.

———. 1989. *An Act to Amend Sections 8680.2, 8680.3, 8680.4, 8685, 8685.7, 8685.8, 8686, 8587.2, 8690, 8690.4 and 164818 of the Government Code, to Amend Section 17207 of, to add Chapter 5 (Commencing with Section 194) to Part 1 of Division 1 of, the Revenue and Taxation Code, and to Add Chapter 5.8 (Commencing with Section 13600) to Part 3 of Division 9 of the Welfare and Institutions Code, Relating to Natural Disaster Assistance, and Making an Appropriation Therefore*. S.B. 1910, 1987–88 Regular Session.

Cigler, Beverly A. 1987. "Political and Organizational Considerations in Infrastructure Investment Decision-Making," in Thomas Johnson, ed., *Local Infrastructure Investment Decisionmaking*. Boulder,CO: Westview Press, pp. 201–213.

———. 1988a. "Current Issues in Mitigation," in Louise K. Comfort, ed., *Managing Disaster*. Durham, NC: Duke University Press, pp. 39–52.

———. 1988b. "Emergency Management and Public Administration," in Michael Charles, ed., *Crisis Management: A Casebook*. Springfield, IL: Charles C. Thomas Publishing, pp. 5–19.

———. 1989. "Redefined Challenges for Local Administrators," in James L. Perry, ed., *Handbook of Public Administration*, San Francisco: Jossey-Bass Publishers.

Cigler, Beverly, Bruce Stiftel, and Raymond J. Burby. 1987. "Rural Community Responses to a National Mandate: An Assessment of Floodplain Land-Use Management," *Publius: The Journal of Federalism* 17, 4: 113–130.

Comptroller General of the United States. 1975. *National Attempts to Reduce Losses from Floods by Planning for and Controlling the Use of Flood-Prone Lands*. Washington: U.S. General Accounting Office.

———. 1980. *Federal Disaster Assistance: What Should the Policy Be?* Washington: U.S. General Accounting Office.

———. 1981. *Requests for Federal Disaster Assistance Need Better Evaluation.* Washington: U.S. General Accounting Office.

———. 1982. *Improved Administration of Public Disaster Assistance Can Reduce Costs and Increase Effectiveness.* Washington: U.S. General Accounting Office.

Conservation Foundation. 1977. *Physical Management of Coastal Floodplains: Guidelines for Hazards and Ecosystems Management.* Washington, DC: The Foundation.

———. 1980. *Coastal Environmental Management: Guidelines for Conservation of Resources and Protection Against Storm Hazards,* Washington, DC: The Foundation.

Cragg, Lauren C., and H. Felix Kloman. 1985. "Risk Management: A Developed Discipline," *In Risk Management Today,* Natalie Wasserman and Dean G. Phelus, eds. Washington, DC: International City Management Association, pp. 7–21.

Dacy, D. C., and Howard Kunreuther. 1969. *The Economics of Natural Diasters: Implications for Federal Policy.* New York: The Free Press.

Dalton, Linda C. 1989. "The Limits of Regulation: Evidence from Local Plan Implementation in California," *Journal of the American Planning Association* 55 (Spring): 151–168.

Davis, J.F., et al. 1982a. *Earthquake Planning Scenario for a Magnitude 8.3 Earthquake on the San Adreas Fault in southern California.* Special Publication No. 60. Sacramento, CA: California Department of Conservation, Division of Mines and Geology.

———. 1982b. *Earthquake Planning Scenario for a Magnitude 8.3 Earthquake on the San Adreas Fault in the San Francisco Bay Area.* Sacramento, CA: California Department of Conservation, Divison of Mines and Geology.

Deb, Arun. 1982. *Alternative Technologies for Small Water System Management.* National Science Foundation Grant ISP 80 15075, Washington, DC.

Denenberg, Herbert, S., Robert D. Eilers, G. Wright Hoffman, Chester A. Kline, Joseph J. Melone, and H. Wayne Snider. 1964. *Risk and Insurance.* Englewood Cliffs, NJ: Prentice-Hall, Inc.

Diggins, William, James D. Wright, and Peter H. Rossi. 1979. "Local Elites and City Hall: The Case of Natural Disaster Risk-Mitigation Policy," *Social Science Quarterly* 60 (September): 203–217.

Dillman, Don A. 1978. *Mail and Telephone Surveys: The Total System Design.* New York: John Wiley and Sons.

Dillon, Robert M. 1985. "Development of Seismic Safety Codes," in *Societal Implications: Selected Readings.* Earthquake Hazard Reduction Series 14. Washington, DC: Federal Emergency Management Agency.

Drabek, Thomas E. 1986. *Human Systems Responses to Disaster.* New York: Springer-Verlag.

Drabek, Thomas E., Alvin H. Mushkatel, and Thomas E. Kilijanek. 1983. *Earthquake Mitigation Policy: The Experience of Two States,* Boulder: Institute of Behavioral Science, The University of Colorado.

Dubnick, Mel, and Lynne Holt. 1985. "Industrial Policy and the States," *Publius: The Journal of Federalism* 15,1: 113–129.

Dye, Thomas R., and Virginia Gray, eds. 1980. *Determinants of Public Policy.* Lexington, MA: D.C. Heath, Lexington Books.

Dynes, Russell R., Enrico L. Quarantelli, and Gary A. Kreps. 1972. *A Perspective on Disaster Planning.* Columbus, OH: Disaster Research Center, Ohio State University.

Elliott, Curtis M., and Emmett J. Vaughan. 1972. *Fundamentals of Risk and Insurance.* New York: John Wiley and Sons, Inc.

Federal Emergency Management Agency. 1986. *A Unified National Program for Floodplain Management.* Washington, DC: Federal Emergency Management Agency.

Federal Highway Administration. 1980. *The Design of Encroachments on Flood Plains Using Risk Analysis.* Hydraulic Engineering Circular 17. Washington: The Agency.

Federal Register. Vol. 52, No. 39. Friday, February 27, 1987, pp. 5979.

Fleming, Robert W., and Fred A. Taylor. 1980. *Estimating the Costs of Landslide Damage in the United States.* USGS Circular 832. Reston, VA: U.S. Geological Survey.

Forester, John. 1982. "Critical Reason and Political Power in Project Review Activity: Serving Freedom in Planning and Public Administration," *Policy and Politics* 10 (1): 65–83.

Forsythe, J. E., and W. Steve Harriman. 1989. *A Summary of the October 17, 1989 Loma Prieta Earthquake.* Prepared Under the Direction of Professor Steven P. French. San Luis Obispo, CA: Department of City and Regional Planning, California Polytechnic State University.

Frank, James, Elizabeth R. Lines, and Paul B. Downing. 1987. *Impact Fees.* Chicago, IL: Planners Press.

Fratto, Edward S. 1987. "Legal Issues and Regulatory Approaches in Abatement of Seismic Hazards to Transportation Systems," in *Abatement of Seismic Hazards to Lifelines. Proceedings of a Workshop and Development of an Action Plan, Volume 6: Papers on the Political, Economic, Social, Legal, and Regulatory Issues and General Workshop Presentations.* Prepared for Buildings Seismic Safety Council. Washington, DC: Federal Emergency Manaement Agency.

French, Steven P., and Deborah Harmon. 1982. "Current Land Use Planning for Seismic Safety in California," San Luis Obispo, CA: School of Architecture and Environmental Planning, California Polytechnic State University, May.

French, Steven P., and Mark S. Isaacson. 1984. "Applying Earthquake Risk Analysis Techniques to Land Use Planning," *Journal of the American Planning Association* 50 (Autumn): 509–522.

French, Steven P., and Gary G. Rudholm. Forthcoming 1990. "Damage to Infrastructure and Public Property in the Whittier Narrows Earthquake," *Earthquake Spectra* 6 (February).

French, Steven P., and Lyna L. Wiggins. 1989. "Computer Adoption and Use in California Planning Agencies: Implications for Education," *Journal of Planning Education and Research* 8 (2).

Friesma, H. Paul, James Caporaso, Gerald Goldstein, Robert Lineberry, and Richard McCleary. 1979. *Aftermath: Communities After Natural Disasters.* Beverly Hills: Sage.

Fritz, Charles E. 1961. "Disaster," in Robert K. Merton and Robert A. Nisbet, eds., *Contemporary Social Problems.* New York: Harcourt, Brace and World, Inc., pp. 651–694.

Gates, James T. 1987. "Techniques for Design and Construction of New Transportation Facilities in California," in *Abatement of Seismic Hazards to Lifelines. Proceedings of a Workshop and Development of an Action Plan, Volume 2: Papers on Transportation Lifelines and Special Workshop Presentations.* Prepared for Buildings Seismic Safety Council. Washington, DC: Federal Emergency Management Agency, pp. 1–14.

Getter, R. W., and Nick Elliot. 1976. "Receptivity of Local Elites Toward Planning," *Journal of the American Institute of Planners* 42 (January): 419–424.

Godschalk, David R., and David J. Brower. 1985. "Mitigation Strategies and Integrated Emergency Management," *Public Administration Review* 45 (January): 64–71.

Godschalk, David R., David J. Brower, and Timothy Beatley. 1989. *Catastrophic Coastal Storms: Hazard Mitigation and Development Management.* Durham, NC: Duke University Press.

Gordon, Peter. 1987. "Political, Economic and Social Problems in Abatement of Seismic Hazards to Urban Passenger Transportation Facilities," in *Abatement of Seismic Hazards to Lifelines. Proceedings of a Workshop and Development of an Action Plan, Volume 6: Papers on the Political, Economic, Social, Legal, and Regulatory Issues and General Workshop Presentations.* Prepared for Buildings Seismic Safety Council. Washington, DC: Federal Emergency Management Agency, pp. 3–16.

Graham, John D. 1982. "Some Explanations for Disparities in Lifesaving Investments," *Policy Studies Review* 1 (May): 692–704.

Griggs, Gary B., and John A. Gilchrist. 1977. *The Earth and Land Use Planning.* North Scituate, MA: Duxbury Press.

Hogarth, R., and H. Kunreuther. 1988. *Risk, Ambiguity and Insurance.* Chicago: University of Chicago, Center for Decision Research.

Hutton, Janice R., Dennis S. Mileti, with William B. Lord, John H. Sorensen, and Marvin Waterstone. 1979. *Analysis of Adoption and Implementation of Community Land Use Regulations for Floodplains.* San Francisco: Woodward-Clyde Consultants.

Insurance Services Office. 1983. *Guide for Determination of Earthquake Classifications.* New York: Insurance Services Office.

International City Management Association. 1987. *Management Policies in Local Government Finance.* Washington, D.C.: ICMA.

International Congress of Building Officials. 1985. *Uniform Building Code.* Whittier, CA: ICBO.

Jaffe, Martin. 1981. *Reducing Earthquake Risks: A Planner's Guide.* Chicago, IL: American Planning Association. PAS Reprot #354.

Jaffe, Martin, Joann Butler, and Charles Thurow. 1984. *Reducing Earthquake Risks: A Planners Guide.* Chicago: American Planning Association.

James, L. Douglas. 1977. "Information Needs to Facilitate Implementation of Non-structural Alternatives," in Waldon R. Kerns, ed. *Implementation of Non-Structural Alternatives in Flood Damage Abatement.* Blacksburg, VA: Virginia Polytechnic Institute and State University, pp. 16–28.

Jones, Barclay G., and Costakis N. Nicolaides. 1988. "The Whittier Narrows, California Earthquake, October 1, 1987—Buildings at Risk," *Earthquake Spectra* 4 (February).

Kahneman, Daniel, Paul Slovic, and Amos Tversky, eds. 1982. *Judgment Under Uncertainty: Heuristics and Biases.* New York: Cambridge University Press.

Kaiser, Edward J., and Raymond J. Burby. 1988. "Exactions in Managing Growth: The Land Use Planning Perspective," *New York Affairs* 10 (Winter): 113–126.

Kartez, Jack, and William Kelley. 1988. "Research-based Disaster Planning: Conditions for Implementation," in Louise Comfort, ed., *Managing Disaster: Strategies and Policy Perspectives.* Durham, NC: Duke University Press.

Kartez, Jack, and Michael Lindell. 1987. "Planning for Uncertainty: The Case of Local Disaster Planning," *Journal of the American Planning Association* 53, 4: 487–498.

———. 1990. "Adaptive Planning for Community Disaster Response," in R. Sylves and W. Waugh, eds., *Cities and Disaster.* Springfield, IL: Charles C. Thomas Publishing.

Kiesler, S., and L. Sproull. 1982. "Managerial Response to Changing Environments: Perspectives on Problem Sensing from Social Cognition," *Administrative Science Quarterly* 27: 548–70.

Kockelman, William J. 1975. *Use of U.S. Geological Survey Earth-Science Products by City Planning Agencies in the San Francisco Bay Region, California.* U.S.G.S. Open File Report 75–276. Menlo Park, CA: USGS.

———. 1976. *Use of U.S. Geological Survey Earth-Science Products by County Planning Agencies in the San Francisco Bay Region, California.* U.S.G.S. Open File Report 76–547. Menlo Park, CA: USGS.

———. 1979. *Use of U.S. Geological Survey Earth-Science Products by Selected Regional Agencies in the San Francisco Bay Region, California.* U.S.G.S. Open File Report 79–221. Menlo Park, CA: USGS.

Koe, Charles K. 1980. *Understanding Risk Management.* Athens, GA: Institute of Government, University of Georgia.

Krutilla, John V. 1966. "An Economic Approach to Coping with Flood Damage," *Water Resources Research* 2 (2): 183–190.

Kunreuther, Howard. 1974. "Economic Analysis of Natural Hazards: An Ordered Choice Approach," Pp. 206–214 in *Natural Hazards: Local, National, Global,* Gilbert F. White, ed., New York: Oxford University Press.

Kunreuther, Howard., Ralph Ginsberg, Louis Miller, Phillip Sagi, Paul Slovic, P. Borkan, and Norman Katz. 1978. *Disaster Insurance Protection: Public Policy Lessons.* New York, New York: John Wiley & Sons.

Kusler, Jon A. 1976. *A Perspective on Flood Plain Regulations for Flood Plain Management.* Washington, DC: Department of the Army.

———. 1982a. *Innovation in Local Floodplain Management: A Summary of Community Experience. Appendix B, Regulation of Flood Hazard Areas to Reduce*

Flood Losses, Volume 3. Boulder: Natural Hazards Research and Applications Information Center, University of Colorado.

———. 1982b. *Regulation of Flood Hazard Areas, Vol. 3.* Prepared for the U.S. Water Resources Council. Boulder: Natural Hazards Research and Applications Information Center, University of Colorado.

Kusler, Jon A., and Thomas Lee. 1972. *Regulations for Flood Plains.* Planning Advisory Service Report No. 277. Chicago: American Society of Planning Officials.

Lamont, William. 1979. "Subdivision Regulations and Land Conversion," in So, Frank, Israel Stollman, Frank Beal, and Arnold, *The Practice of Local Government Planning.* Washington, D.C.: International City Managers Association.

LeMond, Don. 1986. "What States Should Do For Themselves," *State Government News,* (March/April): 16–17.

Leopold, Luna B. 1968. *Hydrology for Urban Land Planning—A Guidebook on the Hydrologic Effects of Urban Land Use.* Geological Survey Circular 554. Washington: U.S. Geological Survey.

Lester, James P., et al. 1987. "Public Policy Implementation: Evolution of the Field and Agenda for Future Research," Paper prepared for presentation at the 1987 Annual Meeting of the American Political Science Association.

"Liability Crisis Eases as Debate Continues." 1986. *Public Administration Times* (November 15): 3.

Lind, C. Robert. 1967. "Flood Control Alternatives and the Economics of Flood Protection," *Water Resources Research* 3 (2): 345–357.

Liu, Ben-chieh, with Chang-Tseh Hsieh, Robert Goftafson, Otto Nuttli, and Richard Gentile. 1981. *Earthquake Risk and Damage Functions: Applications to New Madrid.* Boulder, CO: Westview Press.

L. R. Johnston Associates. 1989. *A Status Resport on the Nation's Floodplain Management Activity: An Interim Report.* Prepared for the Interagency Task Force on Floodplain Management. Washington, DC: Interagency Task Force on Floodplain Management, Federal Emergency Management Agency.

Luloff, A. E., and Kenneth P. Wilkinson. 1979. "Participation in the National Flood Insurance Program: A Study of Community Activeness," *Rural Sociology* 44 (Spring): 137–152.

Mader, George, et al. 1980. *Land Use Planning and Earthquakes.* Portola Valley, CA: William Spangle Associates, Inc.

March, James, and Herbert Simon. 1958. *Organizations.* New York: John Wiley.

Martin, Geoffrey R., Ignatius (Po) Lam, and C. B. Crouse. 1987. "Seismic Retrofit for Geotechnical Components of Transportation Systems," *Abatement of Seismic Hazards to Lifelines. Proceedings of a Workshop and Development of an Action Plan, Volume 2: Papers on Transportation Lifelines and Special Workshop Presentations.* Prepared for Buildings Seismic Safety Council. Washington, DC: Federal Emergency Manaement Agency, pp. 39–48.

May, Peter J. 1985. *Recovering From Catastrophes: Federal Disaster Relief Policy and Politics.* Westport, CT: Greenwood Press.

May, Peter J., and Patricia Bolton. 1986. "Reassessing Earthquake Hazard Reduction Measures," *Journal of the American Planning Association* 52: 443–451.

May, Peter J., and Walter Williams. 1986. *Disaster Policy Implementation: Managing Programs Under Shared Governance*. New York: Plenum.

Mazmanian, Daniel, and Paul Sabatier. 1980a. "A Multivariate Model of Public Policy-Making," *American Journal of Political Science* 34 (August): 439–468.

_____. 1980b. *Effective Policy Implementation*. Lexington, MA: Lexington Books, Heath.

_____. 1983. *Implementation and Public Policy*, Glenview, IL: Scott, Foresman.

Merriam, Dwight, and Christine I. Andrew. 1988. "Defensible Linkage," *Journal of the American Planning Association* 54 (2): 199–209.

Milliman, Jerome W. 1983. "An Agenda for Economic Research on Flood Hazard Mitigation," in Stanley A. Chagnon, Jr., ed., *A Plan for Research on Floods and Their Mitigation in the United States*, Champaign, IL: Illinois Department of Energy and Natural Resources, State Water Survey, pp. 83–104.

Milliman, Jerome W., and R. Blaine Roberts. 1985. "Economic Issues in Formulating Policy for Earthquake Hazard Mitigation," *Policy Studies Review* 4 (May): 645–654.

Mintier, J. Laurence. 1982. *General Plan Guidelines*. Sacramento, CA: Office of Planning and Research, State of California.

Mintier, J. Laurence, and Peter Arne Stromberg. 1983. "Seismic Safety at the Local Level: Does Planning Make a Difference?" *California Geology* 36 (7): 148–154.

Mittler, Elliott. 1988. "Agenda-setting in Nonstructural Hazard Mitigation Policy," in Louise Comfort, ed., *Managing Disaster: Strategies and Policy Perspectives*. Durham, NC: Duke University Press.

Mittler, Elliott. 1989. *Natural Hazard Policy Setting: Identifying Supporters and Opponents of Nonstructural Hazard Mitigation*. Program on Environment and Behavior Monograph No. 48. Boulder, CO: Institute of Behavioral Science, University of Colorado.

Murphy, Francis C. 1958. *Regulating Flood Plain Development*.Department of Geography Research Paper No. 56. Chicago: Department of Geography, University of Chicago.

Mushkatel, Alvin H., and Dennis R. Judd. 1981. "The States' Role in Land Use Policy," *Policy Studies Review* 1: 263–274.

Mushkatel, Alvin H., and Joanne Nigg. 1987. "Effect of Objective Risk on Key Actors' Support for Seismic Mitigation Policy," *Environmental Management* 11: 77–87.

Mushkatel, Alvin H., and Louis F. Weschler. 1985. "Intergovernmental Implementation of Building Codes with Lateral Force Provisions," *Policies Studies Review* 4: 680–688.

National Association of State Budget Officers. 1985. *Budgeting Amid Fiscal Uncertainty*. Washington, DC: National Association of State Budget Officers.

National Governors' Association. 1985. *State of the States*. Washington, DC: National Governors' Association.

National Infrastructure Advisory Committee to the Joint Economic Committee of Congress. 1984. *Hard Choices: A Report on the Increasing Gap Between America's Infrastructure Needs and Our Ability to Pay for Them*, Committee

Print, Subcomittee on Economic Goals and Intergovernmental Policy of the Joint Economic Committee, Congress of the United States. Washington, DC: U.S. Government Printing Office.

National Research Council. 1989. *Estimating Losses from Future Earthquakes.* Washington, D.C.: National Academy Press.

Nelson, Ivan, and Melvin L. Baron. 1981. "Earthquakes and Underground Pipelines," in *Earthquakes and Earthquake Engineering: The Eastern United States*, James E. Beavers, ed. Ann Arbor: Ann Arbor Science Publishers, Inc.

New York State Legislature, Assembly Ways and Means Committee. 1980. *Municipal Insurance Pools.* Albany, NY: State of New York.

Nichols, D.R., and J. M. Buchanan-Banks. 1974. *Seismic Hazards and Land-Use Planning.* Washington, DC: U.S. Geological Survey, Circular #690.

Nigg, Joanne M. 1986. "Factors Affecting the Improvement of Seismic Hazard Abatement Practices in Public Works Departments and Utility Companies." Working Paper 108. Tempe, AZ: Office of Hazards Studies, School of Public Affairs, Arizona State University.

Nigg, Joanne M., and Ronald W. Perry. 1988. "Influential First Sources: Brief Statements with Long-Term Effects," *International Journal of Mass Emergencies and Disasters* 6 (November): 311–343.

Nilson, Douglas C., and Linda B. Nilson. 1981. "Seismic Safety Planning Strategies: Lessons from California," Pp. 1113–1135 in *Earthquakes and Earthquake Engineering–Eastern United States*, Vol. 2, Ann Arbor, MI: Ann Arbor Science Publishers, Inc.

O'Brien, L.E., and Duane E. Wilcox. 1985. "Risk Management Organization and Administration," in *Risk Management Today*, Natalie Wasserman and Dean G. Phelus, eds. Washington, DC: International City Management Association, pp. 22–31.

Office of Planning and Research, State of California. 1982. *General Plan Guidelines.* Sacramento, CA: The author, 1400 Tenth Street.

Olshanshy, Robert B., Howard Foster, and Thomas G. Dickert. 1987. "Seismic Microzonation and Land Use Planning: A Summary of the Current State of Relevant Technical Knowledge." Berkeley: University of California, Center for Environmental Design Research.

Olson, Richard Stuart, and Douglas C. Nilson. 1982. "Public Policy Analysis and Hazards Research: Natural Complements," *The Social Science Journal* 19 (January): 89–103.

Osborne, David. 1988. *The Next Agenda: Lessons from the Laboratories of Democracy.* Cambridge: Harvard Business School Press.

Owen, H. James, and Glen R. Wall. 1981. *Floodplain Management Handbook.* Washington, DC: U.S. Government Printing Office.

Perrow, Charles. 1984. *Normal Accidents.* New York, New York: Basic Books.

Petak, William J. 1973. *Guidelines for Developing a Seismic Safety Element for the General Plan.* PAS Report No. M–12. Chicago: American Society of Planning Officials.

―――. 1984. "Natural Hazard Mitigation: Professionalization of the Policy Making Process," *International Journal of Mass Emergencies and Disasters* 2 (August): 285–302.

Petak, William J., and Arthur A. Atkisson. 1982. *Natural Hazard Risk Assessment and Public Policy: Anticipating the Unexpected.* New York: Springer-Verlag.

Platt, Rutherford H., et al. 1980. *Intergovernmental Management of Floodplains.* Boulder: Institute of Behavioral Science, University of Colorado.

Pouzar, Edward A. 1985. "A Risk Management Strategy for the Hard Insurance Market," *Government Finance Review* (December): 15–18.

Prosser, Jim. 1985. "Taming the Insurance-Rate Roller Coaster with a Risk Management Agency," *Government Finance Review* (August): 6–7.

Puddington, Elizabeth D. 1987. "How To Start an Intergovernmental Pool." Presented to the Public Risk and Insurance Management Association's The Government Risk Management Seminars, Tucson, AZ, February 16–20.

Rabe, Barry G. 1986. *Fragmentation and Integration in State Environmental Management.* Washington, DC: Conservation Foundation.

Rakich, Ronald. No date. "Before You Jump Into the Pool—Check the Water!" Mimeo supplied by PRIMA.

Reitherman, Robert. 1985. "A Review of Earthquake Damage Estimation Methods," *Earthquake Spectra* 1(4) (August).

Rettger, Michael J., and Richard N. Boisvert. 1979. "Flood Insurance or Disaster Loans: An Economic Evaluation." *American Journal of Agricultural Economics* 61 (3).

Ricci, P.F., L.A. Sagan, and C.G. Whipple, eds. 1984. *Technological Risk Assessment.* Boston, MA: Martinus Nijhoff Publishers.

Rose, Adam. 1981. "Mandating Local Government Emergency Services," *Urban Interest* 65–73

Rosenberg, Philip, and Sally Rood. 1985. "The Realities of Our Infrastructure Problem." *Municipal Management* 7,3: 84–88.

Rossi, Peter H., James D. Wright, and Eleanor Weber-Burdin. 1982. *Natural Hazards and Public Choice: The State and Local Politics of Hazard Mitigation.* New York: Academic Press.

Rossi, Peter H., et al. 1983. *Victims of the Environment: Loss from Natural Hazards in the United States, 1970–1980.* New York: Plenum Press.

Rubin, Claire B., with Martin D. Saperstein, and Daniel G. Barbee. 1985. *Community Recovery from a Major Natural Disaster.* Boulder: Institute of Behavioral Science, University of Colorado.

Sabatier, Paul A. 1986. "Top-Down and Bottom-Up Approaches to Implementation Research: A Critical Analysis and Suggested Synthesis," *Journal of Public Policy* 6 (1): 21–48.

Scawthorn, Charles. 1986. "Rapid Assessment of Seismic Vulnerability" in *Techniques for Rapid Assessment of Seismic Vulnerability,* Charles Scawthorn, ed., New York: American Society of Civil Engineers.

Schenker, Allan. 1986. "Zero Employment Governments: Survival in the Tiniest Towns." *Small Town* 16: 4–11.

Scott, Stanley. 1979. *Policies for Seismic Safety: Elements of a State Government Program.* Berkeley, CA: Institute of Governmental Studies, University of California, Berkeley.

Settle, Allan K. 1985. "Financing Disaster Mitigation, Preparedness, Response, and Recovery." *Public Administration Review* 45: 101–106.

Settle, Allan. 1990. "Disaster Assistance: Securing Presidential Declarations," in R. Sylves and W. Waugh, eds.. *Cities and Disaster.* Springfield, IL: Charles C. Thomas Publishing.

Shah, Haresh C., and J. R. Benjamin. 1977. "Lifeline Seismic Criteria and Risk: A State of the Art Report," in *The Current State of Knowledge of Lifeline Earthquake Engineering.* New York: American Society of Civil Engineers.

Sheaffer, et al. 1976. *Flood Hazard Mitigation Through Safe Land Use and Construction Practices.* Chicago.

Sheaffer and Roland, Inc. 1981. *Evaluation of the Economic, Social and Environmental Effects of Floodplain Regulations,* Federal Insurance Administration. Washington: Federal Emergency Management Agency.

Sheaffer, John R., and Louis Rozaklis. 1980. "Barrier Islands Purchase: A Cost-Effective Approach to Management," Presented to the House Committee on Interior and Insular Affairs, Subcommittee on National Parks and Insular Affairs, on H.R. 5981, March 27.

Shenkel, William M. 1977. *Modern Real Estate Principles.* Dallas: Business Publications, Inc.

Shrader-Frechette, K. S. 1985. *Risk Analysis and Scientific Method: Methodological and Ethical Problems With Evaluating Societal Hazards.* Boston, MA: D. Reidel Publishing Company.

Singer, Saul Jay. 1986. "The Hydrologic Method of Calculating Flood Insurance Rates." *The Flood Report.* SMMA Inc. 4 March.

Slovic, Paul, Baruch Fischoff, and Sarah Lichetenstein. 1987. "Behavioral Decision Theory Perspectives on Protective Behavior," in Neil D. Weisnstein, ed., *Taking Care: Understanding and Encouraging Self-Protective Behavior.* Cambridge, UK: Cambridge University Press, pp. 14–41.

Slovic, Paul, Howard Kunreuther, and Gilbert F. White. 1974. "Decision Processes, Rationality, and Adjustment to Natural Hazards," in Gilbert F. White, ed., *Natural Hazards: Global, National, and Local.* New York: Oxford Press.

Sokolow, Alvin D., and Beth Walter Honadle. 1984. "How Rural Local Governments Budget: The Alternatives to Executive Preparation," *Public Administration Review* 44, 5: 373–383.

Sylvester, Kathleen. 1987. "Do-It-Yourself Insurance (Or Learning to Live with the Risk)," *Governing* (October): 56–63.

Thomas, William A. 1983. "Legal Aspects of Mitigating Flood Damages," in Stanley Chagnon, ed., *A Plan for Research on Floods and Their Mitigation in the United States.* Champaign, IL: Illinois State Water Survey, pp. 157–170.

Turner, Ralph H., et al. 1980. *Community Response to Earthquake Threat in Southern California: VII Vulnerability Zones and Earthquake Subculture.* Los Angeles, CA: Institute for Social Science Research, University of California, Los Angeles.

Tversky, A., and Kahneman, D. 1981. "The Framing of Decisions and the Psychology of Choice," *Science* 211: 453–458.

U.S. Bureau of the Census. 1983. *Statistical Abstract of the United States: 1984* (104th Edition). Washington: U.S. Government Printing Office.

U.S. Congress, Committee on Banking and Currency, United States Senate. 1966. *Insurance and Other Programs for Financial Assistance to Flood Victims*, Committee Print. Washington: U.S. Government Printing Office.

U.S. Congress, Committee on Banking, Housing and Urban Development, United States Senate. 1975. *Oversight on Federal Flood Insurance Programs*. Washington, DC: U.S. Government Printing Office.

U.S. Department of Justice. 1986. "Report of the Tort Policy Working Group on the Causes, Extent and Policy Implications of the Current Crisis in Insurance Availability and Affordability." (February).

U.S. Environmental Protection Agency. 1980. *Construction Costs for Municipal Wastewater Treatment Plants: 1973–1978*. Denver, CO: General Services Administration.

U.S. House of Representatives. Document No., 99–17, 99th Cong., 1st Sess. (February 4, 1985). (Part 5, page 85–President's FY 1986 budget submission).

Waller, Ray A., and Vincent T. Covello, eds. 1984. *Low-Probability High-Consequence Risk Analysis: Issues, Methods, and Case Studies*. New York: Plenum Press.

Ward, Delbert B. 1985. "Management of Earthquake Safety Programs by State and Local Governments," in *Societal Implications: Selected Readings*. Earthquake Hazards Reduction Series 14. Washington, DC: Federal Emergency Management Agency.

Wasserman, Natalie. 1986. "What States Should Do to Avoid the Next Insurance Crisis," *State Government News* (March/April): 12–14. Young, Robert L. 1985. "Self Insurance," in *Risk Management Today*, Natalie Wasserman and Dean G. Phelus, eds. Washington, D.C.: International City Management Association, pp. 59–64.

White, Gilbert F. 1936. "Notes on Flood Protection and Land-use Planning," *Planners Journal* 3 (May-June): 57–61.

_____. 1945. *Human Adjustment to Floods*. Department of Geography Research Paper No. 29. Chicago: Department of Geography, University of Chicago.

_____. 1974. "Natural Hazards Research: Concepts, Methods and Policy Implications," Pp. 3–16 in *Natural Hazards: Local, National, Global and Policy Implications*, Gilbert F. White, ed., New York: Oxford University Press.

_____. 1975. *Flood Hazard in the United States: A Research Reassessment*. Boulder: Institute of Behavioral Science, University of Colorado.

White, Gilbert F., and J. Eugene Haas. 1976. *Assessment of Research on Natural Hazards*, Cambridge, MA: The MIT Press.

White, Gilbert F., et al. 1976. *Natural Hazard Management in Coastal Areas*. Washington, DC: National Oceanic and Atmospheric Administration.

Working Group on Earthquake Hazard Reduction. 1978. *Earthquake Hazard Reduction: Issues for an Implementation Plan*. Washington, DC: Executive Office of the President, Office of Science and Technology Policy.

Wright, James D., and Peter H. Rossi. 1981. *Social Science and Natural Hazards*. Cambridge, MA: Abt Books.

Wright, James D., Peter H. Rossi, Sonia R. Wright, and Eleanor Weber-Burdin. 1979. *After the Clean-Up: Long-Range Effects of Natural Disasters.* Beverly Hills, CA: Sage.

Wyner, Alan J. 1984. "Earthquakes and Public Policy Implementation in California," *International Journal of Mass Emergencies and Disasters* 2 (August): 267–284.

Wyner, Alan J., and Dean E. Mann. 1983. "Seismic Safety Policy in California: Local Governments and Earthquakes," Santa Barbara, CA: Department of Political Science, University of California, Santa Barabara.